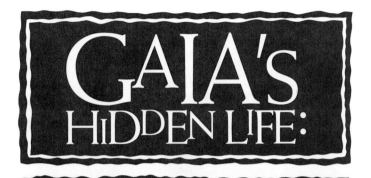

GAIA'S HIDDEN LIFE:

THE UNSEEN INTELLIGENCE OF NATURE

Compiled by SHIRLEY NICHOLSON & BRENDA ROSEN

*This publication made possible with
the assistance of the Kern Foundation*

QUEST BOOKS
The Theosophical Publishing House
Wheaton, Ill. U.S.A.
Madras, India/London, England

Copyright 1992 by The Theosophical Publishing House
A Quest original. First Edition 1992.
All rights reserved. No part of this book may be
reproduced in any manner without written permission
except for quotations embodied in critical articles
or reviews. For additional information write to:

The Theosophical Publishing House
P.O. Box 270
Wheaton, IL 60189-0270

A publication of the Theosophical Publishing House,
a department of the Theosophical Society in America.

Library of Congress Cataloging-in-Publication Data

Gaia's hidden life : the unseen intelligence of nature / compiled by
Shirley Nicholson & Brenda Rosen.
    p. cm.
    ISBN 0-8356-0685-6 (pbk.) : $14.00
    1. Religion and science.   2. Nature — Religious aspects.
3. Earth — Religious aspects.   4. Gaia hypothesis.   I. Nicholson,
Shirley J.   II. Rosen, Brenda.
BL240.2.G35   1992
291.2'12 — dc20   92-50143
                                                                    CIP

9 8 7 6 5 4 3 2 1 * 92 93 94 95 96 97 98 99

This edition is printed on acid-free paper that meets the
American National Standards Institute Z39.48 Standard

Printed in the United States of America by Bookcrafters

I did not merely come to believe, but I saw that the universe is not composed of dead matter but is, on the contrary, a living Presence.

Richard M. Bucke

Contents

Acknowledgments

"What Is Gaia?" is reprinted from *The Ages of Gaia, A Biography of Our Living Earth,* by James Lovelock, by permission of W. W. Norton & Company, Inc. Copyright © 1988 by The Commonwealth Fund Book Program of Memorial Sloan-Kettering Cancer Center.

"The New Story" is reprinted from *To Care for the Earth: A Call to a New Theology* by Sean McDonagh. Copyright © 1986 by Sean McDonagh. Reprinted by permission of Bear & Co., Inc., PO Drawer 2860, Santa Fe, NM 87504.

"The Celtic Fairy-Faith" is reprinted from *The Fairy-Faith in Celtic Countries* by W. Y. Evans-Wentz, © 1966 by University Books, Inc. Published by arrangement with Carol Publishing Group.

"The Deva Consciousness" from *The Findhorn Garden* by The Findhorn Community. Copyright © 1975 by The Findhorn Community. Reprinted by permission of HarperCollins Publishers.

"Wizard of Tuskegee" from *The Secret Life of Plants* by Peter Tomkins and Christopher Bird. Copyright © 1973 by Peter Tomkins. Reprinted by permission of HarperCollins Publishers.

"The World an Organism" from *The Death of Nature* by Carolyn Merchant. Copyright © 1980 by Carolyn Merchant. Reprinted by permission of HarperCollins Publishers.

"The Elements and Their Inhabitants" from Manly P. Hall, *The Secret Teachings of All Ages,* copyright Philosophical Research Society. Reprinted by permission.

"The Dance of Life" from *Gaia: The Human Journey from Cosmos to Chaos* by Dr. Elisabet Sahtouris. Copyright © 1989 by Dr. Elisabet Sahtouris. Reprinted by permission of Pocket Books, a division of Simon & Schuster, Inc.

Contributing Authors

THOMAS BERRY, PH.D., is a historian and a writer with special concern for the foundation of cultures in their relation to the natural world. His doctoral degree in history is from the Catholic University of America. He has taught the cultural history of India and China at various universities and was director of the graduate program in the History of Religions at Fordham University from 1966 until 1979. He is founder and director of the Riverdale Center of Religious Research in Riverdale, New York. His recent writings have centered on human-earth relations.

CHRISTOPHER BIRD is a biologist, anthropologist, and expert on the Soviet Union. Coauthor with Peter Tompkins of *The Secret Life of Plants,* he frequently contributes articles to leading magazines.

KENNETH COOPER, Cha-Das-Ska-Dum, is a member of the Lummi tribe of Washington state and a member of the Seyowen traditional religious society. He teaches young people how to "listen with their third ear"—the heart. He is also a singer and a maker of traditional instruments.

PAMELA KENT DEMERS holds a degree in molecular biology from the University of Washington. She worked for eleven years in medical laboratories, in a cancer research center, and for a genetic engineering company. She has also been a student of theosophy for fifteen years.

W. Y. EVANS-WENTZ, M.A., D. LITT., formerly of Jesus College, Oxford, was a student of occult doctrines and traditions. A noted translator and editor, he conducted extensive research in India and Sikkim during the early years of this century. In addition to his pioneering work on the fairy-faith in Celtic countries, he is noted for his early translation of the *Tibetan Book of the Dead.*

JOAN HALIFAX, PH.D., is an author, teacher, medical anthropologist, and founder of the Ojai Foundation, an educational center which merges Western academics and world cultural traditions. A protégée of the late Joseph Campbell, she has studied native cultures in Africa, the Americas, the Caribbean, and Asia. She is author of *Shamanic Voices, Shaman: The Wounded Healer,* and *The Human Encounter with Death* (with Stanislav Grof). She has practiced Buddhism for many years under Zen Master Thich Nhat Hanh.

MANLY P. HALL, D. LITT., was president of the Philosophical Research Society, a group dedicated to the dissemination of knowledge of philosophy, comparative religion, and psychology. Widely known as a lecturer, he authored over one hundred and fifty books and essays. Editor of the *PRS Journal,* Hall was also instrumental in the establishment of the PRS Library, a public research facility that houses rare materials in many obscure fields of learning.

GEOFFREY HODSON was a gifted and noted clairvoyant who cooperated with physicists, archaeologists, physicians, and other scientists to demonstrate the research potential of superphysical faculties. Born and educated in England, Hodson served with distinction in the British army during World War I. He authored over forty books, including *The Christ Life from Nativity to Ascension, The Hidden Wisdom of the Holy Bible,* and *Kingdom of the Gods.*

CLARA SUE KIDWELL, PH.D., is associate dean of the Graduate Division and associate professor of Native American Studies at the University of California, Berkeley. She is a Chippewa-Choctaw Native American.

SERGE KAHILI KING, PH.D., is the *kumu* (teaching master) of *Halau Kupua o Kaua'i,* a traditional Hawaiian shaman guild. He trained from an early age in the *kahuna* tradition of Hawaii and studied shamanism for seven years in West Africa. He also holds a doctorate in psychology. He is executive director of Aloha International, an organization dedicated to using the principles of Hawaiian shamanism to bring about personal, social, and environmental harmony. He is author of *Kahuna Healing, Imagineering for Health, Mastering Your Hidden Self, Urban Shaman,* and *Earth Energies.*

DORA VAN GELDER KUNZ was born with clairvoyant faculties. She has been associated for many years with alternative healing methods, developing with Dr. Dolores Krieger the technique known as Therapeutic Touch. She is author of *The Personal Aura,* coauthor of *The Chakras and the Human Energy Fields* (with Shafica Karagulla, M.D.), and editor of the anthology *Spiritual Aspects of the Healing Arts.* She is past president of the Theosophical Society in America.

CHARLES W. LEADBEATER developed clairvoyant abilities as an adult. A clergyman in the Church of England as a young man, Leadbeater became a Theosophist in 1883, traveling to India to assist H. P. Blavatsky, the principal founder of the movement. A teacher and worldwide lecturer, Leadbeater authored many books, including *Man Visible and Invisible, The Inner Life,* and *The Chakras.*

JAMES LOVELOCK, PH.D., was educated at the University of London and Manchester University and holds a doctorate in medicine. He has taught at Yale, the Baylor University College of Medicine, and at Harvard as a Rockefeller Fellow. An independent scientist, Lovelock works out of a barn-turned-laboratory at Coombe Mill in Cornwall, England. He is author of *The Ages of Gaia: A Biography of Our Living Earth, Gaia: A New Look at Life on Earth,* and *Healing Gaia: A New Prescription for the Living Planet.*

DOROTHY MACLEAN has been involved in human and planetary transformation all of her life. Cofounder of the Findhorn community in Scotland, she has used her gift of clairvoyant perception to help others learn the benefits of mutual contact and cooperation with the beings inhabiting the spiritual realms.

DAVID P. MCALLESTER, PH.D., was educated at Harvard and at Columbia University. He has conducted field research in Native American music, religious literature, and ceremony among the Hopi, Navajo, Penobscott, Passmaquoddie, Apache, Zuni, Comanche, Laguna, and Menomoni peoples. He founded the Department of Anthropology at Wesleyan University and cofounded the Society for Ethnomusicology. He has taught at major universities in the United States and Australia, is author or editor of numerous books, and has produced some eighty articles, three recordings, and one film.

SEAN MCDONAGH is an Irish Columban missionary who worked for many years on the island of Mindanao in the Philippines. He has studied theology and anthropology and has lectured at the Pacific Mission Institute in Sydney, Australia. He is author of *To Care for the Earth*, a passionate appeal for a new Christian theology which appreciates the sacredness of the Earth.

CAROLYN MERCHANT, PH.D., is professor of environmental history, philosophy, and ethics in the Department of Conservation and Resource Studies at the University of California, Berkeley.

PATRICK MILBURN is a biologist committed to a liberal arts perspective on the sciences. Educated at Stanford and Princeton, he served as program director for the Center for Integrative Education in New Rochelle, New York. A longtime student of Jungian and archetypal psychology, he is exploring the role of storytelling in establishing a living relationship with nature. He is currently a research associate of the Terra Foundation.

SHIRLEY NICHOLSON is former senior editor of Quest Books. She has lectured in both the U.S. and abroad on theosophical ideas and is author of *Ancient Wisdom, Modern Insight*. She is also compiler of two anthologies, *The Goddess Reawakening* and *Shamanism* and co-compiler of *Karma: Rhythmic Return to Harmony*.

BRENDA ROSEN, M.A., is senior editor of Quest Books. She is a former high school English teacher. A student of Tibetan Buddhism, she is editor of *Lighting the Lamp: An Approach to the Tibetan Path* by Alfred Woll.

ELISABET SAHTOURIS, PH.D., abandoned academia for a simple lifestyle on a Greek Island, where she worked to develop her own optimistic conception of Gaia through a synthesis of scientific knowledge and personal experience of nature. She is author of *Gaia: The Human Journey from Cosmos to Chaos* and the forthcoming *Eagle Man and Crow Woman: Science Meets the Sacred* (with Ed McGaa).

JOHN SEED is an environmental activist who travels around the world organizing and leading groups called the Council of All Beings, which he developed with Joanna Macy. His workshops use ritual, visualization, movement, and breath work to help people experience interconnectedness with the earth and other life forms. He is author of *Thinking Like a Mountain: Toward a Council of All Beings.*

HENRYK SKOLIMOWSKI, PH.D., received his doctorate in philosophy from Oxford University. Since 1971 he has been professor of philosophy in the Department of Humanities at the University of Michigan. He has consulted with the U.S. Congress and with UNESCO on the impact of science and technology on development and cultural values. He is author of six books, including *Eco-Philosophy: Designing New Tactics for Living, The Theatre of the Mind: Evolution in the Sensitive Cosmos,* and several hundred articles.

JAMES A. SWAN, PH.D., is co-producer of The Spirit of Place symposiums, associate professor of anthropology at the California Institute of Integral Studies, and president of the Institute for the Study of Natural Systems, in Mill Valley, California. His books include *Sacred Places: How the Living Earth Seeks Our Friendship* and *The Power of Place & Human Environments.*

PETER TOMKINS is the author of *Mysteries of the Mexican Pyramids* and *Secrets of the Great Pyramid.* He is coauthor with Christopher Bird of *Secrets of the Soil* and *The Secret Life of Plants.*

DAVID VALBRACHT, M.A., is a landscape architect. He is a graduate of the United States Military Academy and holds a masters degree in public administration and landscape architecture from Harvard University.

MACHAELLE SMALL WRIGHT is a nature researcher, teacher, flower essence practitioner, and cofounder of Perelandra, a nature research center in the Virginia countryside. She is author of *Behaving As If the God in All Life Mattered* and *The Perelandra Garden Workbook.*

Introduction

JAMES A. SWAN

I live in the middle of a giant love story. The town I live in is Mill Valley, California, and my neighbor, Mount Tamalpais, which rises up from the Pacific Ocean through some of the tallest trees in the world—the towering redwoods of Muir Woods National Park—is nearly half a mile in elevation. The Miwok Indians who once lived here say Tamalpa is a reclining maiden patiently awaiting her suitor. The gentleman in question is named Mount Diablo, a straw-colored peak of similar size bulging up out of the drier Berkeley Hills thirty-five miles to the east. Legend has it that it acquired the name "Mountain of the Devil" because when the Spanish were attacking the Indians of this area, a band led by a powerful shaman retreated to Diablo to perform ceremonies with the aid of the spirit of the mountain. Through the power of human beings and nature working together, it is said that whenever Spanish soldiers approached the mountain, they had visions of a fire-breathing dragon coming out of the mountain to devour them. The soldiers left in fear, sparing the Indians and the mountain, at least for a time.

Joseph Campbell has noted that mythic sentiments are often linked to places, for reasons which may not be apparent to the rational mind. About two miles to the east lies Ring Mountain, a grassy mound which flanks out from the east arm of Mount Tamalpais. Just below the crest of Ring Mountain is a two-car-garage-sized, dark green serpentine stone. A careful inspection of the south face of this soft stone reveals Indian petroglyphs—oval-shaped indentations with a central core about the size of a softball. The Miwok Indians who carved these forms hundreds of years ago are long gone, but we know today that these simple forms were scratched from the rock in a ceremony to pray for a woman to have safe childbirth and a healthy child. The carved forms are said to represent the dilated cervix. Once the carving was done, dust from the rock was rubbed on the woman's body to strengthen the power of the ceremony. Since some of these petroglyphs are an inch deep, it seems likely that the tradition passed from mother to daughter for many generations.

Modern mechanistic science looks at this stone and declares it an archeological treasure, implying that it is a thing from the past. Today, the stone is in danger from vandalism. Strangely enough, the favorite type of graffiti is lovers' names enclosed in hearts. Other stones are located nearby, and there is no sign telling people that this particular stone's power is associated with fertility. Yet a mind that can stretch beyond the boundaries of materialism might understand that couples instinctively know that the spirit of this place is especially suited to honoring women, children and love.

Off to one side of the stone, a dark green swatch of sedges reveals an artesian spring bubbling up to the surface of the ground. Shamans around the world say that spirits often live near springs. Several sinuous trails also converge on the stone from the surrounding hillside, made originally by the frequent travels of sheep and deer. A dowser would recognize these trails as "track lines," special currents of earth energies which animals recognize and follow. Perhaps track lines extend even above the ground, for nearly every time I come to this stone in the daylight, one or two ravens swoop by, playfully calling out "ork, ork, ork." When one is in accord with nature, nothing happens by chance. An earthwise mind would understand that these ravens are the physical guardians of this mountain, for around the world the raven is known to be the symbol of the wise guide, leading one to the right place at the right time.

Sometimes when the moon is full, bathing the grassy summit of Ring Mountain in shimmering, luminous pale light, friends and I hike to this rock to sit and watch the parade of lights across the bay in San Francisco. All around us, smaller rocks join in the watch, making us feel as if in a crowd watching a giant concert. Upon returning home, more than one visitor to the rock has reported a dream in which an Indian woman appears and sings a soft lullaby.

Modern science insists we have five senses to perceive the world—touch, taste, smell, sight and sound. Master Thomas Lin Yun, a Chinese Feng Shui geomancer, insists we have at least one hundred senses through which we perceive and understand the world around us. Reviewing my description of the stone on Ring Mountain, I note that I have talked about subtle energies of place, unusual dreams, special animal behavior and unconscious behavioral patterns of a consistent nature without visual cues that correspond to the subtle spirit of a place. People today increasingly recognize that ancient peoples cultivated an extraordinary sense of place. However, we often fail to understand that the human species has not evolved away from the ability to sense the subtle voices of nature; we simply have not allowed ourselves to learn to listen to what our host, Gaia, is trying to teach us.

Gaia's Hidden Life is an important collection of essays on coming to our senses and realizing that earth kinship requires a dialogue with nature. Intellectual concepts and principles can help create contexts for understanding, but without the actual perception of nature's messages to us—what Piaget called the "continuity of exchanges" with the environment, which goes on twenty-four hours a day—we live in dangerous alienation from ourselves, as well as from nature.

People are increasingly recognizing that they have lost touch with nature and that the ancient wisdom of the indigenous peoples holds a treasure chest of knowledge about right livelihood. But learning the languages of the creatures of all the communities of life—material and spiritual—is a process that is less understood, especially among those of us who have been educated not to listen and feel. A case in point is the mistaken view that a root cause of today's environmental crisis is an "anthropocentric," or human-centered worldview. The ravens flapping past me on Ring Mountain understand that they are both part of a great web of life and the center of their own perceptual process. They assure me that we humans are no different.

I do not know if ravens dream, but seeing one asleep, up close, and noting its rapid eye movements in deep sleep, I suspect they do. Humans most definitely do dream. My friends, the Native American shamans who speak with ravens frequently and more fluently than I, agree that there are two main types of dreams. Dreams of the body pertain to mundane personal matters—the kind of thing Freud helped us to understand. Dreams of the spirit, however, are extraordinarily vivid technicolor ventures into the timeless world where myths come to life.

People have prayed for dreams of the spirit on mountain tops and in caves for thousands of years. Shamans say that if you are blessed by such a dream, in which you meet a creature half-animal and half-human, or one that changes back and forth from human to animal form, you have met an animal of great totemic power. Such beliefs are also an example of "anthropomorphism," the primary perceptual mechanism of anthropocentric thinkers. The ravens tell me that shamans are the best psychologists. If I believe the ravens, which I frequently find more helpful than two-leggeds, I would have to say that anthropocentrism is a false demon, as it is very natural for humans to see the world as an image of themselves. In fact, if we deny such perception, we castrate our personal power in the name of self-righteousness. "Truth will get you to righteousness, but righteousness will never get you to truth," Ram Dass has often reminded us. Environmental pollution starts in the human mind, and the real eco-villain of perception is egocentrism, which leads to delusions of divinity and frequently to what we call "power trips."

For the past twenty years I have been conducting research on people who seem to have achieved an extraordinary state of harmony with nature.[1] Some are dedicated environmentalists who walk the streets in suits and dresses and have impressive titles after their names. Others are rattle-shaking shamans. While their lifestyles are often different, they share the view that they achieve most of their personal power not from ego dominance, but from surrendering to forces beyond their control. Their ability to win legal battles about preserving the wilderness, write moving ecological books, paint or photograph nature with extraordinary talent, or heal seemingly incurable patients is ultimately due to achieving a state of mind in which they slip into oneness with nature and become an agent able to focus and facilitate natural forces into actions which result in greater ecological harmony and balance. People who are deeply committed to conservation share the ability to be voices for a species or a place. In return for helping protect a species or place, they are seemingly honored by the universe. James Lovelock, developer of the Gaia hypothesis (see Chapter 6) is a case in point. Lovelock acknowledges that the wellspring for his living earth thesis, as well as for his extraordinary environmental leadership, has been his visits to a special hill near his home in England. The ancient Church of St. Michel de Rupe sits on top of this hill in the town of Brentor. Lovelock says that the mood on this hill is special and inspiring.[2]

Lovelock supports his view that Gaia is alive by noting that we can see that the earth is a self-regulating, homeostatic system. If Gaia is alive, and we are, then we both must be parts of a larger self-regulating system, for in a systems paradigm, all things are interconnected. The record of history shows us that pilgrimages to special places, such as Lovelock's sacred hill in Brentor or the fertility stone on Ring Mountain, serve as touchstones of inspiration for the great religions of the world. Thus it would seem that one integral, self-regulating act involving people and nature is for humans to visit special places which inspire them to let go of their egos and, in so doing, gain greater recognition of the unity of all things. The Sufis say that if a good man undertakes a pilgrimage, things will get better, but if an evil man does the same thing, things will become better or worse. Perhaps this rule helps us understand why Joseph Campbell concluded that a fundamental homeostatic quality in human life is the recognition and cultivation of what Rachel Carson called "a sense of wonder"—the emotion of awe.[3]

The Achilles heel of ancient cultures is superstition, belief not founded in reality. Many skeptics today assert that Gaia is not alive nor that it has any special voice or intelligence. Such a philosophy leads us to conclude that we can mold nature into whatever shape we want, without incurring consequences. This belief eases our ecological guilt, for the more our actions impinge upon creatures like us the more guilt we feel for them. The decline of ozone in the upper atmosphere, the destruction of the tropical rainforests, acid rain, air and water pollution, mountains of garbage and toxic contamination of the biosphere are all examples of egocentric thinking—of failure to look and listen for feedback from the world around us. True systems all have feedback mechanisms; the challenge is to learn to recognize and understand the messages we are being given.

This collection of essays is exciting to me because of the diversity of the authors and the similarity of their views. Scientists, theologians, architects, scholars and shamans all write that life is an interconnected web of intelligence which can be—no, must be—recognized to avert ecological catastrophe. Shamans are masters of perception, but we must also remember that they are tricksters. Raven can laugh and play games as well as speak the truth. Sometimes the human mind has to be tricked into realizing its blindness, because the ego is defensive, as the shaman understands. And so, just to make sure that the shamans are not pulling our leg, in the future, science and shamanism must learn to work together.

My patient raven friends now sitting on top of the stone and preening their silky black coats also remind me of the possibility of interspecies communication. Anyone who owns a dog or a cat or works on a farm knows such communication takes place. Some animal rights people today suggest that an animal should have the same legal rights as a "retarded child."[4] My ravens report this statement makes them furious, since shamans understand that animals can be the wisest of all creatures, if you know how to communicate with them. As the work of Michael Harner amply shows, when humans need information about a decision, they can and readily do undertake psychic journeys to worlds in which they can converse with animals, who provide them with important information about life.[5]

In a similar fashion, shamans pray and perform rituals in hopes of inducing dreams and visions in which they speak with animal spirits, who often have humanlike qualities. Once a person has journeyed to another realm and has made mind-to-mind contact with another species, that person can never see living animals in the same way, for such contact leads to understanding the ancient shamanic teaching that all members of a species are joined in a great tribe which reaches into the spirit world, in which a spirit keeper of that species resides. (Rupert Sheldrake calls such a grouping a "morphogenetic field.") Some who have reason to know might argue that we nearly hairless two-leggeds have about the same intelligence as a "retarded" raven.

Such speculations lead us to the question posed by the title of this book—what is the intelligence of Gaia? We can only answer this question with accuracy if we have tried to converse with Gaia. Humans invented English and the printed word. What is Gaia's language? It would be egocentric to suppose that Gaia should speak our language. A tradition among the Pueblo Indians, reported by Frank Waters in his book *The Man Who Killed the Deer*, is that as children come of age, they are led into an underground room called a *kiva* where they sit in silence for up to nine months. Emerging from this womb, the children are said to be "born to the second mother, the earth." During their nine months in incubation, the children are taught by wise elders to listen to the quiet voices of Gaia, their new mother. In the subdued light in which days merge with nights, dreaming and the para-senses become the primary means of perception. The consciousness and subtle energies of nature coming from Gaia permeate their consciousness, and like normal, healthy humans, they create a language of symbols to make sense of what they are experiencing. Imagine how our world might be different if we had spent such a time in contemplation of Gaia instead of say, a year in junior high school. Consider the psychic connections that would have been made apparent and which forever after would be part of the flow of information available to us. Earth wisdom arises from careful reflection on sensory experiences, which is translated into paradigms of understanding. Today educators argue the need for teaching the concepts of ecology to all students. Hopefully, this soon will be a requirement in all schools. But if we teach only the intellectual concepts of ecology, we will never comprehend fully how to live joyfully in harmony with Gaia. Think of how different cities might be if architects and designers were required to spend nine months learning to communicate with Gaia! We humans must all cultivate the ability to share information directly with the wise, patient, and loving being who carries us through space.

The ravens have just flapped off, swooping and chortling, reminding me that I should now practice what I preach. The soft voice of the stone on Ring Mountain sends out an enchanting lullaby, perhaps Tamalpa and Diablo hear it and will meet here someday to consummate their love, with raven, of course, singing their wedding song. In anticipation of this moment, I return to that soft stone to listen.

Notes

1. James A. Swan. *Nature As Teacher and Healer*. New York, NY: Villard-Random House, 1992.
2. James Lovelock. *Healing Gaia*. New York, NY: Harmony Books,1991.
3. Joseph Campbell. *The Masks of God*. New York, NY: Penguin Books, 1976.
4. Alex Pacheco, quoted in the *New York Times*, January 14, 1989.
5. Michael Harner. *The Way of The Shaman*. New York, NY: Bantam, 1982.

Part One
Worldviews of a Living Cosmos

O Hidden Life! vibrant in every atom;
O Hidden Light! shining in every creature;
O Hidden Love! embracing all in Oneness;
May all who feel themselves as one with Thee,
Know they are also one with every other.

Annie Besant

The Western scientific worldview—the dominant view of Western civilization since the Renaissance—holds that human beings are the most important creatures in the universe. Everything else—plants, animals, rocks, and rivers—exists to serve the needs of humanity. Followed to its logical conclusion, this view deems the harvesting of rainforests, the damming of wild rivers to generate electricity, and the decimation of animal species for their horns and hide as unassailable human rights.

Yet native peoples, mystics, yogis, and other thinkers able to penetrate the veil of appearances have always known that human beings are only one participant in a much larger dance, in which all of nature, in both its material and spiritual manifestations, is joined in a deep and purposeful pattern of unfolding.

The worldviews explored in Part One, drawn from a variety of traditional and contemporary sources, share the conviction that the cosmos and everything in it are alive and significantly interconnected. The cyclic evolution of life and human consciousness postulated by Western esotericists like H. P. Blavatsky and Rudolf Steiner parallels the speculations of Christian mystics Pierre Teilhard de Chardin and Hildegarde of Bingen, who recognized and celebrated the universe's psychic dimension. The view that the earth itself is a living being, popularized by scientist James Lovelock, strikingly echoes the ancient Native American belief that stones, storms, and animals are embued with volition and life.

The essays in this section challenge us to reevaluate humanity's place in the web of life. It reviews growing evidence from both traditional and contemporary sources that a "hidden life" shines in every atom and in every creature of the visible and invisible world.

1

The Living Cosmos

SHIRLEY NICHOLSON

> *Everything in the universe, throughout all its kingdoms, is conscious, i.e., endowed with a consciousness of its own kind and on its own plane of perception. We . . . must remember that simply because we do not perceive any signs which we can recognize—of consciousness— say, in stones, we have no right to say that* no consciousness exists there. *There is no such thing as either "dead" or "blind" matter.*
>
> The Secret Doctrine 1:274

The Secret Doctrine, H. P. Blavatsky's source book of esoteric philosophy, came out in 1888. In it she gathered ideas of an esoteric philosophy that, she said, has been with humanity since before recorded history. Its wisdom has sometimes been expressed openly, as in ancient Greece, and sometimes found only in secret societies and mystery schools.

Since its publication, *The Secret Doctrine* has fed many streams of esoteric thought. Some of its ideas, startling in the nineteenth century, have become mainstream by now. Others remain revolutionary even near the twenty-first century. The essays in this volume corroborate some ideas of the ancient wisdom or theosophy as expressed by Blavatsky and later writers, as well as in ancient sources.

The fundamental basis on which all esoteric philosophy rests is widely discussed today, though it clashed with the materialistic worldview current when Blavatsky proposed it. It is unity, the recognition that the cosmos is one and we are all interconnected. Today we are confronted with this inter-connection in global affairs from business and economics to ecological concerns. We are acutely aware that all humankind shares one planet and that effects in distant parts of that planet influence life everywhere. Acid rain and the hole in the ozone layer dramatize such connections. No one can deny that we are all interdependent with each other and with all of nature.

Esoteric philosophy, or theosophy, one of its names since the time of Ammonius Saccas in the third century, takes the idea of interdependence to a deeper level than does current ecological and economic thinking. Blavatsky spoke of "the radical unity of the ultimate essence of each constituent part of compounds in Nature—from Star to mineral Atom, from the highest Dhyan Chohan (angel) to the smallest infusoria" (S.D. 1:120). That is, everything emerges from "One homogeneous living Substance-Principle, the one radical cause." According to this doctrine, which has been corroborated by generations of seers, sages, and mystics, all nature, including ourselves, is rooted in one essence that is its basic being. In the light of this age-old insight, all that exists emerged from and is permeated and sustained by one Life, one Source, one Divine essence. The rather recent discovery that we are interwoven with nature and cannot abuse it without abusing ourselves is but one of the consequences of this radical unity that lies at the heart of the cosmos.

Esoteric philosophy further holds that this one fundamental Substance-Principle has two aspects—spirit or consciousness and matter. Consciousness is related to intelligence, not only in humans but as universal intelligence that pervades all nature. The term *Divine Mind* signifies the intelligence of nature, an aspect of the Consciousness that inheres in the one Source of all. The term *Spirit* has been used in many ways, but theosophical writers including Blavatsky often use it as synonymous with Consciousness in this wider sense. According to the ancient wisdom, our individual consciousness, one aspect of which is mind, is also rooted in universal Consciousness and Intelligence.

Consciousness and matter always occur together, and neither is superior to the other. As Blavatsky said, "Spirit (or Consciousness) and Matter are . . . to be regarded not as independent realities but as the two facets or aspects of the Absolute, . . . which constitute the basis of conditioned Being, whether subjective or objective" (S.D. 1:15). In other words, everything that exists anywhere in the cosmos has both a material and a conscious side.

The implications of this concept are enormous. It means that every pebble, every mountain, every stream, moon, black hole, or quasar is conscious. That is not to say that seemingly inanimate things are self-conscious as are humans or that they have human capacities for thought and feeling. But it makes clear that there is some quality and degree of consciousness, awareness, sensitivity, and intelligence in everything in the cosmos. We do not respond to nonhuman forms of consciousness; we are usually locked into the one familiar to us. But the cosmos is teeming with expressions of consciousness and intelligence.

Teilhard de Chardin was aware of the life in all nature when he spoke of "the within of things." He held that, as electricity is perceptible in the eel and exists in a lower degree everywhere, so consciousness, perceptible in humans, exists everywhere in nature. Gardner Murphy, the late psychologist, felt that the notion of human consciousness arising from the "primal ooze" does not diminish humans but glorifies the ooze. Erich Jantsch, biologist, wrote, "If consciousness is defined as the degree of autonomy a system gains in the dynamic relations with its environment, even the simplest . . . systems such as chemical . . . structures have a primitive form of consciousness" (*The Self-Organizing Universe* 1980, p. 40). Many nature-lovers feel that it is possible to enrich our being and expand our consciousness immensely by opening to the wider life around us.

Many ecologically aware people today are groping toward recognizing the conscious, living aspect of nature as understood by ancient cultures and simpler peoples. For instance, Native Americans speak of Sister Stream or Grandfather Eagle, acknowledging the life of natural entities. Shamanistic, nature-centered cultures see natural objects as infused with consciousness, intelligence, and power. The spirits of trees, mountains, rocks have been revered in many Eastern cultures from ancient times. More recent experiments such as those at Findhorn tend to confirm that there is indeed consciousness and intelligence in the natural world. The concept of the Earth as a living, regulating intelligence, Gaia, is gaining acceptance today.

Theosophy adds still another dimension to the idea of consciousness and life in nature. Blavatsky, Geoffrey Hodson, Rudolph Steiner and many other exponents of esoteric philosophy have written of an unseen hierarchy of beings that guide nature from an inner level. In the Kabbalah these are called *Sephiroth*; in Judaism, *Elohim*; in Christianity, *angels, archangels, seraphim*; in Hinduism, *devas*. According to theosophy, they are expressions of the One Life and the Divine Mind that fashion and guide the cosmos from within. As Blavatsky put it, "The universe is worked and guided from within outward" (S.D. 1:274).

These Intelligences embody universal archetypes that mold material forms. The shape and pattern of a pine tree, for instance, seems to follow an archetype, an "idea in the mind of God," as it has been called. Experiments show that if pine branches are tied to the trunk of a young tree, they will grow out from the tie at exactly the same angle at which free branches grow. The growth seems to follow a pattern imposed from within the tree. According to esoteric philosophy, unseen intelligences orchestrate the growth and infuse the forms with their own life and intelligence. They guide evolution, the development and decline of living species. "The whole Kosmos is guided, controlled, animated by almost endless series of Hierarchies of sentient beings, each having a mission to perform" (S.D. 1:274).

These beings vary in degree of consciousness and intelligence —from vast Dhyan Chohans, who are the architects of the universe, to local nature spirits involved with tending a single garden plot of a few plants. Esoteric philosophy holds that they live at subtle, superphysical levels that our senses cannot detect. But sensitives, clairvoyants, and shamans, who have perception beyond the physical senses, describe such beings and report communicating with them. Tribal people that live in tune with nature speak of these beings and cultivate a relation with them. Cultures such as the Celtic have reported contact with beings such as "little people" since ancient times.

For some centuries the Western world has considered nature as a material phenomenon not connected with human consciousness and has shut out awareness of unseen intelligence around us. In recent decades we have been forced to recognize our dependence and interconnection with all peoples and with nature. Perhaps the next step for us is to awaken the archaic awareness of the living intelligence inherent in nature and to learn to cooperate with it for the good of the planet and all peoples.

There are many ways we can deliberately interact with the consciousness and intelligence of nature, not the least of which is to expand and enrich our own consciousness to include the life of nature. We get intimations of nature's life when we stand on a mountaintop and sense its massive, uplifting presence, or feel the fury in a storm, or absorb the dynamic peace of a forest. We can learn from Native Americans and other nature-based cultures how to cultivate this awareness. We can try to sense the life in a tree, a lake, a mountain, or a crystal.

Blavatsky gives us a hint about the state of mind needed to begin to realize the life in nature: " 'Man can neither propitiate nor command the *Devas*' it is said. But by paralysing [quieting] his lower personality, and arriving thereby at the full knowledge of the *non-separateness* of his higher Self from the One absolute Self, man can, even during his terrestrial life, become as 'One of Us.' " By centering in the One Life, we can learn to cooperate and cocreate with its agents, the devas and nature spirits, in building a world based on harmony with nature and its unseen life.

2

The Dance of Life

ELISABET SAHTOURIS

It was in the search for life on other planets that we discovered what a live planet is—and that we ourselves are part of the only live planet in our solar system.

The first astronauts to see the whole earth with their own eyes were astonished by what they saw. Although they couldn't see any of the living creatures they knew to be on it, the earth itself looked very much alive—like a beautiful glowing creature pulsing or breathing beneath its swirling, veillike skin.

Scientists, of course, cannot simply trust the way things *look.* After all, science was built on the discovery that the earth is *not* the unmoving center of the universe, much as it looks to be just that. Nevertheless, it was seeing our planet from afar for the first time and noting how very different from other planets it appeared that inspired new ideas and studies of Earth.

Long before we saw our planet in this new way, scientists had adopted the view that the earth with its various environments is a nonliving geological background for life, living creatures having evolved upon it by accident and having adapted to it by natural selection. The Scottish scientist James Hutton, who is remembered as the father of geology, seems to have been virtually ignored when, in 1785, he called the earth a living superorganism and said its proper study should be physiology. A century later the Russian philosopher Y. M. Korolenko told his nephew, Vladimir Ivanovitch Vernadsky, that the earth was a live being, and though it is not clear that Vernadsky believed this himself, his studies of earth took a very different view of life than did those of other scientists.

Vernadsky called life "a disperse of rock," because he saw life as a chemical process transforming rock into highly active living matter and back, breaking it up, and moving it about in an endless cyclical process. The Vernadskian view is the concept of life as rock rearranging itself, packaging itself as cells, speeding its chemical changes with enzymes, turning cosmic radiation into its own forms of energy, transforming

16

itself into ever evolving creatures and back into rock. This view of living matter as continuous with, and as a chemical transformation of, nonliving planetary matter is very different from the view of life developing *on* a nonliving planet and adapting to it.

While this Vernadskian view is stimulating much research in the Soviet Union, it never became widely known in the West. The biologist G. E. Hutchinson was one of the very few Western scientists of this century who took an interest in and promoted Vernadsky's view that life is a geochemical process of the earth.

Then the independent English scientist James Lovelock, at NASA during the search for life on Mars, knowing nothing of Vernadsky's work, shocked the world of science by suggesting that the geological environment is not only the product and remainder of past life but also an active creation of living things. Living organisms, said Lovelock, continually renew and regulate the chemical balance of air, seas, and soil in ways that ensure their continued existence. He called this idea—that life creates and maintains precise environmental conditions favorable to its existence—the Gaia hypothesis, at the suggestion of his Cornwall neighbor, the novelist William Golding.

The Gaia hypothesis is now recognized as Gaia theory, but it is still controversial among scientists. Lovelock, like his predecessor Hutton, calls Earth-as-Gaia an organism or superorganism and claims its proper study is physiology. Yet he also calls Gaia a self-stabilizing mechanism made of coupled living and nonliving parts—organisms and physical environments—which affect one another in ways that maintain Earth's relatively constant temperature and chemical balance within limits favorable to life. Lovelock describes this mechanical system as a *cybernetic device* working by means of feedback among its coupled parts to maintain Earth's stable conditions in the manner of a thermostat-controlled heating system that maintains house temperature, or an automatic pilot that keeps an airplane on course. This concept of Gaia as a cybernetic device is far more acceptable within the mechanical worldview that still dominates science than is the concept of Gaia as a live organism.

For Lovelock "organism" and "mechanism" are equally appropriate concepts, but in fact the two concepts contradict each other logically, and this causes confusion around the whole issue of Gaia theory. The concept of life—by any definition, including the autopoietic definition of self-producing and self-renewing living systems—is not logically consistent with the concept and reality of mechanism.

For one thing, life cannot be part of a living being; life is the essence or process of the whole living being. If Gaia is the living earth, then it would be as meaningless to say that life creates its own environments or conditions on earth as it would be to say that life creates its own environments or conditions in our bodies. Life *is* the process of bodies, not one of their parts, and we maintain that the same is true for Gaia-Earth—that life is its process, its particular kind of working organization, not one of its parts. We can still say that organisms within Gaia create their environments and are created by them, in the sense that we say cells create their own environments and are created by them in our bodies. In other words, there is continual and mutually creative interaction between holons and their surrounding holarchies. But we do not divide living bodies or holarchies into "life" and "non-life."

If we accept the autopoietic definition of life, we see another contradiction between Gaia as a living being and Gaia as a mechanical system in which life and non-life are coupled parts. An autopoietic system is self-producing and self-maintaining. It must constantly change or renew itself in order to stay the same—your body renews most of its cells within each seven years of your life, for instance. No mechanism has ever done this, because a mechanism is not self-ruled but other-ruled—produced and repaired (or programmed for repair) from the outside. It cannot, and therefore does not, change itself by its own rules, and that one fact points out the essential difference between living systems and mechanical ones including even the most sophisticated computers and cybernetic robots. A contradiction arises if we define Gaia at once as a living organism and as a cybernetic device—a contradiction that is causing confusion about Gaia theory among scientists.

Our position then, is that the earth meets the biological definition of a living organism as a self-creating autopoietic system, and that only limited aspects of its function—never its essential self-organization—may be usefully modeled by cybernetic systems, just as we can usefully model aspects of our own physiology (for instance, temperature regulation) as cybernetic feedback systems.

*   *   *

Let us look now at the planet Earth as a self-producing living organism, which we call Gaia to distinguish it from a nonliving planet with life upon it. Lovelock's first clue to Gaia came to him when he was comparing the atmospheres of different planets. The atmospheres of the other planets in our solar system all make sense chemically—they are stable mixtures of gases. Only Earth has an atmosphere that is quite impossible by the laws of chemistry. Its gases should have burned each other up long ago!

Yet if they had, Earth would have no living creatures. And of course it *does*. They make and use almost the entire mixture of gases we call the atmosphere, ever feeding it new supplies as they use it and as it burns itself up chemically. This activity of living things always keeps the atmosphere in just the right balance for the life of Earth to continue. We can compare it to the activity of our cells in producing, using, and renewing the blood, lymph, and intercellular fluids flowing around them.

Living creatures, for example, produce four billion tons of new oxygen every year to make up for use and loss. They also make huge amounts of methane, which regulates the amount of oxygen in the air at any time, and they keep the air well diluted with harmless nitrogen. In fact, the Gaian atmosphere is held at very nearly 21 percent oxygen all the time. A little more and fires would start all over our planet, even in wet grass. A little less and we, along with all other air-breathing creatures, would die.

Every molecule of air you breathe, with the exception of trace amounts of inert gases such as argon and krypton, has actually been recently produced inside the cells of other living creatures. Thus the atmosphere is almost entirely the result of the constant production of gases by organisms. If these smaller organisms within the great Gaian organism stopped making and balancing the gases of our air, the atmosphere would burn itself up rather quickly. And if living things didn't turn salty nitrates into nitrogen and pump that nitrogen into the air, the seas would become too salty for life to go on in them, and the atmosphere would lose its balance. The right balance of chemicals and acid in the seas and in the soil, and even the balance of temperature all over the earth—all of the conditions necessary for the life of our planet, that is—are regulated within the planet as they are in our bodies.

Our sun has been growing larger and hotter ever since the earth was formed, yet the earth has kept a rather steady temperature—in much the same way that a warm-blooded animal keeps a steady temperature while things get cooler or hotter around it.

Old attempts to explain how geological mechanisms might regulate the earth's temperature are giving way to new explanations of how a live planet does it. Part of the complicated system involves regulating "greenhouse gases" such as carbon dioxide and methane, which trap solar heat; another part involves controlling the amount of cloud cover to let in more or less sunlight. Perhaps the earth even creates ice ages to cool its fevers.

In our own bodies, there are always things going on to upset the balance of oxygen or salt or acid in our blood and cells. Yet the parts of our living body work together constantly against these upsets of balance. Just so, it seems that the parts of the earth work together to help it recover from its own imbalances, though as yet we know little about how this is done.

Although we have learned much about how the complex coordinated systems of our own bodies function, we can hardly even dream of knowing everything involved in building and running such systems. We seldom reflect on the fact that our bodies work without asking anything of our conscious, thinking minds. We need not even be aware of what is going on, much less having to think or plan or *do* anything about it. And a good thing this is, because we would most certainly mess up our bodies' wonderful work if we interfered in it in an attempt to control it ourselves. Lewis Thomas, an American scientist who is best known for his popular essays on science, has said that for all his physiological knowledge, he would rather be put behind the controls of a jumbo jet than be put in charge of running his liver. Any one of our organs is more complicated by far than the most complicated computer we've invented—and it knows how to run itself, repair itself, and work in harmony with all other organs.

In some sense, even if not in the sense of conscious minds, our bodies and other living cells and bodies *know* what is good for them—they know just how they should be balanced as well as how to do the balancing. Physiologists call this still mysterious property of life "body wisdom." It is clear that such wisdom, or intelligence, can evolve without conscious mind or conscious purpose. So if we see our Gaian planet acting "intelligently" or "wisely" in its own interest, without planning ahead or being aware, without having anything like a mind in the human sense, it should not seem strange to us. We would do well to acknowledge and respect Gaian wisdom in the sense that Thomas suggests we respect the wisdom of our bodies.

The sooner we recognize and respect Gaia as an incredibly complex self-organized living being, the sooner we will gain enough humility to stop believing we know how to manage the earth. If we stay on our present course and cling to our present belief in our ability to control the earth while knowing so little about it, our disastrously unintelligent interference in its affairs will not kill the planet, as many people believe, but it *will* very likely kill us as a species.

*   *   *

Starting with physicists' current view of cosmic beginnings, we have seen that the universe has tremendous energy to spend—and that it spends this energy evolving itself into ever more complicated patterns, including those we recognize as alive. We have come to believe that the total useful, or working, energy of the universe—according to the laws of physics, in particular the law of entropy—is gradually running down. Yet living creatures collect, store, and increase working energy wherever they find it, violating this law. To keep the laws of physics consistent, scientists believe that in increasing energy locally living beings must be decreasing the energy of their environment at an even greater rate. Only thus would they satisfy the overall demands of the entropy law, otherwise known as the second law of thermodynamics—the law which says that things are running down as a whole. This implies that living things must use up and thereby degrade their environment, making it ever less useful to other living things.

On our planet this would mean that each form of life gradually uses up or degrades its environmental supplies until it chokes itself off and dies. Indeed it seems that some living creatures sometimes behave in just that way, as did the first bacteria, which used up the ready-made sugars and acids in their environment, and as we humans do when we use up and destroy our natural resources. But when one kind of organism creates such a crisis, the living Gaian system as a whole seems to find a solution. On a planetary scale we find the enrichment of species and their environments in variety and complexity—a single system recycling its supplies without running down the way mechanical systems do.

What about the planet as a whole living being, then? Does it degrade its environment as it organizes itself? Over billions of years—surely a more than adequate test for the law of entropy—our Gaian planet has continued to self-organize in ever greater complexity. It lives off the sun, to be sure, but the sun does not burn up faster because the earth uses its energy, and the waste heat given off by the earth cannot be construed as degrading its cold space environment. It would seem that the entropy law, which is one of the laws of thermodynamics, and was "discovered" to explain how certain nonliving mechanical systems such as steam engines work, can tell us nothing about living systems.

Again we run into a contradiction between mechanics and organics. Many non-scientists, many readers of this book, probably find it strange that scientists *do* try to explain life in mechanical terms, feeling intuitively (and rightly) that there is something wrong with the whole idea.

* * *

Recent discoveries in physics strongly suggest that the nature of the universe was from the beginning such that it would come alive however and wherever possible. Perhaps planets are to our galaxy something like seeds and eggs are to multicelled earth creatures in that far more of them are produced than can actually form new living beings. And perhaps, like the cells in our own bodies, the "cells" of the universe, in the form of star systems or planets, may be alive for a time and then die; after death, their components may be recycled—in other words, the energy locked up in their atoms and molecules may be used again by some other part coming alive and needing supplies to develop. Those parts of the universe that seem most lifeless to us may be something like its skeleton—providing a framework as does the core of the earth in supporting its living surface, or the deadwood forming most of a redwood tree under its living surface.

If we agree that nature is not mechanical but organic, why should we not understand the energetic motion of the very first whirling shapes in the early universe as the first stirrings of that self-organizing process leading to living organisms?

The spiraling pregalactic clouds, composed of spiraling atoms, held themselves together, drew in more matter-energy from their surroundings, built it into themselves, and lost energy again to their surround. In this process of energy exchange they evolved into new, more complicated forms. By the time we get to galaxies and to fully formed stars within them, the dance toward life has become quite complicated already. We are only beginning to discover how complicated are the structure and process of our own sun star, and we still have much to learn about the way our own planet rearranges its matter into those lively chemical patterns we all agree to call living organisms.

Earth, we now know, is the only planet in our solar system that had just the right size, density, composition, fluidity of elements, and just the right distancing and balancing of energy with its sun star and satellite moon to come alive and stay so. Yet its life *is* a result of this fortunate confluence of conditions, just as the development of a plant or animal embryo is. Our living earth is likely no more a freak accident than is the seedling that grows or the frog egg that matures. All are the inevitable result of right compositions and conditions. Some scientists believe the conditions were so special that Earth is a rare phenomenon, perhaps the only such planet in the universe. But there is no better reason to believe this than there is to believe that living planets are as common in the universe as are the successful seedlings and hatchlings of Earth. And if this is so, there are billions of other live planets in the billions of galaxies, each with billions of star systems.

The only part of the earth that is more energetic than living creatures is the lava erupting or oozing through its crust, but most of that energy is quickly lost as heat pouring into the atmosphere, while living things recycle their energy within and among themselves and from one generation to another. On the whole, the living matter of the earth, as Vernadsky would call all its living creatures taken together, is up to a thousand times more active, more energetic, than the rocky crust from which it and they evolved. Hardly an example of the decreasing energy predicted by the entropy law! Where did all this energy come from?

The giant molecules from which the first creatures formed themselves were produced by powerful solar and lightning energy, some of which got locked up in them. The creatures formed from these molecules released this energy by breaking up other big molecules, or learned to use solar energy directly as we have seen, maintaining themselves and producing an oxygen-rich atmosphere in the process. Oxygen-burning respirers get their energy by consuming fermenters, photo-synthesizers, and one another. Organisms can thus convert stored energy or direct solar energy into other useful forms of energy—the energy of motion, of heat, of chemical reaction, even of electricity—while the atmosphere regulates the kinds and amounts of solar radiation available, keeping it within appropriate bounds. As Lewis Thomas has said, earth seems to be a creature "marvelously skilled in handling the sun."

Meanwhile, the raw materials of the earth's interior spew or well up as new rock to be transformed into living matter, while old living matter, dead and compressed back into rock, sinks back into the soft mantle at the edges of tectonic plates. On the earth's surface scientists have a hard time finding any rock that has not been part of living organisms, that was not transformed into living matter before it became rock again.

Thus virtually all of the atmosphere and all of the rocks have been through at least one phase in which they were living matter. The same is true of the soil and the seas. It is easier to distinguish between life and death than between the domains of life and nonlife we have assigned to biologists and geologists. In fact, virtually every geological part or feature of earth we can find is a product of our planet's life activity. Further, living organisms have "invented" 99.9 percent of all kinds of molecules we know, almost all of them back when bacteria were the only creatures around. This is auto-poiesis—the self-production we take, in this book, as the definition of living beings.

* * *

What confused us for so long—kept us from seeing that our planet is alive as a whole—is at least in part our own human space (size) and time perspective. Since we easily see ourselves and many kinds of plants and animals as wholes separate from one another and from their surround, we have had as hard a time recognizing ourselves or them as parts of a single being as we had recognizing that we ourselves are made of separate cells. In one instance we saw the parts more easily than the whole; in the other we saw the whole more easily than the parts.

If we had a magnifying glass powerful enough to let us see

everything in the world around us at the level of molecules, we would see life in the energetic molecular dance of chemical reactions and recombinations—the dance that weaves molecules into new patterns, some livelier than others. But instead, our experience comes through eyes that see life as a collection of separate plants and animals. This makes it hard for us to see them as parts of their environment, much less as parts of a whole living planet. Yet when we see the whole earth from far enough away to show it on a movie screen and speed up its rotations, it *does* look alive, though we can no longer see its "separate" plant and animal parts. We have no way of seeing our world of life-within-life at all its size levels at once, but we *can* use our minds to put information about different levels together and understand its living holarchy of holons.

The smaller living holons or organisms within Gaia grow and reproduce, so we have come to think of growth and reproduction as essential features of living beings. The autopoietic definition of life, however, does not include them as essential or defining features; rather, they are consequences of the autopoietic life process—something that may or may not happen, as when people do or do not reproduce. Therefore, the argument that the earth cannot be alive because it does not grow or reproduce does not hold.

Cells are the "packages" in which living matter housed itself when our planet came alive; they contain and connect autopoietic systems by enclosing them in open boundaries— membranes of their own making that allow materials and energy to be exchanged with the environment, as does the self-produced atmospheric membrane of the earth. In a sense, the whole earth is a giant cell within whose boundary membrane other smaller cells multiply, die, and are recycled in such a way that the whole need not grow. This is a wonderfully efficient way to make living beings (planets) possible in cosmic deserts with only stars for nourishment. Because our perception has been so focused on separate organisms in their physical or social environments, we tend to see insect, animal, and human societies, as well as whole ecosystems, as collections of individuals that have come to live and function together. It is actually more appropriate to see that such collections have always functioned as wholes which were never separated into completely individual beings. Individual creatures surely exist within and across species, but none could ever become completely independent, though some are relatively more or less independent than others. All their complex forms and ways have evolved within a single system, just as our cells evolved their separate functions within an inseparable whole. Their connections with their species fellows and with their ecosystem are as holons within holarchies up to the whole Gaian organism—connections that were never broken and cannot be, just as our cells cannot break their connections with their organs or their/our whole bodies.

Scientists who try to understand Gaia as a collection of separate organisms mechanically coupled to nonliving environments get bogged down in arguments about whether the organisms—collectively called the *biota*, or "life"—could actually have joined forces on purpose to "control" the conditions of their *abiotic*, or nonliving, environment in their own interest. How could all bacteria—assuming the Gaian mechanism was formed when there were no other creatures—get together, they ask, to work cooperatively and purposively for their own good?

This argument, like the other confusions previously discussed, is another result of seeing Gaia as a mechanism. Purpose is an essential aspect of machinery, all machines being built to serve the purposes of their inventors and users. Thus, machines are "other-ruled," as we said earlier. And so, seeing Gaia as a mechanism raises the question of purpose. But purpose is a taboo in scientific descriptions of nature, because God, whom Renaissance scientists saw as the Grand Engineer of natural mechanism, is no longer part of scientific explanation. Scientists thus argue a logical contradiction: that nature is mechanical but has no creator and no purpose.

If we see natural organisms as self-ruled autopoietic systems that evolved without benefit of a purposive God, we see that they simply evolve wherever they are not prevented from so doing, wherever their energetic development is mutually consistent with whatever else is going on around them. No one argues about whether or not our bodies regulate our temperature "on purpose"—we simply accept that they do so because they evolved that way, "purpose" being limited to the relatively recent (in evolution) conscious mind, about which we will say more later.

The answer to the question of whether bacteria assembled purposively to control their environments is thus that they did *not* "get together" any more than did the cells of our bodies assemble themselves after they had formed. All bacteria are living matter transformed from earth's rocky crust and packaged in open boundaries that keep them functioning as a single system. They are not separate from one another or from the crust; they are not parts of an assembled mechanism but part of a single Gaian life process we can call *geobiological.* The Gaian organism has evolved to do what it needs to do in order to preserve itself as naturally as we do and with no more purpose than we find in our own bodies.

If Gaia is a single live planet or organism, why did its rock rearrange itself into such an astounding variety of individual creatures? Why not just a planet holon, instead of a planetary holarchy of holons?

We might as well ask why the first gas clouds sorted themselves into individual galaxies, and the galaxies into stars and planets and other space bodies. The answer, as we now begin to understand, is that life becomes ever more stable as it becomes more complex! Mechanical systems may be more vulnerable to breakdown as they become more complex, but this seems not to be true of living systems. The Gaian division of labor or function among different species—different *kinds* of creatures—makes possible a division of labor similar to that of our bodies, which function efficiently through the combined work of many different kinds of organs. No place, or environment, on earth—from the barest mountaintop to the deepest part of the sea—has fewer than a thousand different life species, mostly microbial, forming it and doing different things to keep it alive and evolving. If a planet does come alive, it would seem that it must come alive everywhere, not just in patches.

Scientists are only now beginning to work out the physiology of our Gaian planet—to understand why the introduction of a single new species into a complex environment can make that environment ill, just as the introduction of a single species of disease microbe into our bodies can make *us* ill; they are only now coming to understand why the destruction of an environment such as tropical forest can unbalance the whole planet, just as removing an organ from our bodies can unbalance us. Yet we are also discovering that Gaia's incredible complexity makes her tougher and more resourceful than we are. We are far more likely to choke our own species off by destroying our environment than we are to kill Gaia. Gaia's evolving dance of life will continue with or without us.

The word "evolution," when used in talking about human

dancing, means the changing patterns of steps in any particular dance. A dance thus evolves when its step patterns change into new ones as the dance goes on. In exactly this sense, the evolution of Gaia's dance—of Earthlife—is the changing patterns of steps in the interwoven self-organization of creatures and their habitats over time.

We see that Gaia's dance is endlessly inventive. Trying out new step patterns in a dance is called *improvising*, as a creative dance is not planned out in advance. Rather the dancers improvise as they go, testing each new step for its fit with other steps and with the whole dance pattern. Gaia's dance seems to have evolved by such improvisation, the working out of basic steps used over and over in new combinations.

In Gaia's dance, all organisms smaller than Gaia, from the first bacteria to ourselves, have been built from DNA and protein molecules. The very complex patterns of these giant molecules are almost entirely made of only six kinds of atoms—hydrogen, carbon, nitrogen, oxygen, phosphorus, and sulfur. And as we saw, *all* kinds of atoms other than hydrogen were created all over the universe under pressure inside stars as combinations of the original hydrogen atoms, which were combinations of the original subatomic particles.

There are very few kinds of protein or other molecules on earth today whose patterns the ancient bacteria had not already invented billions of years ago. Nor have any new basic life processes been developed since bubblers, blue-greens, and breathers invented the three ways of making ATP energy molecules: fermentation, photosynthesis, and respiration. In other words, evolution since then has been a matter of rearranging not only the same atoms but also the same molecules and life processes into an endless variety of new creature patterns. This, then, is Gaia's dance—the endless improvisation and elaboration of elegantly simple steps into the awesomely beautiful and complex being of which we are the newest feature.

3

The New Story: A Christian Mystical View of Nature

SEAN McDONAGH

How, we may ask, can the human community free itself from the grip of the machine metaphor? Its many benefits have seduced and dazzled us. Unfortunately, those of us who have benefitted most from the labour-saving inventions of modern technology are often not conscious of the negative aspects of technology. We fail to record accurately what the ever-increasing web of technology has done to the vast majority of people in Third-World countries and to the Earth itself. We need a much deeper understanding of technology before we let loose its power in our world. In other words, we need a new context of meaning for technology which will allow us to pinpoint those technologies which enhance life on Earth and those which retard it. In order to do this effectively, we need a new understanding of the story of life on Earth and the creative role which human beings and their artifacts must play in that story.

In a word, there is a need for a new story or myth of the emergence of the Earth. Since the dawn of human consciousness, story has been the basic vehicle of human understanding and meaning. In every culture, throughout history, storytellers have enthralled and delighted people and brought joy and meaning to their lives.

The 'story' which I will present here is a story of our universe which comes to us through modern ways of knowing. Strange as it might seem, since storytelling is not often associated with the discourse of science, the tellers of this story are the scientists. They have shaped and refined an intelligible and exciting new story of our universe. The sequence of the story is not the work of any single scientist but is the cooperative venture of many individual scientists and scientific disciplines. The astronomers who have gazed with wonder on the night sky with their ever more powerful telescopes have joined with physicists who have studied the minute particles of matter. To clarify important elements of the story, biologists and geneticists have spent long hours examining living tissue. Sometimes the whole scientific community has moved forward, piecing together the most fascinating and stupendous story ever told.

The task of fashioning the story continues. Even with satellite probings of the heavens and explorations into the depths of the oceans, the picture is by no means complete. Nevertheless, the broad outlines are there, and the story is revealing itself as one of extraordinary creativity, variation, abundance and beauty.

More important, this is our story, one which gives the Earth community, and especially human beings, a breadth and depth hitherto undreamed of. It is truly a revolutionary story and confirms, without a shadow of doubt, that the universe does not run on mechanistic principles. All the processes of nature, from the emergence of life itself to the cycle of the seasons and the metabolic processes of living forms, are intimately related. This new story is a powerful antidote to the mechanistic story of the past four hundred years. It shows the old story to be shallow in comparison to the new one's magnificent span of twenty billion years. It also tells us that unless we abandon mechanistic science and technology we place in jeopardy the future florescence of this beautiful Earth. It tells us that to attempt to understand human beings outside the context of the emergent universe is to restrict ourselves unduly and to hamper any genuine effort at self-understanding, either as individuals or as a species. This new story must, more and more, begin to shape our lives, even our religious sensibilities, and it must provide norms of behaviour for human activity. Above all it provides the spiritual energies for the whole human community to begin to live according to the dictates of the story.

We have seen that the physical and biological articulation of the story gradually emerged from the scientific community during the later part of the nineteenth century and the early twentieth century. Partly because of the antipathy and mis-understanding between the scientific community and most religious people, one essential dimension was missing. The story lacked spiritual understanding.

It took the genius and courage of Pierre Teilhard de Chardin (1881-1955)—a priest and paleontologist—to bridge this gap. Teilhard insisted that any complete telling of the story of the

mythology—has mechanisms which optimize the conditions suitable for life. Evidence in this direction is the fact that the oxygen content of the air was stabilized at about twenty-one percent and the temperature of the Earth has remained stable for hundreds of millions of years.

So from a variety of sources this vision of an evolving Earth must today become the norm of what is real and worth striving for within every institution on the planet. Human beings must enter as creatively as possible into the processes of the planet in order to discern the true role of the human within the Earth's story. This emergent story will give the human community basic norms to guide the human-Earth relationship in a way that will be mutually enriching and enhancing. These norms must be enshrined in our political, economic, social, commercial and religious institutions so that these enhance the Earth community and do not impoverish it.

Hildegarde of Bingen: The Greening of the Earth

The approach of Hildegarde of Bingen (1098-1178) adds a unique dimension. Unfortunately, her writings are not widely known. Selections from her writings have only been published in English in the last few years. This remarkable woman—poet, musician, painter, visionary, botanist, herbalist, counsellor to the popes, princes and councils of the Church—has a unique contribution to make to the western Christian's appreciation of the natural world. Her approach to the Earth delights in the 'greening of the Earth.'

The Divine is present in the 'greening' of the Earth in a way reminiscent of the fertility poetry of the pre-Christian Celtic religion of much of Europe. Hildegarde captures and celebrates in her writings the uniquely feminine experience of the most intimate processes of the natural world. The taming, organizing skills of Benedict and even the fraternal solicitude for all creatures of Francis are valuable elements of a masculine approach to reality. But Hildegarde celebrates the feminine, fertility dimension. Her poetry pulsates with a rapturous, sensuous love for the Earth. It is full of ardour and passion. In the following poem she delights in the love of the Creator for the creation and does not feel constrained to shy away from explicitly sexual language. 'I compare the great love of Creator and creation to the same love and fidelity with which God binds man and woman together. This is so that together they might be creatively fruitful.'[7]

There is no ambiguity towards creation in Hildegarde; no revulsion at the mention of earthly, bodily or inanimate nature. She does not see the world as evil or corrupting, to be subdued and tamed through ascetical practices. Unlike the writings of many Christian mystics before and since, the person seeking sanctity is not encouraged to run away from the natural world. Hildegarde insists that 'holy persons draw to themselves all that is earthly.' For her, the natural world is not an area of chaos or wilderness which humans must either avoid or do battle with in order to conquer and domesticate. Nature evokes joy, wonder, praise, awe and especially love. She is so beautifully adorned that even her creator approaches her in the guise of a lover to embrace her with a kiss.

> As the Creator loves his creation
> so creation loves the Creator.
> Creation, of course, was fashioned to be adorned
> to be showered
> to be gifted with the love of the Creator
> The entire world has been embraced by this kiss.[8]

Many cultures around the world revere the Earth as mother and celebrate her fruitfulness. It is not surprising then that Hildegarde takes up this image. The nourishing role of the Earth is not confined to our biological needs but includes our emotional and spiritual well-being. Finally, the Earth is most creative in moulding the very flesh of the Son of God.

> The Earth is at the same time mother
> She is mother of all
> For contained in her
> are the seeds of all
> The Earth of humankind
> contains all moistness
>   all verdancy
>   all germinating power
> It is in so many ways fruitful
> Yet it forms not only the basic
> raw material for humankind
> but also the substance of God's Son.[9]

Hopefully, when her writings are better known, Hildegarde will assume her rightful place in Christian spirituality. In her company we may be able to overcome the deep-seated fear and hostility for the natural world which is found so frequently in Christian spiritual guides, ancient and modern. With her we can leave aside the gloom, pessimism and guilt that commonly haunt Christian spirituality and joyfully recognize God's presence in the world around us.

In the modern world, women are often to the fore in both the peace movement and the ecological movement. They can more easily identify with the pain and destruction which the Earth is experiencing at the hands of a male-dominated world since they have also been victims. One thinks, for example, of the women camped for a number of years at Greenham Common in England, protesting against the installation of Cruise and Pershing II missiles in western Europe. It is a pity the creation-affirming writings of Hildegarde are not more readily available to them as they protest on behalf of all peoples and the Earth herself at the stupidity of pretending that anyone's security rests in weapons which, if ever used, will bring death to everything on Earth.

Notes

1. Eliade, M., 1976. *Occultism, Witchcraft and Cultural Fashions. Essays in Comparative Religion,* University of Chicago Press, p. 12.
2. Huxley, J. Introduction to Teilhard de Chardin, *The Phenomenon of Man.* Fontana Books, p. 21.
3. *Phenomenon of Man,* p. 329.
4. *Ibid.,* p. 244.
5. *Ibid.,* p. 243.
6. Lovelock, J. E., 1979. *Gaia: A New Look at Life on Earth.* Oxford University Press.
7. Hildegarde of Bingen, *Meditations with Hildegarde of Bingen,* translated by Uhlein, Gabriele, 1982, p. 56. Bear and Company, P. O. Santa Fe, NM 87504-2860.
8. *Ibid.,* p. 65.
9. *Ibid.,* p. 51.

4

1492 and After:
Native American and European
World Views

CLARA SUE KIDWELL

When Christopher Columbus first set foot on the island of Hispaniola in October of 1492, two cultures with fundamentally different world views confronted one another. The Greco-Roman, Judeo-Christian, Western European world view and the Native American world view were based on radically different assumptions about the nature of the physical world. The former is most often characterized as scientific, the latter as magical or religious.

The Native Americans believe in a transcendent power underlying physical reality, a power not understood in rational terms but rather one that arouses feelings of awe and occasionally fear. In the Native American belief system, the forces of nature are manifestations of a transcendent power that has will or volition. Physical forces in nature demonstrate powers of self-movement and choice, and these attributes remove nature from the realm of pure rationality. The European scientific view, on the other hand, presupposes a natural world of physical forces acting according to laws. Those forces have no personal aspect; they can be understood rationally because their behavior is lawful, rather than willful.

There was also common ground between these two quite different traditions. Both Europeans and Native Americans were keen observers of natural phenomena, and both proposed ways of understanding, controlling, and predicting the effects of their actions in the natural environment. The Hopi in the Southwest, for instance, had to produce corn successfully during a very short growing season. They could predict the coming of the seasons and the rains through their observations of the sun's path, and they performed ceremonies timed by the solstices. Columbus was able to chart his voyage to the New World based on his knowledge of the positions of celestial bodies.

Prediction is an essential element in both of these instances; the difference between the European and the Native American approaches is in the underlying assumptions about the nature of the physical world. European science is based on a belief in the lawful behavior of natural forces and the rational understanding of laws. Native Americans look toward personal interaction with the forces of nature through dreams, visions, and ceremonies, and through intuitive ways of comprehending and controlling those forces.

The Native American view is based on the perception that natural forces are powerful because of their ability to change. Power is the ability to move, to have volition, and to make independent choices. The power of will and movement is apparent to the Native Americans in the forces of the environment. Sudden storms, lightning, winds, flash floods—all are dramatic demonstrations of the power of nature to impinge upon the plans of human beings. Forests, mountains, and rivers are sources of power because they are not under the control of humans and because the forces that dwell in them are mysterious. In the Native American mode of thought, these aspects of nature have volition of their own.

The event or object that is powerful cannot be explained by the cycles of ordinary behavior. Stones may have power if they demonstrate the ability to move, or to speak, or to assume a form other than that which they ordinarily have. The Lakota—the western division of the Sioux nation of the Great Plains—attributed power to some stones. It is said that a stone once entered a lodge and struck a man, and people spoke of the stones sending in "rattles through the smoke hole of a lodge."

At one point in the course of his field work among the Saulteau people, a band of the Ojibwa, or Chippewa, tribe living in the Berens River area in Canada, anthropologist A. Irving Hallowell asked a man, "Are all the stones that we see around us alive?" The man thought about the question and then replied, "No, but some are." The question and the answer illustrate a difference between Western science and the Native American view. Hallowell was interested in a general principle that could be applied to all stones. The Salteau man was not interested in all stones, but only in the particular ones that exhibited unusual behavior marking them as powerful. These stones could move, had been heard to talk, and were thus imbued with power.

Indeed, the essence of power in American Indian societies is the event or thing that cannot be explained by the circumstances of everyday life. In this respect there is a profound difference between Native American and European world views. The one is concerned with the unique or unusual event as a sign of power, while the other focuses on the replicable event, the pattern that establishes a generalizable law of nature.

Another example from Hallowell's studies indicates the Native American perception of a connection between observable patterns in the physical world and unusual or seemingly capricious activity. The thunderbird of Ojibwa belief is the great bird whose darting eyes produce lightning and whose flapping wings produce thunder. In the northern woodlands, birds appear in the spring, arriving from the south, and summer storms also move from the south. Throughout the summer the birds and storms are present. In the fall, the birds begin to move south, and the storms begin in the north and also move south. The conjunction of birds and storms can be explained in a scientific manner as the result of climatic patterns, or in the Native American view as the physical manifestation of the great thunderbird spirit.

Certainly Native Americans perceived patterns in their environment. They knew that crops grew because of rain and sun at appropriate times, that animals could be expected at certain places and times, and that the wild rice would begin to ripen when the bear berry bushes bore ripe fruit. All of these events occurred in recognizable and predictable cycles, and knowledge of these cycles was essential to human survival.

The objective of both Europeans and Native Americans was control over the environment. For Europeans, the laws of nature could be understood; they made possible the prediction of natural phenomena. For Native Americans, natural phenomena, despite their changeability which demonstrated the willfulness of nature, were susceptible to human influence and even control.

The personal relationship between Native Americans and the natural world was vitally important. In many tribes, the vision quest provided individuals access to knowledge about the spirits of nature. For other tribes, the initiation into a group of people controlling esoteric knowledge established a sense of relationship with spiritual forces. Ceremonies could be used to assure the coming of rain, if proper ritual activities and human purification were observed. The placement of tobacco on a post could ward off destructive wind storms. Through the knowledge of the spiritual world that they imparted, ceremonies made it possible for people to have a sense of power over the environment.

Physical evidence of the methods by which native people in the New World understood and controlled their environments shows how native and European world views were similar, and ethnographic evidence demonstrates the differences between the two cultures' world views.

Both Europeans and Native Americans had a long tradition of observing and systematizing the movements of celestial bodies. Most Europeans in the sixteenth century believed that the earth was the center of the universe. The Catholic Church cited biblical passages to support this concept. The Bible says, for example, that before the Battle of Jericho, Joshua successfully ordered the sun to stand still in the sky.

In the southwestern part of the United States, the Pueblo Indians believed that the sun was a being who traveled across the sky from his house in the south to his house in the north and then back again. Pueblos had sun watchers who positioned themselves at certain points when they knew the sun would reach one house or the other. These were the times, at the summer and winter solstices, when the sun appeared to rest at a given point on the horizon for several days. Ceremonies in the yearly cycle that dominated Pueblo life were timed according to the solstices, and it was thought that these ceremonies were necessary to assure that the sun would reverse his journey through the sky.

Contemporary Hopi still perform such ceremonies, as do many other Pueblo groups. Many still depend upon the traditional dry farming techniques practiced by their ancestors. They are keenly aware of the short growing season and the possibility of frost. The solstice ceremonies mark not only the sun's journey, but also critical points in the seasons and therefore in the agricultural cycle.

Among agricultural peoples such as the Iroquois in the northeast woodlands, the Pleiades were a marker of seasons. Their first appearance in the evening sky in October signaled the end of the agricultural season. Their disappearance in May marked the time of planting. The Iroquois midwinter ceremony, a time of thanksgiving and social activity, was timed by the appearance of the Pleiades directly overhead. Stories of the Pleiades described them as a group of young people whose unrestrained dancing had led them into the sky.

One of the most dramatic ceremonies associated with the Pleiades was that of the Aztecs, who celebrated the end of a fifty-two-year cycle of celestial events at the time when the Pleiades were directly overhead at midnight. All fires in the city of Tenochtitlán were put out and in one of the temples a captive was put to death, his heart plucked from his chest cavity, and a new fire kindled therein.

This gruesome ceremony was based on sophisticated observation of the movements of celestial bodies. The ceremony was held when the Pleiades and the sun were directly opposite each other—the Pleiades overhead and the sun directly below the earth. It was a marker for the conjunction of the starting points of the 260-day ceremonial calendar and the 365-day solar calendar. The Aztecs believed that both calendars had begun together in the past and that they revolved separately, their beginning points coinciding once every fifty-two years.

A stone formation called the Medicine Wheel on a slope of the Bighorn Mountains in Wyoming is thought to give further evidence of the ability of native peoples to recognize cycles of nature. The Medicine Wheel is a circle of stones with radiating spokes and cairns around its perimeter. Certain alignments of the twenty-eight spokes appear to mark the summer solstice and the rising of stars that mark seasonal changes. The formation is something of an enigma; it is located on an isolated mountainside, often covered with snow at the time of the summer solstice, and undated. Considered along with other such structures throughout North America, it hints at the possibility that hunters, too, were concerned about the celestial world and what its movements meant for the seasonal cycles that governed their lives, and that they had devised ways, through systematic observation of the physical world around them, to predict patterns of those cycles.

Native people in the New World also observed and predicted the actions of their environment through their relationship with plants. The use of plants in Native American societies was based upon close observation of the natural environment and knowledge of the physical effects that plants had on the human body. Plants were used extensively for curing illness, and their physical effects were obvious—emetic, purgative, diuretic, fever-reducing. Peyote, a powerful psychoactive plant, was used in connection with some Native American religious practices. When Jacques Cartier and his men were trapped on their ice-bound ships in the St. Lawrence River in the winter of 1543-44 and many were dying of scurvy, Native Americans found them, recognized their symptoms, and prepared an herbal tea that cured them.

The underlying premise for the efficacy of plants was that the plants had their own powers, manifested in their ability to grow. Plants were considered sentient beings. A medicine person gathering plants acknowledged their abilities and requested, rather than demanded, their healing power.

The use of plant medicines also had a long tradition in Europe and was indeed still a prevailing form of treatment when the New World was discovered by Europeans. Physicians dispensed medicinal simples, herbal remedies based upon the similarity of form between the plant and the Galenic humor —blood, bile, or phlegm—that was believed to be the source of illness. Ginseng, with its forked root that resembles the form of the human body, was widely used. Plants with red juice were prescribed for tonics because of the resemblance to human blood.

Europeans were extraordinarily interested in the wealth of unfamiliar plants and animals that existed in the New World. They were particularly concerned with the curative powers of New World plants, especially as these could be applied to diseases that appeared to originate in the New World. Francisco Hernandez, personal physician to Philip II of Spain, was sent to the New World in 1571 to gather information on the plants and animals there, and his description of native plants include their medicinal properties. His observations of the natural world were within the European intellectual tradition of interest in natural history during the sixteenth century.

In both Europe and the New World, then, systematic observation of natural events was taking place, and systems of explanation were being derived. The Europeans' quest for knowledge was based on close observation of the physical environment and the desire to understand its operation. Throughout the New World, native tribes also sought to understand the powers of their environment and the cycles of the natural world around them. In Europe, although the ideas of Aristotelian natural place, circular motion, and biblical interpretation served to maintain the earth-centered universe, the systematic observation of celestial phenomena provided the body of data that would ultimately lead to the challenging of that concept. The Old World increasingly accepted the immutability of nature and the concept of natural law. In the New World, the concept of the sun as a deity, a sentient being, led to ceremonies designed to influence the sun's actions. Through these ceremonies, Native Americans maintained personal relationships with what they perceived to be the powers of nature.

Concepts of power in Native American societies derive from those societies' close contact with the phenomena of the physical world. Any perceived phenomena, or being, can influence the activities of another being by providing or withholding something essential to survival, whether physical or social.

Hallowell, in his work with the northern Ojibwa in Canada during the 1930's, described the Native American idea of personhood. Persons, in this context, are not only humans, but those aspects of nature that have volition and the ability to control physical forces.

The concept of personhood is important to understanding the concept of power in Native American societies. Since the definition of power includes the ability of forces to interact with one another and to influence each other's behaviors, some way of identifying those forces must be established. To personify them, not in an animistic sense but in the sense of identifying their modes of action, provides a way of examining the relationships among them. To assign each being, human and non-human, an identifiable mode of action is to provide a way to see how Native American people related with each other and with the physical world.

This concept of personhood was certainly foreign to the world view of the Europeans who arrived in the New World in 1492. It was a strikingly different way of explaining the natural environment, which the Europeans approached scientifically. The native world of North and South America was populated not only with humans but with a myriad of other "persons." Their existence was determined by close and systematic observation of both the predictable and un-predictable aspects of nature.

For any group of people who live in close contact with the forces of the environment, who derive their food, clothing, and shelter from the environment directly through their own energies, the power of the forces of nature is obvious. Yet these powers of nature are not idealized in the minds of native people. They are the experience of everyday life, and people realize their dependence upon the actions of the natural environment for their existence. Rather than the primacy of any religious doctrine, then, it is the experience of the environment that furnishes the substance of Native American belief.

5

The Evolution of the Earth and Humanity: A View Based on the Work of Rudolf Steiner

DAVID VALBRACHT

For the peoples of the past, the gods walked on earth. Cultures throughout history have perceived the spiritual nature of the earth and accepted the presence of spirits residing at particular places on the landscape. Spirit of place was accepted as literal truth, not simply as a personification of environmental forces. Spirit beings were recognized, and temples marked their presence on the landscape. Yet gradually these spirits have disappeared from an increasingly industrialized and mechanized landscape. Humanity no longer consults the seers or priests when decisions are made on the use of land. Beliefs and practices concerning nature spirits have been driven underground and remain only in mythology and folklore. Decisions about the use of land are based on economic, legal, and political considerations alone.

The capacity to recognize the spiritual, supersensible nature of the earth is retained by traditional peoples who continue to live in unbroken connection with their lands. These people accept the participation of unseen beings in the activities of the human community and in nature. However, for the peoples of most of the earth, such a connection no longer exists. Separated from the land, employed in jobs having little direct connection with the earth, and educated to ignore the possibility of the spiritual, much of the earth's population can no longer consciously recognize the spirits of the earth. Modern societies have either driven the spirits away or are blind to their presence.

Beliefs in spirits may be dismissed as superstition or interpreted as a primitive way of describing subtle physical forces. By such thinking, we discount the experiences of the past and affirm our cultural superiority. We can, however, choose to respect the beliefs of the past and seek to comprehend objectively the phenomena they have described. In so doing, we take a step towards rediscovering the forces and beings behind the observable workings of nature.

Recognizing and honoring the connection between traditional peoples and their lands is important. Traditional cultures have maintained the tenuous link between humanity and the earth, and we have much to learn from them. Recognizing this, those of us who are not part of such a society must now ask how a connection can be reestablished. We need to find impulses arising out of our own cultural framework which recognize the importance of spirit of place.

A View Based on Rudolf Steiner

The work of Rudolf Steiner suggests ways for recognizing and working with the spiritual forces of the earth. This view is based on an understanding of the evolution of the earth and humanity. Steiner believed that the condition of the earth is a direct reflection of the mode of consciousness of the human societies which now dominate it. The present consciousness of humanity has itself developed as part of the evolution of the earth. Our present separation from the spirits of place has been the inevitable result of the development of modern consciousness. We can improve the condition of our land and our own health by striving to recognize once more the spiritual nature of our earth and to become reintegrated with its processes.[1]

A current influential view is that life resulted from the interaction of randomly occurring physical processes. Religious views suggest a spiritual origin for humanity, yet fail to account for the physical evidence of evolution. Rudolf Steiner's description explains the physical and cultural evidence of evolution and assists in understanding humanity's relationship to the spirits of place. The separation of humanity from an awareness of the spirits of place is a significant and relatively recent phenomenon in the overall evolution of the earth.[2]

The present form of the earth can be understood to be the result of a process of condensation from a spiritual state into an increasingly dense and physical one. This condensation occurred in a series of cycles, each of which resulted in the emergence of a kingdom of nature and a characteristic mode of consciousness. In each cycle, old capacities were sacrificed for the development of new ones. The present dense, material state of the earth has become the basis for the next, critical step in the evolution of human consciousness.

As the earth gradually condensed into a solid state, it lost much of its original vitality. The earth's life forces gradually diminished as the earth became more mature. This same phenomena is observed in the growth pattern of other organisms, including human beings. Living organisms generally grow more rapidly and exhibit more vitality when young. Rapid early growth gradually slows until the organism reaches normal size. Life forces continue to diminish slowly until the physical death of the organism. Projecting the growth rate of a mature human back to birth confuses organic and physical processes and results in calculating an exaggerated estimated age.

As a living organism, the earth is going through a similar cycle of development. Early conditions of the earth were far different than those which can be observed today. Present mineral substances are, in reality, the results of early organic processes. The rocks of the earth are similar to the bark of a tree, which itself is no longer alive, but which is a product of life. The earth's life forces are weaker now than in earlier eons, and geological processes now occur far more slowly and only under conditions of extreme heat and pressure. The organic origin of the earth and its history have been hidden by this slowing of biological activity. Present geological theories assume that the upbuilding and erosional forces of today are identical to those of the distant past. By not recognizing the organic nature of the earth and the similarity of its life cycle to that of human beings, we overlook the possibility of different rates of growth in different organisms.[3]

In the gradual condensation of the earth, physical substances gradually precipitated out, much as the bones of a developing human being form out of the fluid embryo. The simplest, least evolved substances precipitated out first. The mineral kingdom therefore appeared earliest. Later the more developed plant and animal kingdoms appeared in physical form, emerging out of the more spiritualized, rarefied substances of the earth. These kingdoms resulted not from natural selection over great geological eras, but through gradual emergence from the surrounding spirit substance. Once they appeared on the earth, the relative density of physical matter and the slowing of organic activity made further change in their physical forms difficult.

Each kingdom of nature possesses a distinctive form of

consciousness which emerged during the great cycles of earth evolution. The mineral kingdom, as the simplest and therefore the youngest kingdom, though the first to emerge on earth, possesses a relatively undeveloped consciousness—the consciousness of deep sleep. This consciousness is so dull that most observers conclude that this kingdom is totally lacking in consciousness. The plant kingdom represents a decisive step up in consciousness, in that plants respond to outside stimula, though compared to human consciousness, plants possess the consciousness of sleep. The consciousness of the animal kingdom might, in turn, be compared to the dream consciousness of humans. Humanity has developed more fully; its clear, objective consciousness can relate to the world through powers of thinking. Human beings also have the ability to withdraw from the influences of the outer world and to develop an inner life. The emergence of human consciousness has been an ongoing process of evolution. As the kingdom with the most developed form of consciousness, humanity is revealed as the oldest of the kingdoms, though the latest to emerge into the present physical conditions of earth.[4]

As the most highly developed kingdom, humanity was able to remain within the finer spiritual substances of the earth longest. Humanity did not evolve physically from previous animal forms. It initially emerged without the bony structures which now characterize both animals and human beings. For this reason, fossil remains providing evidence of physical links to animal forms cannot be discovered. Humanity's subsequent evolution on earth continued this gradual densification and the modification of the sense organs until they were fully adapted to the physical world. Capacities for perception of the spiritual world were gradually replaced by capacities for perceiving physical surroundings. Humanity has progressed furthest in achieving independence from the earth; its technological development represents the latest stage in this process.[5]

Though humanity emerged as the final kingdom to enter into physical existence, the earth continues to be interpenetrated by other spiritual beings which influence the condition of the earth and humanity. Some beings are of kingdoms more advanced than humanity, recognized by earlier peoples as guardian spirits or as gods residing in a higher world. Other beings were seen as primarily active in earthly nature. Such elemental beings have played an important part in legends and stories in all cultures, as elves, gnomes, or leprechauns. They are depicted as having a protective and nurturing relationship to the physical world. Stories of such beings did not arise out of naive imagination but out of the perceptions of cultures which relied on their keen senses for survival.

Other beings were recognized as having a special relationship with the kingdoms of nature which surrounded humanity. These were the higher spiritual parts of the plant and animal kingdoms which did not enter physical existence. Members of traditional peoples continue to meet the spirits of Bear or Eagle or other animal species. Likewise the archetypal Plant which stands behind all plants was perceived by Goethe after he had prepared himself through careful study of their physical form.[6]

The descent out of the spiritual world into physical matter provided humanity with the necessary opportunity to develop self-conscious thinking. The development of this form of consciousness required separation and stability. The head is hard and relatively isolated from the rest of the body. Separated from contact with the environment, the head provides a basis for the independent power of thinking. It provides protection for the brain, the most insulated, least vital major organ in the body. This stability provides the support for the new order of vitality and mobility represented by our capacity for thought. In contrast, the physically mobile limbs learn with great difficulty, through repetition and hard work.

The earth itself has also gradually developed from a highly animate organism into one possessing a higher consciousness. The earth has contracted into a hard, headlike form and has lost much of its earlier vitality. This deadening of the earth was necessary so that humanity could emerge as independent of the earth. The conditions of the primeval world were too intensely vital for the human form to develop. A deadening of the earth was essential for the next stage of evolution. With the emergence of humanity into physical form, the evolution of the earth continued through the development of human consciousness. The basis for this evolution is provided by the emergence of the human brain—human consciousness progresses towards independent, self-conscious thought. With the emergence of self-consciousness, evolution becomes deliberate. The earth no longer has its early life forces. The nature of the relationship has changed; responsibility for the care of the earth has shifted to humanity.

The Evolution of Human Consciousness

The gradual evolution of human consciousness can be traced through history. Each great human cultural epoch has had a distinctive form of consciousness. Yet understanding how peoples of the past experienced the world is a challenge for modern humanity. Just as we have assumed that the primeval earth must have been very similar to the present earth, we assume that earlier humanity had a perception of their world similar to our own. So absorbed are the people of the modern world in their own unique way of perception that they often lose the understanding that there are other valid forms of perception. This is illustrated by the difficulties travelers have when they visit countries where cultural values differ from their own. The problems of understanding the way that peoples of the past experienced the world are far greater than the culture shock of tourists.

Cultures of today feel their form of consciousness is either identical to that of earlier peoples or superior in every way. However, in some respects, the consciousness of the past was far more penetrating, deep, and comprehensive. It was a consciousness far more able to see beyond the surface appearances of things, more capable of understanding humanity's place in a universe of life and consciousness. Lacking our characteristic modern self-consciousness, early peoples felt no separation from their environment. Their consciousness was less attuned to the physical world than our own. Thus, it provided them with the access to the world of the spirits.[7]

This consciousness of the early peoples was similar to our present state of dreaming. In dreaming, we experience a loss of self and feel ourselves flowing into the surrounding world. In dream consciousness we perceive less clearly than in our waking state, but we penetrate the boundaries of waking perception. Physical limits to our perception are dissolved. The consciousness of earlier peoples permitted penetration into worlds beyond the limitations of the senses. People were able to live in intimate contact with nonphysical entities through this dreamlike consciousness. Beings met in dreams were often described in physical terms, since the dividing line between the physical and spiritual world was less defined than it is in our day. Mythology is the record of this relationship of humanity with the gods. To the consciousness of early humanity, spiritual beings were more real than those of the physical world around them. Dreaming is still important to traditional peoples, who possess a form of this early consciousness.

As humanity evolved, its consciousness and relation to the spiritual world changed. The gods walked among the peoples of ancient India. The spiritual world provided guidance and direction for human activities. The physical world, in contrast, was considered illusionary—as Maya. The gods were found in the physical world in places of their own choosing, Shiva on the inaccessible peaks of the Himalaya, Krishna among the herds.

For the Egyptian people, the earth was also full of spirits, many of whom were connected to particular places. The earth was less a physical place than a community of spirits. The land was seen as the body of Osiris; the Nile was a god. Provinces were recognized, not only for their physical characteristics, but for their resident spirit beings. These identifications were in accord with a mode of consciousness attuned to spiritual reality. In later periods the intimate connection with this world began to weaken.[8]

The Greek civilization marks the beginning of a modern consciousness. While the Greek gods might at times walk among the people, increasingly the presence of the gods could be recognized only by specially prepared individuals able to regain momentarily the consciousness that was once the common heritage of all humanity. In such places such as Delphi, trained men and women might serve as oracles and temporarily regain a connection to the gods. The location of these important spots was not selected arbitrarily. Each sacred place was characteristic of the god who dwelt there. The selection of the spots for the mysteries reflects not a choice in the physical world but a choice based on spiritual perception of the gods themselves.

Humanity gradually became unable to perceive the spirit powers of the earlier ages. As individuals became aware of their physical bodies, they experienced separation from the world, which was increasingly experienced in physical terms. Humanity's developing senses were now oriented to the physical world. The spirit beings, in turn, withdrew from active participation in the earth. While earlier peoples saw spirit beings, later societies perceived only forces or the seemingly divine laws of nature. Their experience of the world had decisively changed due to a new mode of consciousness. Human beings also experienced a freedom that was impossible when humanity received its insights through the spirit beings under whose charge they had long remained.

Humanity now found its connection to the world through thought and reason. The traditional connection with the spiritual world was prolonged through the efforts of individuals who, through special preparation, could continue the relationship with the spiritual world. Initiates, those persons schooled in esoteric knowledge, guided humanity in that period in which most people lived solely within the physical world. Eventually even this guidance became increasingly distorted. This withdrawal from the spiritual world and its guidance was an essential element in evolution.

Conflicts arose during this period of separation between those who represented the fading methods of the past and those who typified the emerging powerful, if limited, modes of consciousness of the new scientific age. After centuries of struggle the scientific approach triumphed. The only remaining challenges to this mode of consciousness were the scattered representatives of the old order and emerging new forms of consciousness. Humanity had developed an independent life of thought, separate from the thoughts of the sustaining spirit beings which had accompanied its evolution and had provided guidance.

This passage into material consciousness was inevitable, an essential development that allowed humanity to develop new forces with which to continue evolution. These forces of independent thinking could not develop without separation from the spiritual world. Humanity was in the position of the adolescent who requires separation from its parents in order to reach independent, productive adulthood. Humanity and the earth have both suffered from this turbulent transition.

Though losing their spiritual perception, humanity gained the advantages of an increased self-consciousness and clarity of perception through immersion in the physical world. Modern consciousness has permitted humanity to gain new abilities to perceive, conceptualize, and act independently of race, nation, and family. The evolution of races and nations was replaced by the evolution of individuals. Each individual can, through individual effort, expand perceptive capacities and so provide a base for creative activity. Once achieved, these new forces may then be put to the service of all of creation.

Humanity's power to alter the environment has resulted in the impoverishment and destruction of the earth; modern technology has profoundly disturbed the natural balance of the planet. Yet humanity remains in connection with the earth and cannot free itself from a relation of interdependence with the other kingdoms of nature. Now that humanity has emerged as independent, we cannot assume that the earth has the capacity to continue to balance environmental conditions. Humanity can no longer remain a passive participant in the process of evolution. Having achieved a new degree of independence, it must now consciously participate in evolution. Humanity has reached a point at which it must become a cocreator with the other spiritual forces of the earth. Without the emergence of such free action, the evolution of all of creation will be retarded. Humanity is the means by which freedom can emerge within the cosmos.

The earth has become a seed. Though appearing less alive than the growing plant, the seed contains all the new possibilities for future development. Although the seed seems hard and lifeless, this dimming of external life masks an inner vitality. It awaits the forces that can awaken it into new life. Like the human head, the seed's solidity allows the future to develop secure and protected. In this period of contraction, our task as human beings is to protect this earth-seed and encourage the necessary forces that are preparing it for the next stage of evolution.[9]

Notes

1. Rudolf Steiner (1861-1925) was, by the turn of the century, a respected writer and scholar, particularly known for his work on Goethe's scientific work. His efforts were increasingly applied to the extension of the modern scientific method of research to a study of the spiritual nature of mankind and the earth. The results of his methods of spiritual scientific research was termed "Anthroposophy," and is described in his published works, including over six thousand lectures in a wide variety of fields. The practical results of this research include the Waldorf School movement, the biodynamic agricultural method, and initiatives in medicine, curative education and the arts. As both a scientist and man of his age, Steiner worked to develop a modern path of spiritual training. The philosophical basis for these activities was his first major work, *The Philosophy of Freedom*, which affirmed the importance of clear, conscious thinking as the first step towards comprehension of the supersensible world. His methods of research were based

on an understanding of the present stage of human consciousness and the importance of human freedom.

Biographies of Steiner include *Rudolf Steiner: Herald of a New Epoch* by Stewart Easton and *Rudolf Steiner: Life, Work, Inner Path and Social Initiatives* by Rudi Lissau. Stewart Easton has also written an introduction to Steiner's life and work, *Man and the World in the Light of Anthroposophy*. A valuable introduction to Steiner's work, including an extensive annotated bibliography, is *The Essential Steiner: Basic Writings of Rudolf Steiner,* edited by Robert McDermott. The works of Rudolf Steiner and other anthroposophical authors are available from Anthroposophic Press, Bell's Pond Road, Star Route, Hudson, NY 12534 and the Rudolf Steiner Library, RD2 Box 215, Ghent, NY 12075. Rudolf Steiner's work in the United States is continued by the Anthroposophical Society in America, 529 W. Grant Pl., Chicago, IL 60614.

2. Rudolf Steiner's fundamental description of evolution is contained in *An Outline of Occult Science.* In this work Steiner explains the nature of spiritual scientific research and its relation to natural science and gives some of the results of this research. In later years Steiner continued to speak about this process of evolution in lectures on a variety of subjects. He repeatedly stated that such an understanding of the relationship of man and the earth must be the foundation of practical work. Kees Zoetman discusses the relationship between Rudolf Steiner's descriptions of evolution and contemporary theories in *Gaiasophy.*

3. An examination of the geology of the earth from this organic perspective is provided by Walther Cloos in *The Living Earth: The Organic Origin of Rocks and Minerals.*

4. Rudolf Steiner's description of the consciousness of the different kingdoms and the relation to human consciousness is contained in his early work *Theosophy* as well as in many subsequent lectures.

5. The relationship between humanity and the animal kingdom is examined in *A New Zoology* by Hermann Poppelbaum. Dr. Poppelbaum uses a study of the forms of the various animals and of man to confirm Steiner's description of evolution.

6. A translation of *Goethe's Metamorphosis of the Plants* has been published with an introduction by Rudolf Steiner. Goethe's writings on botany have been collected in *Goethe's Botanical Writings,* edited by Bertha Mueller. The emergence of the modern scientific approach and the alternative proposed by Goethe is described by Ernst Lehrs in *Man Or Matter.*

7. Descriptions of earlier modes of consciousness are contained in both *An Outline of Occult Science* and in various later lecture courses.

8. A course of lectures by Rudolf Steiner entitled *Egyptian Myths and Mysteries* describes the mode of consciousness of the Egyptians and other earlier civilizations and their relationship to their land.

9. Rudolf Steiner's description of the earth as seed is discussed by Cloos in *The Living Earth.*

David Valbracht

Bibliography

Cloos, Walter. *The Living Earth: The Organic Origin of Rocks and Minerals.* Lanthorne Press, 1977.

Easton, Stewart. *Man and the World in the Light of Anthroposophy.* Spring Valley, NY: Anthroposophic Press.

Rudolf Steiner: Herald of a New Epoch. Spring Valley, NY: Anthroposophic Press.

Lissau, Rudi. *Rudolf Steiner: Life Work, Inner Path and Social Initiatives.* Hawthorn Press, 1987.

McDermott, Robert. *The Essential Steiner: Basic Writings of Rudolf Steiner.* New York: Harper and Row, 1985.

Poppelbaum, Hermann. *A New Zoology.* Dornach, Switzerland. Philosophic-Anthroposophic Press, 1961.

Schiller, Paul Eugen. *Rudolf Steiner and Initiation.* Spring Valley, NY: Anthroposophic Press, 1981.

Steiner, Rudolf. *Agriculture.* London: Bio-Dynamic Agricultural Association, 1972.

Steiner, Rudolf. *Knowledge of the Higher Worlds and Its Attainment.* Spring Valley, NY: Anthroposophic Press, 1947.

Steiner, Rudolf. *An Outline of Occult Science.* Spring Valley, NY: Anthroposophic Press, 1972.

Steiner, Rudolf. *The Philosophy of Freedom.* Spring Valley, NY: Anthroposophic Press, 1970.

Steiner, Rudolf. *Theosophy: An Introduction to Supersensible Knowledge and the Destiny of Man.* Spring Valley, NY: Anthroposophic Press, 1971.

Zoetman, Kees. *Gaiasophy.* Hudson, NY: Lindisfarne Press, 1991.

Part Two
Ecological and Scientific Perspectives

When the animals come to us,
   asking for our help,
   will we know what they are saying?
When the plants speak to us
   in their delicate, beautiful language,
   will we be able to answer them?
When the planet herself
   sings to us in our dreams,
   will we be able to wake ourselves, and act?

                                        Gary Lawless

Ecologists, biologists, physicists, and psychologists are, in some senses, moving backwards—towards regaining a philosophic perspective we have lost over the past thousand years. The mechanistic, scientific worldview long-dominant in Western culture has led, we are coming to realize, to the loss of a felt-sense of the aliveness of the world. Yet even Aristotle, the father of modern scientific methodology, believed that everything in the universe is alive with spirit. As theologian J. Ronald Halvern explained at a recent conference on "The Reunion of Science and Spirit":

> *Aristotle believed that everything has an essence, each object contains a spirit within itself. That essence has an energy and a volition: It moves toward a future and a goal. The energy within an acorn gathers earth around it and creates an oak tree.*

Just because Aristotle's view of nature as alive has been eclipsed, Halvern continues, "does not mean that it cannot today be regained."

The essays in Part Two, by contemporary scientists, ecologists, and philosophers, explore the extent to which we have succeeded in regaining the ancient perspective. Two essays address the question "What is Life?" and conclude that the traditional divisions between what is alive and what is not alive are today breaking down. Boundaries are coming down as well between objective and subjective views—in physics as well as in philosophy. As a result, the traditional alienation between human beings and nature is dissolving, and we are increasingly able to hear the "delicate, beautiful language" of the animals, the plants, and of Mother Earth herself.

6

What Is Gaia?

JAMES LOVELOCK

You must not . . . be too precise or scientific about birds and trees and flowers. . . .

Walt Whitman, *Specimen Days*

Travel back in your memory to the time when you first awoke, that exquisite moment of childhood when first you came alive— the sudden rush of sound and sight, as if a television receiver had been switched on and was about to bring news of vast importance. I seem to recall sunlight and soft fresh air; then suddenly knowing who I was and how good it was to be alive.

To reminisce about the first memory of my personal life may seem irrelevant in our quest to understand Gaia. But it isn't. As a scientist I observe, measure, analyze, and describe phenomena. Before I can do these things I need to know what I am observing. In a broad sense it may be unnecessary to recognize a phenomena when observing it, but scientists almost always have preconceived notions of the object of their study. As a child I recognized life intuitively. As an adult wondering about the Earth's strange atmosphere—a mixture made of incompatible gases such as oxygen and methane coexisting like foxes and rabbits in the same burrow—I was forced to recognize Gaia, to intuit her existence, long before I could describe her in proper scientific terms.

The concept of Gaia is entirely linked with the concept of life. To understand what Gaia is, therefore, I first need to explore that difficult concept, life. They hate to admit it, but the life scientists, whether the natural historians of the nineteenth century or the biologists of the twentieth, cannot explain what life is in scientific terms. They all know what it is, as we have done since childhood; but in my view no one has yet succeeded in defining life. The idea of life, the sense of being alive, are the most familiar and the most difficult to understand of the concepts we meet. I have long thought that the answer to the question "What is life?" was deemed so important to our survival that it was classified "top secret" and kept locked up as an instinct in the automatic levels of the mind. During evolution, there was great selection pressure for immediate action: crucial to our survival is the instant distinction of predator from prey and kin from foe, and the recognition of a potential mate. We cannot afford the delay of conscious thought or debate in the committees of the mind. We must compute the imperatives of recognition at the fastest speed and, therefore, in the earliest-evolved and unconscious recesses of the mind. This is why we all know intuitively what life is. It is edible, lovable, or lethal.

Life as an object of scientific inquiry requiring precise definition is much more difficult. Even scientists, who are notorious for their indecent curiosity, shy away from defining life. All branches of formal biological science seem to avoid the question. In the *Dictionary of Biology* compiled by M. Abercrombie, C. J. Hickman, and M. L. Johnson, these three distinguished biologists succinctly define all manner of words like *ontogeny* (development), *Pteridophyta* (ferns), and *ecdysis* (a stage in insect development). Under the letter *L* there is *Leptotene* (the first sign of chromosome pairing in meiosis) and *limnology* (the study of lakes), but nowhere is life mentioned. When the word *life* does appear in biology it is in rejection, as by the philosophically inclined N. W. Pirie who, in 1937, published an article entitled "The Meaninglessness of the Terms 'Life' and 'Living.' "

The Webster and the Oxford dictionaries are not much more help. Both remind of the word's origin from the Anglo-Saxon *lif*. This may explain some of the reluctance of academic biologists to tangle with so elemental a concept as life. The tribal war between the Normans and the Saxons was long enduring; the medieval schoolmen, knowing where power and preference lay, chose to support the victorious Norman establishment and to keep Latin as their language. Life was another of those rude uncivilized Anglo-Saxon words, best avoided in polite company. The Latin equivalent of lif, *anima*, was even less help. It was close in meaning to that other four-letter Gothic word, *soul*.

To go back to the Webster dictionary, it defines life as:

> That property of plants and animals (ending at death and distinguishing them from inorganic matter) which makes it possible for them to take in food, get energy from it, grow, etc.

The Oxford dictionary says much the same:

The property which differentiates a living animal or plant, or a living portion of organic tissue, from dead or nonliving matter; the assemblage of the functional activities by which this property is manifested.

If such manifestly inadequate definitions of life are all I have to work with, can I do much better defining the living organism of Gaia? I have found it very difficult, but if I am to tell you about it I must try. I can start with some simpler definitions and classifications. Living things such as trees and horses and even bacteria can easily be perceived and recognized because they are bounded by walls, membranes, skin, or waxy coverings. Using energy directly from the Sun and indirectly from food, living systems incessantly act to maintain their identity, their integrity. Even as they grow and change, grow and reproduce, we do not lose track of them as visible, recognizable entities. Although there are uncountable millions of individual organisms all growing and changing, their traits in common allow us to group them and recognize that they belong to species such as peacocks, dogs, or wheat. About ten million species are estimated to exist. When any individual fails to get energy and food, fails to act to maintain its identity, we realize it is moribund or dead.

An important step in our understanding is to recognize the significance of collections of living things. You and I are both composed of a collection of organs and tissues. The many beneficiaries of heart, liver, and kidney transplants testify eloquently that each of these organs can exist independently of the body when kept warm and supplied with nutrients. The organs themselves are made up of billions of living cells, each of which can also live independently. Then the cells themselves, as Lynn Margulis has shown, are communities of microorganisms that once lived free. The energy-transforming entities of animal cells (the mitochondria) and of plants (the mitochondria and the chloroplasts) both were once bacteria living independently.

Life is social. It exists in communities and collectives. There is a useful word in physics to describe the properties of collections: *colligative*. It is needed because there is no way to express or measure the temperature or the pressure of a single molecule. Temperature and pressure, say the physicists, are the colligative properties of a sensible collection of molecules. All collections of living things show properties unexpected from a knowledge of a single one of them. We, and some other animals, keep a constant temperature whatever the temperature of our surroundings. This fact could never have been deduced from the observations of a single cell from a human being. The tendency to constancy was first noted by the French physiologist Claude Bernard in the nineteenth century. His American successor in this century, Walter Cannon, called it *homeostasis* or the wisdom of the body. Homeostasis is a colligative property of life.

We have no trouble with the idea that noble entities such as people are made up from an intricate interconnected set of cell communities. We don't find it too difficult to consider a nation or a tribe as an entity made up of its people and the territory they occupy. But what of large entities, like ecosystems and Gaia? It took the view of the Earth from space, either directly through the eyes of an astronaut, or vicariously through the visual media, to give us the personal sense of a real live planet on which the living things, the air, the oceans, and the rocks all combine in one as Gaia.

The name of the living planet, Gaia, is not a synonym for the biosphere. The biosphere is defined as that part of the Earth where living things normally exist. Still less is Gaia the same as the biota, which is simply the collection of all individual living organisms. The biota and the biosphere taken together form part but not all of Gaia. Just as the shell is part of a snail, so the rocks, the air, and the oceans are part of Gaia. Gaia, as we shall see, has continuity with the past back to the origins of life, and extends into the future as long as life persists. Gaia, as a total planetary being, has properties that are not necessarily discernible by just knowing individual species or populations of organisms living together.

The Gaia hypothesis, when we introduced it in the 1970s, supposed that the atmosphere, the oceans, the climate, and the crust of the Earth are regulated at a state comfortable for life because of the behavior of living organisms. Specifically, the Gaia hypothesis said that the temperature, oxidation state, acidity, and certain aspects of the rocks and waters are at any time kept constant, and that this homeostasis is maintained by active feedback processes operated automatically and unconsciously by the biota. Solar energy sustains comfortable conditions for life. The conditions are only constant in the short term and evolve in synchrony with the changing needs of the biota as it evolves. Life and its environment are so closely coupled that evolution concerns Gaia, not the organisms or the environment taken separately.

Most of my working life has been spent on the fringes of the life sciences, but I do not think of myself a biologist, nor do I believe would biologists accept me as one of them. When seen from outside, much of biology appears to be the building of data bases—making the "whole life catalog." Sometimes, in a pensive mood, I fancy that to biologists the living world is a vast set of book collections held in interconnected libraries. In this dream, the biologists are like competent librarians who devise the most intricate classification of every new library they discover but never read the books. They sense that something is missing from their lives, and this feeling intensifies as new collections of books grow hard to find. I see the biologists expressing an almost palpable sense of relief when joined by molecular biologists who dare to start the even greater task of classifying the words the books contain. It means that the search for the answer to the awesome question of what the books are about can be put off until the new and infinitely detailed molecular classification is complete.

My imaginary world, populated by biologists as book collectors, is in no way intended as a slur on the life sciences. Left to my own devices in such a world I should have been much less constructive. Impatient of waiting for an answer to the question, "What is the meaning of the books?" I would have seized some of them for experimental tests—for example, burning them in a calorimeter and measuring, accurately, the heat released. My sense of frustration would not have lessened when I discovered that the densely packed pages of an encyclopedia give no more heat than the same mass of plain paper. Like the biologists' classification, this physical experiment would have been profoundly unsatisfying because it would have put to Nature the wrong question.

Can we scientists, any of us, do better in our quest to understand life? There are three equally powerful approaches: molecular biology, the understanding of those information-processing chemicals that are the genetic basis of all life on Earth; physiology, the science concerned with living systems seen holistically; thermodynamics, the branch of physics that deals with time and energy and that connects living processes to the fundamental laws of the Universe. Of these sciences, the latter is the one that may go furthest in the quest to define life, yet so far has made the least progress. Thermodynamics grew from down-to-earth origins, the quest of engineers to make steam engines more efficient. It flourished in the last century, both taxing and entertaining the minds of the greatest scientists.

The first law of thermodynamics is about energy, or in other words, the capacity to do work. Energy, says the first law, is conserved. Energy in the form of sunlight falling on the leaves of a tree is used in many ways. Some is reflected so that we see the leaves as green, some is absorbed and warms them, and some is transformed to food and oxygen; ultimately, we eat the food, consume it with the oxygen we breathe, and so use the Sun's energy to move, to think, and to keep warm. The first law says that this energy is always conserved and that no matter how far it is dispersed the total always remains the same. The second law is about the dissymmetry of Nature. When heat is turned to work, some of it is wasted. The redistribution of the total quantity of energy in the Universe has direction, says the second law. It is always running down. Hot objects cool, but cool objects never spontaneously become hot. The law can appear to be broken when some metastable store of internal energy is tapped, as when a match is struck, or a piece of plutonium experiences nuclear fission, but once used up the energy cannot be recovered. The law was not broken, the energy was merely redistributed and the downward path maintained. Water does not flow up the rivers from the sea to the mountains. Natural processes always move towards an increase of disorder, and this disorder is measured by entropy. It is a quantity that always and inexorably increases.

Entropy is real, not some hazy notion invented by professors to make it easier to challenge students with difficult examination questions. Like the length of a piece of string or the temperature of wine in a glass, it is a measurable physical quantity. Indeed, like temperature, the entropy of a substance is, in a practical sense, zero at the absolute zero of $-273°C$. When heat is added to a material substance, not only the temperature increases but also the entropy. Unfortunately there is a complication: whereas temperature can be measured with a thermometer, entropy cannot be measured directly with an "entropometer." Entropy, measured in the units calories per gram per degree, is the total quantity of heat added, divided by the temperature.

Consider the lifeless perfection of a snowflake, a crystal so exquisitely ordered in its fractal pattern that it is one of the most intricate of nonliving things. The quantity of heat needed to melt a snowflake to a raindrop is 80 times larger than the quantity needed to warm the raindrop by a single degree of temperature. The increase of entropy when snowflakes melt is 80 times larger than when they warm from $-1°C$ to the melting point. Alternatively, the formation of ice that expresses the ordered perfection of a snowflake represents a decrease of entropy of the same amount. Entropy is connected in quantitative terms with the orderliness of things. The greater the order, the lower the entropy.

I like to think of entropy as the quantity that expresses the most certain property of our present Universe: its tendency to run down, to burn out. Others see it as the direction of time's arrow, a progression inevitably from birth to death. Far from being something tragic or a cause of sorrow, this universal tendency to decay benefits us. Without the decay of the Universe there could have been no Sun, and without the superabundant consumption of its energy store the Sun could never have provided the light that let us be.

The second law is the most fundamental and unchallenged law of the Universe; not surprisingly, no attempt to understand life can ignore it. The first book I read on the question of life was by the Austrian physicist, Erwin Schrödinger. He was curious about biology and wondered if the behavior of the fundamental molecules of life could be explained by physics and biology. His famous little book, entitled *What Is Life?*, is a collection of the public lectures on this topic that he gave in Dublin during his exile there in the Second World War. He describes his objective on the first page:

> The large important and very much discussed question is: How can the events in space and time which take place within the spatial boundary of a living organism be accounted for by physics and chemistry?

He goes on to write:

> The obvious inability of present-day physics and chemistry to account for such events is no reason for doubting that they can be accounted for by those sciences.

In those times, physicists were accustomed to exploring the dead, near-equilibrium world of "periodic crystals"— crystals whose regularity is predictable, one atom of one kind always following another of a different kind in a repeating pattern. Even these comparatively simple structures were enough to stretch to the limit the simple equipment then available. Organic chemists were discovering the intricate structures of the "aperiodic crystals" from living matter, such as the proteins, polysaccharides, and nucleic acids. They were still far from the present-day understanding of the chemical nature of genetic material. Schrödinger concluded that, metaphorically, the most amazing property and characteristic of life is its ability to move upstream against the flow of time. Life is the paradoxical contradiction to the second law, which states that everything is, always has been, and always will be running down to equilibrium and death. Yet life evolves to ever-greater complexity and is characterized by an omnipresence of improbability that would make winning a sweepstake every day for a year seem trivial by comparison. Even more remarkable, this unstable, this apparently illegal, state of life has persisted on the Earth for a sizable fraction of the age of the Universe itself. In no way does life violate the second law; it has evolved with the Earth as a tightly coupled system so as to favor survival. It is like a skilled accountant, never evading the payment of required tax but also never missing a loophole. Most of Schrödinger's book is an optimistic prediction of how life is knowable. The eminent molecular biologist, Max Perutz, has recently commented that little in Schrödinger's book is original, and what is original is often wrong. This may be true; but I, like many of my colleagues, still acknowledge a debt to Schrödinger for having set us thinking in a productive way.

The great physicist Ludwig Boltzmann expressed the meaning of the second law in an equation of great seemliness and simplicity: $S = k(lnP)$, where S is that strange quantity entropy; k is a constant rightly called the Boltzmann constant; and lnP is the natural logarithm of the probability. It means what it says—the less probable something is, the lower is its entropy. The most improbable thing of all, life, is therefore to be associated with the lowest entropy. Schrödinger was not happy to associate something as significant as life with a diminished quantity, entropy. He proposed, instead, the term "negentropy," the reciprocal of entropy—that is, 1 divided by entropy or $1/S$. Negentropy is large, of course, for improbable things like living organisms. To describe the burgeoning life of our planet as improbable may seem odd. But imagine that some cosmic chef takes all the ingredients of the present Earth as atoms, mixes them, and lets them stand. The probability that those atoms would combine into the molecules that make up our living Earth is zero. The mixture would always react chemically to form a dead planet like Mars or Venus.

Often in science the same idea is thought of in different contexts in different parts of the world. There is nothing occult about this. Ideas are in continuous use as currency in the exchanges between scientists and, like money, can be used to buy many different things. When Schrödinger was lecturing about negentropy in Dublin, Claude Shannon was investigating a similar quantity in the United States, but from a radically different perspective. Shannon, at the Bell Telephone Laboratories, was developing information theory. It started as a plain engineering quest to discover the physical factors that caused a message sent by cable or by radio to lose information as it passed from the sender to the receiver. Shannon soon discovered a quantity that always tended to increase; the size of the increase was a measure of the loss of information. In no experiment was the size of this quantity ever observed to decrease. On the advice of John Von Neumann, a mathematical physicist, Shannon named this quantity entropy because it so much resembled the entropy of the steam engineers. The reciprocal of Shannon's entropy is the quantity often called information. If we assume that the entropy Shannon discovered is the same as the entropy of the steam engineers, then the elusive quantity that Schrödinger associated with the improbability of life—negentropy—is comparable with Shannon's information. In mathematical terms, if S is the entropy then both negentropy and information are $1/S$.

The reward that comes from persevering with thoughts about these difficult concepts is insight to illuminate our quest to understand life and Gaia. The contribution from Shannon's theory is that information is not just knowledge. Information, in thermodynamic terms, is a measure of the absence of ignorance. Better to know all about a simple system than merely a great deal about a complex one. The less the ignorance, the lower the entropy. This is why it is so difficult to grasp the concept of Gaia from the voluminous but isolated knowledge of a single scientific discipline.

If the second law tells us that entropy in the Universe is increasing, how does life avoid the universal tendency for decay? A physicist in Britain, J. D. Bernal, tried to balance the books. In 1951, he wrote in recondite terminology: "Life is one member of the class of phenomena which are open or

continuous reaction systems able to decrease their internal
entropy at the expense of free energy taken from the environment and subsequently rejected in degraded form." Many
other scientists have expressed these words as a mathematical
equation. Among the clearest and most readable are the
statements in a small book, *The Thermodynamics of the Steady
State*, written by a physical chemist, K. G. Denbigh. They can be
restated less rigorously but more comprehensibly as follows.
By the act of living, an organism continuously creates entropy
and there will be an outward flux of entropy across its boundary.
You, as you read these words, are creating entropy by consuming oxygen and the fats and sugars stored in your body.
As you breathe, you excrete waste products high in entropy
into the air, such as carbon dioxide, and your warm body
emits to your surroundings infrared radiation high in entropy.
If your excretion of entropy is as large or larger than your
internal generation of entropy, you will continue to live and
remain a miraculous, improbable, but still legal avoidance
of the second law of the Universe. "Excretion of entropy" is
just a fancy way of expressing the dirty words excrement
and pollution. At the risk of having my membership card of
the Friends of the Earth withdrawn, I say that only by pollution do we survive. We animals pollute the air with carbon
dioxide, and the vegetation pollutes it with oxygen. The
pollution of one is the meat of another. Gaia is more subtle,
and, at least until humans appeared, polluted this region of
the Solar System with no more than the gentle warmth of
infrared radiation.

In recent times, some interesting insights have come from
the investigations of Ilya Prigogine and his colleagues into
the thermodynamics of eddies, vortices, and many other
transient systems that are low in entropy. Things like eddies
and whirlpools develop spontaneously when there is a sufficient flux of free energy. It was in the nineteenth century
that a British physicist, Osborne Reynolds, curious about
the conditions that led to turbulence in the flow of fluids,
discovered that the onset of eddies in a stream or in a flow
of gas takes place only when the flow exceeds a critical value.
A useful analogy here is that if you blow a flute too gently
no sound emerges. But if you blow hard enough, wind eddies
form and are made part of the system that makes sound.
Extending the earlier mathematics of the American physical
chemist Lars Onsager, Prigogine and his colleagues have

applied the thermodynamics of the steady state to develop what might be called the thermodynamics of the "unsteady state." They classify these phenomena by the term "dissipative structures." They have structure, but not the permanency of solids; they dissipate when the supply of energy is turned off. Living organisms include dissipative structures within them, but the class is broadly based. It includes many manufactured things, such as refrigerators, and natural phenomena such as flames, whirlpools, hurricanes, and certain peculiar chemical reactions. Living things are so infinitely complex in comparison with the dissipative structures of the fluid state that many feel that, although on the right track, present-day thermodynamics has far to go in defining life. Physicists, chemists, and biologists, although not rejecting these notions, do not make them part of the inspiration of their working lives. Their response is like that of a wealthy congregation to the exhortations of their priest on the virtues of poverty. It is something felt to be good, but not a way of life for next week.

A crucial insight that comes from Schrödinger's generalizations about life is that living systems have boundaries. Living organisms are open systems in the sense that they take and excrete energy and matter. In theory, they are open as far as the bounds of the Universe; but they are also enclosed within a hierarchy of internal boundaries. As we move in towards the Earth from space, first we see the atmospheric boundary that encloses Gaia; then the borders of an ecosystem such as the forests; then the skin or bark of living animals and plants; further in are the cell membranes; and finally the nucleus of the cell and its DNA. If life is defined as a self-organizing system characterized by an actively sustained low entropy, then, viewed from outside each of these boundaries, what lies within is alive.

You may find it hard to swallow the notion that anything as large and apparently inanimate as the Earth is alive. Surely, you may say, the Earth is almost wholly rock and nearly all incandescent with heat. I am indebted to Jerome Rothstein, a physicist, for his enlightenment on this, and other things. In a thoughtful paper on the living Earth concept (given at a symposium held in the summer of 1985 by the Audubon Society) he observed that the difficulty can be lessened if you let the image of a giant redwood tree enter your mind. The tree undoubtedly is alive, yet 99 percent is dead. The tree is an ancient spire of dead wood, made of lignin and

cellulose by the ancestors of the thin layer of living cells that
go to constitute its bark. How like the Earth, and more so when
we realize that many of the atoms of the rocks far down into
the magma were once part of the ancestral life from which
we all have come.

When the Earth was first seen from outside and compared
as a whole planet with its lifeless partners, Mars and Venus,
it was impossible to ignore the sense that the Earth was a
strange and beautiful anomaly. Yet this unconventional
planet probably would have been kept in the scullery, like
Cinderella, had not NASA in the role of Prince offered a
rescue by way of the planetary exploration program. As we
saw in chapter 1, the questions raised by space science were
at first narrowly focused on a practical question: How is life
on another planet to be recognized? Because that question
could not be explained solely by conventional biology or
geology, I became preoccupied with another question: What
if the difference in atmospheric composition between the
Earth and its neighbors Mars and Venus is a consequence
of the fact that the Earth alone bears life?

The least complex and most accessible part of a planet is
its atmosphere. Long before the Viking spacecraft landed
on Mars, or the Russian Venera landed on Venus, we knew
the chemical compositions of their atmospheres. In the middle
1960s, telescopes tuned to the infrared radiation reflected
by the molecules of atmospheric gases were used to view
Mars and Venus. These observations revealed the identity
and proportion of the gases with fair accuracy. Mars and
Venus both had atmospheres dominated by carbon dioxide,
with only small proportions of oxygen and nitrogen. More
important, both had atmospheres close to the chemical
equilibrium state; if you took a volume of air from either
of those planets, heated it to incandescence in the presence
of a representative sample of rocks from the surface, and
then allowed it to cool slowly, there would be little or no
change in composition after the experiment. The Earth, by
contrast, has an atmosphere dominated by nitrogen and
oxygen. A mere trace of carbon dioxide is present, far below
the expectation of planetary chemistry. There are unstable
gases such as nitrous oxide, and gases such as methane that
react readily with the abundant oxygen. If the same heating-
and-cooling experiment were tried with a sample of the air
that you are now breathing, it would be changed. It would

become like the atmospheres of Mars and Venus: carbon dioxide dominant, oxygen and nitrogen greatly diminished, and gases such as nitrous oxide and methane absent. It is not too far-fetched to look on the air as like the gas mixture that enters the intake of an internal combustion engine: combustible gases, hydrocarbons, and oxygen mixed. The atmospheres of Mars and Venus are like the exhaust gases, all energy spent.

The amazing improbability of the Earth's atmosphere reveals negentropy and the presence of the invisible hand of life. Take for example oxygen and methane. Both are present in our atmosphere in constant quantities; yet in sunlight they react chemically to give carbon dioxide and water vapor. Anywhere you travel on the Earth's surface to measure it, the methane concentration is about 1.5 parts per million. Close to 1,000 million tons of methane must be introduced into the atmosphere annually to maintain methane at a constant level. In addition, the oxygen used in oxidizing the methane must be replaced—at least 2,000 millions tons yearly. The only feasible explanation for the persistence of this unstable atmosphere at a constant composition, and for periods vastly longer than the reaction times of its gases, is the influence of a control system, Gaia.

It is often difficult to recognize the larger entity of which we are a part; as the saying goes, "You can't see the forest for the trees." So it was with the Earth itself before we shared with the astronauts vicariously that stunning and awesome vision; that impeccable sphere that punctuates the division of the past from the present. This gift, this ability to see the Earth from afar, was so revealing that it forced the novel top-down approach to planetary biology. The conventional wisdom of biology on Earth itself had always been forced to take a bottom-up approach by the sheer size of the Earth when compared with us or any living thing we knew. The two approaches are complementary. In the understanding of a microbe, an animal, or a plant, the top-down physiological view of life as a whole system harmoniously merges with the bottom-up view originating with molecular biology: that life is an assembly made from a vast set of ultramicroscopic parts.

Since James Hutton there has been a "loyal opposition" of scientists who doubted the conventional wisdom that the evolution of the environment is determined by chemical and physical forces alone. Vernadsky adopted Suess's concept of the biosphere to define the boundaries of the realm of the biota. Since Vernadsky, there has been a continuous tradition (called biogeochemistry) in the Soviet Union—and, to a lesser extent, elsewhere—that has recognized the interaction between the soils, oceans, lakes and rivers and the life they bear. It is well stated by a Russian, M. M. Yermolaev, in *An Introduction to Physical Geography:* "The biosphere is understood as being that part of the geographical envelope of the Earth, within the boundaries of which the physico-geographical conditions ensure the normal work of the enzymes." More recent members of this scientific opposition have included the following: Alfred Lotka of Johns Hopkins University, and Eugene Odum, who alone among ecologists took a physiological view of ecosystems; two Americans of European origin, the limnologist G. Evelyn Hutchinson and the paleontologist Heinz A. Lowenstam; an oceanographer from Britain, A. Redfield; and a Swedish geochemist, L. G. Sillén. They all have recognized the importance of the participation by life in the evolution of the environment. Most geologists, however, have neglected the presence of living organisms as an active participant in their theories of the Earth's evolution.

The counterpart of this geological apartheid is the failure of most biologists to recognize that the evolution of the species is strongly coupled with the evolution of their environment. For example, in 1982 there appeared a book, *Evolution Now: A Century after Darwin,* edited by John Maynard Smith, which consisted of a collection of essays by distinguished biologists on the most controversial issues of evolutionary biology. In this collection, the only (and enigmatic) mention of the environment is in an essay by Stephen Jay Gould: "Organisms are not billiard balls, struck in a deterministic fashion by the cue of natural selection and rolling to optimal positions on life's table. They influence their own destiny in interesting and complex and comprehensible ways. We must put this concept of organism back into evolutionary biology."

Apart from Lynn Margulis, the only other biologist I know to have taken the environment into account when considering life is J. Z. Young. In 1971, this distinguished physiologist was independently moved to write in a chapter on homeostasis in his book, *An Introduction to the Study of Man:* "The entity that is maintained intact, and of which we all form a part, is not the life of one of us, but in the end the whole of life upon the planet." J. Z. Young's view serves as a link between Gaia theory and the general scientific consensus. Through Gaia theory, I see the Earth and the life it bears as a system, a system that has the capacity to regulate the temperature and the composition of the Earth's surface and to keep it comfortable for living organisms. The self-regulation of the system is an active process driven by the free energy available from sunlight.

The early reaction, soon after the Gaia hypothesis was introduced in the early 1970s, was ignorance in the literal sense. For the most part the Gaian idea was ignored by professional scientists. It was not until the late 1970s that it was subjected to criticism.

Good criticism is like bathing in an ice-cold sea. The sudden chill of immersion in what seems at first a hostile medium soon stirs the blood and sharpens the senses. My first reaction on reading W. Ford Doolittle's criticism of the Gaia hypothesis in *CoEvolution Quarterly* in 1979 was shock and incoherent disbelief. The article was splendidly put together and beautifully written, but this did not lessen its frigidity. Icy waters may be pellucid, but this does not make them warm. After an icy plunge, however, comes that warm sense of relaxation when sunning on the beach. After a while, I began to realize that Ford Doolittle's criticism could be taken not so much as an attack on Gaia but as a criticism of the inadequacy of its presentation.

Gaia had first been seen from space and the arguments used were from thermodynamics. To me it was obvious that the Earth was alive in the sense that it was a self-organizing and self-regulating system. To Ford Doolittle, from his world of molecular biology, it was equally obvious that evolution by natural selection could never lead to "altruism" on a global scale. He was supported in the similarly forceful and effective writings of Richard Dawkins in his book, *The Extended Phenotype* (1982). From their world of microscopes, how could the "selfish" interests of living cells be expressed at the distance of a planet? For these competent and dedicated biologists, positing the regulation of the atmosphere by microbial life seemed as absurd as expecting the legislation of some human government to affect the orbit of Jupiter. I am indebted to them both for having shown clearly that we were taking far too much for granted, and that Gaia lacked a firm theoretical basis.

Not only did molecular biologists object to Gaia. Two other valued critics were the climatologist Stephen Schneider from Colorado, and the geochemist H. D. Holland from Harvard.

They, in common with most of their peers, preferred to explain the facts of the evolution of the rocks, the ocean, the air, and the climate by chemical and physical forces alone. In his book *The Chemical Evolution of the Atmosphere and the Oceans*, Holland wrote: "I find the hypothesis intriguing and charming, but ultimately unsatisfactory. The geologic record seems much more in accord with the view that the organisms that are better able to compete have come to dominate, and that the Earth's near surface environment and processes have accommodated themselves to changes wrought by biological evolution. Many of these changes must have been fatal or near fatal to parts of the contemporary biota. We live on an Earth that is the best of all worlds but only for those who have adapted to it." Stephen Schneider's objection—expressed in his book with Randi Londer, *The Coevolution of Climate and Life*—was to the implication in the early papers on Gaia that homeostasis was the only means of climate regulation. I am indebted to all of these critics for having shown clearly that we were taking too much for granted, and that Gaia lacked a firm theoretical basis. Greater than this is my gratitude to Stephen Schneider who made sure that Gaia was properly debated by the scientific community by calling a Chapman Conference of the American Geophysical Union in March 1988.

To many scientists Gaia was a teleological concept, one that required foresight and planning by the biota. How in the world could the bacteria, the trees, and the animals have a conference to decide optimum conditions? How could organisms keep oxygen at 21 percent and the mean temperature at 20°C? Not seeing a mechanism for planetary control, they denied its existence as a phenomenon and branded the Gaia hypothesis as teleological. This was a final condemnation. Teleological explanations, in academe, are a sin against the holy spirit of scientific rationality; they deny the objectivity of Nature.

But when making this severest of criticisms of Gaia, the scientists may not have noticed the extent of their own errors. The innocent use of that slippery concept "adaptation" is another path to damnation. Earth is indeed the best of all worlds for those who are adapted to it. But the excellence of our planet takes on a different significance in the light of the evidence that geochemists themselves have gathered. Evidence that shows the Earth's crust, oceans, and air to be either directly the product of living things or else massively modified by their presence. Consider how the oxygen and nitrogen of the air come directly from plants and micro-organisms, and how the chalk and limestone rocks are the shells of living things once floating in the sea. Life has not adapted to an inert world determined by the dead hand of chemistry and physics. We live in a world that has been built by our ancestors, ancient and modern, and which is continuously maintained by all things alive today. Organisms are adapting in a world whose material state is determined by the activities of their neighbors; this means that changing the environment is part of the game. To think otherwise would require that evolution was a game with rules like cricket or baseball—one in which the rules forbad environmental change. If, in the real world, the activity of an organism changes its material environment to a more favorable state, and as a consequence it leaves more progeny, then both the species and the change will increase until a new stable state is reached. On a local scale adaptation is a means by which organisms can come to terms with unfavorable environments, but on a planetary scale the coupling between life and its environment is so tight that the tautologous notion of "adaptation" is squeezed from existence. The evolution of the rocks and the air and the evolution of the biota are not to be separated.

It is a tribute to the success of biogeochemistry that most Earth scientists today agree that the reactive gases of the atmosphere are biological products. But most would disagree that the biota in any way control the composition of the atmosphere, or any of the important variables, such as global temperature and oxygen concentration, which depend on the atmosphere. There are two principal objections to Gaia, first that it is teleological, and that for the regulation of the climate, the chemical composition on a planetary scale, a kind of forecasting, a clairvoyance, would be needed. The second objection, most clearly expressed by Stephen Schneider, is that biological regulation is only partial, and that the real world is a "coevolution" of life and the inorganic. The second criticism is the more difficult, and in many ways the purpose of this book is to try to answer it. The first, the teleological criticism, I think is wrong and I will now try to show why.

I knew that there was little point in gathering more evidence about the now-obvious capacity of the Earth to regulate its climate and composition. Mere evidence by itself could not be expected to convince mainstream scientists that the Earth was regulated by life. Scientists usually want to know how it works; they want a mechanism. What was needed was a Gaian model. In those hybrid sciences of biogeochemistry and biogeophysics, models of environmental change do not permit a regulatory role to the biota. The practitioners of these sciences assume that the operating points of the system are fixed by chemical and physical properties. For example, snow melts or forms at 0°C. The reflection of sunlight by snow cover can provide a powerful positive feedback on cooling, and a system for regulating the climate could be based on the melting or formation of snow. But there is no way for the melting point of snow, which is a characteristic of ice as a substance, to change to a more comfortable warmth of, say 20°C. In great contrast, the operating points of a living organism are always set at favorable levels.

In what way do Gaian models differ from the conventional biogeochemical ones? Does the assumption of the close coupling of life and its environment change the nature of the whole system? Is homeostasis a reasonable prediction of Gaia theory? The difficulty in answering these questions comes from the sheer complexity of the biota and the environment, and because they are interconnected in multiple ways. There is hardly a single aspect of their interaction that we can confidently describe by a mathematical equation. A drastic simplification was needed. I wrestled with the problem of reducing the complexity of life and its environment to a simple scheme that could enlighten without distorting. Daisyworld was the answer. I first described this model in 1982 at a conference on biomineralization in Amsterdam, and published a paper, "The Parable of Daisyworld," in *Tellus* in 1983 with my colleague Andrew Watson. I am indebted to Andrew for the clear, graphic way of expressing it in formal mathematical terms in this paper.

Picture a planet about the same size as the Earth, spinning on its axis and orbiting, at the same distance as the Earth, a star of the same mass and luminosity as the Sun. This planet differs from the Earth in having more land area and less ocean, but it is well watered, and plants will grow almost anywhere on the land surfaces when the climate is right. This is the planet Daisyworld, so called because the principal plant species are daisies of different shades of color: some dark, some light, and some neutral colors in between. The star that warms and illuminates Daisyworld shares with our Sun the property of increasing its output of heat as it ages. When life started on

Earth some 3.8 billion years ago, the Sun was about 30 percent less luminous than now. In a few more billion years, it will become so fiercely hot that all life that we know will die or be obliged to find another home planet. The increase of the Sun's brightness as it ages is a general and undoubted property of stars. As the star burns hydrogen (its nuclear fuel) helium accumulates. The helium, in the form of a gaseous ash, is more opaque to radiant energy than is hydrogen and so impedes the flow of heat from the nuclear furnace at the center of the star. The central temperature then rises and this in turn increases the rate of hydrogen burning until there is a new balance between heat produced at the center and the heat lost from the solar surface. Unlike ordinary fires, star-sized nuclear fires burn fiercer as the ash accumulates and sometimes even explode.

Daisyworld is simplified, reduced if you like, in the following ways. The environment is reduced to a single variable, temperature, and the biota to a single species, daisies. If too cold, below 5°C, daisies will not grow; they do best at a temperature near 20°C. If the temperature exceeds 40°C, it will be too hot for the daisies, and they will wilt and die. The mean temperature of the planet is a simple balance between the heat received from the star and the heat lost to the cold depths of space in the form of long-wave infrared radiation. On the Earth, this heat balance is complicated by the effects of clouds and of gases such as carbon dioxide. The sunlight may be reflected back to space by the clouds before it can reach and warm the surface. On the other hand, the heat loss from the warm surface may be lessened because clouds and molecules of carbon dioxide reflect it back to the surface. Daisyworld is assumed to have a constant amount of carbon dioxide, enough for daisies to grow but not so much as to complicate the climate. Similarly, there are no clouds in the daytime to mar the simplicity of the model, and all rain falls during the night.

The mean temperature of Daisyworld is, therefore, simply determined by the average shade of color of the planet, or as astronomers call it, the albedo. If the planet is a dark shade, low albedo, it absorbs more heat from the sunlight and the surface is warmed. If light in color, like fallen snow, then 70 or 80 percent of the sunlight may be reflected back to space. Such a surface is cold when compared with a dark surface under comparable solar illumination. Albedos range from 0 (wholly black) to 1 (wholly white). The bare ground of

Daisyworld is usually taken to have an albedo of 0.4 so that it absorbs 40 percent of the sunlight that falls upon it. Daisies range in shade of color from dark (with an albedo of 0.2) to light (with an albedo of 0.7).

Imagine a time in the distant past of Daisyworld. The star that warms it was less luminous, so that only in the equatorial region was the mean temperature of bare ground warm enough, 5°C, for growth. Here daisy seeds would slowly germinate and flower. Let us assume that in the first crop multicolored, light, and dark species were equally represented. Even before the first season's growth was over, the dark daisies would have been favored. Their greater absorption of sunlight in the localities where they grew would have warmed them above 5°C. The light-colored daisies would be at a disadvantage. Their white flowers would have faded and died because, reflecting the sunlight as they do, they would have cooled below the critical temperature of 5°C.

The next season would see the dark daisies off to a head start, for their seeds would be the most abundant. Soon their presence would warm not just the plants themselves, but, as they grew and spread across the bare ground, would increase the temperature of the soil and air, at first locally and then regionally. With this rise of temperature, the rate of growth, the length of the warm season, and the spread of dark daisies would all exert a positive feedback and lead to the colonization of most of the planet by dark daisies. The spread of dark daisies would eventually be limited by a rise of global temperature to levels above the optimum for growth. Any further spread of dark daisies would lead to a decline in seed production. In addition, when the global temperature is high, white daisies will grow and spread in competition with the dark ones. The growth and spread of white daisies is favored then because of their natural ability to keep cool.

As the star that shines on Daisyworld grows older and hotter, the proportion of dark to light daisies changes until, finally, the heat flux is so great that even the whitest daisy crop cannot keep enough of the planet below the critical 40°C upper limit for growth. At this time flower power is not enough. The planet becomes barren again, and so hot that there is no way for daisy life to start again.

It is easy to make a numerical model of Daisyworld simple enough to run on a personal computer. Daisy populations are modeled by differential equations borrowed from theoretical ecology (Carter and Prince, 1981). The mean temperature of the planet is calculated directly from the balance of the heat it receives from its star and the heat it loses by radiation to the cold depths of space. Figure 1 shows the evolution of the temperature and the growth of daisies during the progressive increase in heat flux from its star according to the conventional wisdom of physics and biology, and according to geophysiology.

When I first tried the Daisyworld model I was surprised and delighted by the strong regulation of planetary temperature that came from the simple competitive growth of plants with dark and light shades. I did not invent these models because I thought that daisies, or any other dark- and light-colored

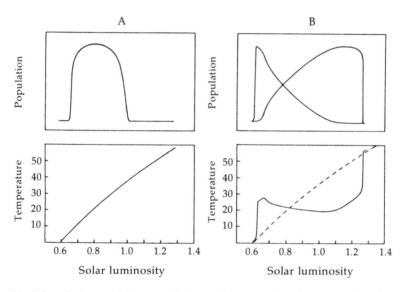

Models of the evolution of Daisyworld according to conventional wisdom (*A*) and to geophysiology (*B*). The upper panels illustrate daisy populations in arbitrary units; the lower panels, temperatures in degrees Celsius. Going from left to right along the horizontal axis, the star's luminosity increases from 60 to 140 percent of that of our own Sun. *A* illustrates how the physicists and the biologists in complete isolation calculate their view of the evolution of the planet. According to this conventional wisdom, the daisies can only respond or adapt to changes in temperature. When it becomes too hot for comfort, they will die. But in the Gaian Daisyworld (*B*), the ecosystem can respond by the competitive growth of the dark and light daisies, and regulate the temperature over a wide range of solar luminosity. The dashed line in the lower panel in *B* shows how the temperature would rise on a lifeless Daisyworld.

plants, regulate the Earth's temperature by changing the balance between the heat received from the Sun and that lost to space. I had designed them to answer the criticism of Ford Doolittle and Richard Dawkins that Gaia was teleological. In Daisyworld, one property of the global environment, temperature, was shown to be regulated effectively, over a wide range of solar luminosity, by an imaginary planetary biota without invoking foresight or planning. This is a definitive rebuttal of the accusation that the Gaia hypothesis is teleological, and so far it remains unchallenged.

So what is Gaia? If the real world we inhabit is self-regulating in the manner of Daisyworld, and if the climate and environment we enjoy and freely exploit is a consequence of an automatic, but not purposeful, goal-seeking system, then Gaia is the largest manifestation of life. The tightly coupled system of life and its environment, Gaia, includes:

1. Living organisms that grow vigorously, exploiting any environmental opportunities that open.

2. Organisms that are subject to the rules of Darwinian natural selection: the species of organisms that leave the most progeny survive.

3. Organisms that affect their physical and chemical environment. Thus animals change the atmosphere by breathing: taking in oxygen and letting out carbon dioxide. Plants and algae do the reverse. In numerous other ways, all forms of life incessantly modify the physical and chemical environment.

4. The existence of constraints or bounds that establish the limits of life. It can be too hot or too cold; there is a comfortable warmth in between, the preferred state. It can be too acid or too alkaline; neutrality is preferred. Almost all chemicals have a range of concentrations tolerated or needed by life. For many elements, such as iodine, selenium, and iron, too much is a poison, too little causes starvation. Pure uncontaminated water will support little; but neither will the saturated brine of the Dead Sea.

Few scientists would object to any of these four conditions, either singly or taken as a group. When they are taken together as a tightly coupled ensemble, they seem to form a recipe for a Gaian system. The ensemble is a fruitful source of models of self-regulating systems like Daisyworld. The fourth condition, which sets the physical and chemical bounds of life, I find the most interesting, unexpected, and full of insight. One has only to think of the social analogue of the family or community that exists with firm but reasonable bounds in comparison with one in which the limits of behavior are ill-defined. Stability and well-defined bounds seem to go together. Physicists are agreed that life is an open system. But like one of those Russian dolls which enclose a series of smaller and still smaller dolls, life exists within a set of boundaries. The outer boundary is the Earth's atmospheric edge to space. Within the planetary boundary, entities diminish but grow ever more intense as the inward progression goes from Gaia to ecosystems, to plants and animals, to cells and to DNA. The boundary of the planet then circumscribes a living organism, Gaia, a system made up of all the living things and their environment. There is no clear distinction anywhere on the Earth's surface between living and nonliving matter. There is merely a hierarchy of intensity going from the "material" environment of the rocks and the atmosphere to the living cells. But at great depths below the surface, the effects of life's presence fade. It may be that the core of our planet is unchanged as a result of life; but it would be unwise to assume it.

In exploring the question, "What is life?" we have made some progress. By looking at life through Gaia's telescope, we see it as a planetary-scale phenomenon with a cosmological life span. Gaia as the largest manifestation of life differs from other living organisms of Earth in the way that you or I differ from our population of living cells. At some time early in the Earth's history before life existed, the solid Earth, the atmosphere, and oceans were still evolving by the laws of physics and chemistry alone. It was careering, downhill, to the lifeless steady state of a planet almost at equilibrium. Briefly, in its headlong flight through the ranges of chemical and physical states, it entered a stage favorable for life. At some special time in that stage, the newly formed living cells grew until their presence so affected the Earth's environment as to halt the headlong dive towards equilibrium. At that instant the living things, the rocks, the air, and the oceans merged to form the new entiry, Gaia. Just as when the sperm merges with the egg, new life was conceived.

The quest to define life might be compared with assembling a jigsaw puzzle, a puzzle where a landscape scene is cut into a thousand small interlocking pieces and the pieces scrambled. Classification is needed to put it together again. The blue sky is easy to separate from the brown earth and green trees. Skilled solvers of the jigsaw puzzle know that a key step is to find and connect the straight-sided pieces that define the edge, the boundary of the scene. The discovery that the outer reaches of the atmosphere are a part of planetary life in a like manner has defined the edge of our puzzle picture of the Earth. Once the edge is completely assembled, at least the size of the picture is known and the placing of the inner groupings made easier. Gaia is no static picture. She is forever changing as life and the Earth evolve together, but in our brief life span she keeps still long enough for us to begin to understand and see how fair she is.

7

Wizard of Tuskegee

PETER TOMKINS
CHRISTOPHER BIRD

That plants were able to reveal their hidden secrets upon request was accepted as normal and natural by a remarkable genius born just before the Civil War, the agricultural chemist George Washington Carver, who overcame the handicap of his slave descent to be heralded in his own lifetime as the "Black Leonardo."

During a stunningly creative career, with methods as incomprehensible to his fellow scientists as were those of his professional forebears the alchemists, Carver turned the lowly peanut, considered useful only as hog food, and the unknown sweet potato into hundreds of separate products, ranging from cosmetics and axle grease to printer's ink and coffee.

From the time he was able to get about by himself in the countryside young Carver began to display an uncanny knowledge of all growing things. Local farmers in Diamond Grove, a tiny community in the foothills of the Ozarks in southwestern Missouri, remembered the weak-looking boy roving for hours through their holdings, examining plants and bringing back certain varieties with which he could miraculously heal sick animals. On his own, the child planted a private garden in a remote and unused bit of bottomland. With the remnants of coldframes and other stray material he built a secret greenhouse in the woods. Asked what he was forever doing all by himself so far from the farmyard, Carver replied firmly if enigmatically, "I go to my garden hospital and take care of hundreds of sick plants."

Farmers' wives from all over the countryside began bringing him their ailing house plants, begging him to make them bloom. Gently caring for them in his own way, Carver often sang to them in the same squeaky voice which characterized him in manhood, put them in tin cans with special soil of his own concoction, tenderly covered them at night, and took them out to "play in the sun" during the day. When he returned the plants to their owners, and repeatedly was asked how he could work his miracles, Carver only said softly: "All flowers talk to me and so do hundreds of little living things in the woods. I learn what I know by watching and loving everything."

Enrolling in Simpson College in Indianola, Iowa, Carver supported himself through his skill as a laundryman by doing shirts for students, then transferred to the Iowa State College of Agriculture. There among his most lasting impressions was the statement of his best-loved teacher, Henry Cantwell Wallace, editor of the popular *Wallace's Farmer*, that "nations endure only as long as their topsoil." Carrying a heavy load of course work and employed by churches as an entirely self-taught organist, Carver found time to take Wallace's six-year-old grandson on long walks into the woods to talk with plants and fairies, little suspecting that the hand he was holding would be that of a Secretary of Agriculture, and later, two years before Carver's own death, Vice President of the United States.

By 1896, Carver had his master's degree and was invited to join the faculty. However, when the founder and president of the Normal and Industrial Institute, Booker T. Washington, who had heard of Carver's brilliance, asked him to come to Tuskegee, Alabama, and run the institute's agricultural department, Carver decided, like Sir Jagadis Chandra Bose, that he could not let the prospect of a comfortable and well-paying post on the Iowa State faculty dissuade him from serving his own people. So he accepted.

Carver had not been back in the South more than a few weeks when he discerned that the main problem facing the flat land spreading out in hundreds of square miles around him was its slow poisoning through monotonous planting year in year out of a single crop, cotton, which for generations had been sucking fertility out of the soil. To counteract the despoliation by thousands of sharecroppers, he decided to set up an experimental station. There he had a private laboratory, christened "God's Little Workshop," in which he would sit for hours communing with plants and into which he never allowed a single book to penetrate.

For his students at Tuskegee he made his lectures as simple and yet as thoroughgoing as possible. When the chancellor of the University of Georgia, W. B. Hill, came to Tuskegee to see for himself if it was true that a Negro professor was as brilliant as rumor had reported, he declared that Carver's presentation on the problem of Southern agriculture was "the best lecture that it has ever been my privilege to attend." Carver's students were greatly impressed that each morning he would rise at four o'clock to walk in the woods before the start of the working day and bring back countless plants with which to illustrate his lectures. Explaining this habit to friends, Carver said, "Nature is the greatest teacher and I learn from her best when others are asleep. In the still dark hours before sunrise God tells me of the plans I am to fulfill."

For more than a decade Carver worked daily on experimental plots of soil trying to discover exactly how to change Alabama's enthrallment by "ol' debbil cotton." On one nineteen-acre plot he put no commercial fertilizer, benefiting it instead with nothing but old dead leaves from the forest, rich muck from the swamps, and barnyard manure. The plot furnished such bountiful harvests of rotated crops that Carver came to the conclusion that "in Alabama the very fertilizers which existed in almost unlimited supply were allowed to go to waste in favor of commercially sold products."

As a horticulturalist, Carver had noticed that the peanut was incredibly self-sufficient and could grow well in poor soil. As a chemist, he discovered that it equaled sirloin steaks in protein and potatoes in carbohydrates. Late one evening while pondering the problem in his workshop Carver stared at a peanut plant and asked, "Why did the Lord make you?" In a flash, he received the briefest of answers: "You have three things to go by: compatibility, temperature, and pressure."

With this slim advice Carver locked himself in his laboratory. There, throughout a sleepless week, he began breaking down the peanut into its chemical components and exposing them by trial and error to different conditions of temperature and pressure. To his satisfaction he found that one-third of the little nut was made up of seven different varieties of oil. Working round the clock, he analyzed and synthesized, took apart and recombined, broke down and built up the chemically differentiable parts of the peanut until at last he had two dozen bottles, each containing a brand-new product.

Leaving his laboratory, he convoked a meeting of farmers and agricultural specialists and showed them what he had been able to do in seven days and seven nights. He begged his audience to plow under the soil-destroying cotton and plant peanuts in its stead, assuring them that it would produce a cash crop far more valuable than its sole existing use as food for pigs might indicate.

The audience was doubtful, the more so when Carver, asked to explain his methods, replied that he never groped for them but that they came to him in flashes of inspiration while walking in the woods. To allay their doubts he began to issue bulletins, one of which stated incredibly that rich, nutritious, and highly palatable butter could be made from the peanut, and that whereas it took one hundred pounds of dairy milk to make ten pounds of butter, a hundred pounds of peanuts could produce thirty-five pounds of peanut butter. Other bulletins showed how a cornucopia of products could also be extracted from the sweet potato, a tropical vine of which most Americans had never heard, that throve in the South's cotton-debased soil. When World War I broke out, and the shortage of dye-stuffs presented itself as a serious national problem, Carver rambled at daybreak through the mist and dew, inquiring of his plant friends which of them could alleviate the deficit. From the leaves, roots, stems, and fruits of twenty-eight volunteers he coaxed 536 separate dyes, which could be used to color wool, cotton, linen, silk, and even leather, producing 49 of them from the scuppernong grape alone.

At last his labors attracted national attention. When it was bruited that at Tuskegee Institute they were saving two hundred pounds of wheat per day by mixing two parts of ordinary flour with a new flour derived from sweet potatoes, a flock of dieticians and food writers interested in cooperating with the wartime drive to economize on wheat came to investigate. They were served delicious breads made from the mixed flours, along with a sumptuous lunch of five courses each made from peanuts or sweet potatoes, or, like Carver's "mock chicken," from the two combined. The only other vegetables on the table were sheep sorrel, pepper grass, wild chicory, and dandelions, served as a salad to illustrate Carver's assertion that plants growing in nature were far better than those from which the natural vitality had been removed in cultivation. The food experts, who realized that Carver's contributions might go a long way to helping the war effort, rushed to telephone their papers, and Carver, who had become known to scientists the year before when he was elected a fellow of Great Britain's famous Royal Society, now appeared in the headlines.

Invited to Washington, Carver dazzled government officials with dozens of products, including a starch valuable to the textile industry which later became a component in the glue of billions of U.S. postage stamps.

Next it came to Carver that peanut oil could help the atrophied muscles of polio victims. Results were so astonishing that he had to set aside one day each month to treat patients who came to his laboratory on stretchers, crutches, or canes. This feat remained as unheralded in medicine as the application of castor-oil packs, recommended about the same time by the "sleeping prophet," Edgar Cayce, with which doctors of an intrepidly investigative frame of mind are only today beginning to achieve startling, and wholly inexplicable cures.

By 1930, the peanut's one-time worthlessness had been converted, through Carver's clairvoyance, into a quarter of a billion dollars for Southern farmers, and had created a huge industry. Peanut oil alone was valued at $60 million a year and peanut butter was establishing itself as one of the favorite foods of even the poorest American child. Not satisfied with his achievements, Carver went on to make paper from a local Southern pine tree which ultimately helped to spur lumberers to cover millions of Southern acres with productive forests where only scrub woods had existed.

In the midst of the depression, Carver was again invited to Washington to testify before the powerful Ways and Means Committee of the U.S. Senate, which was considering the Smoot-Hawley tariff bill designed to protect struggling American manufacturers. Dressed in his usual, seemingly eternally durable, two-dollar black suit, with an ever-present flower in its buttonhole and a home-made necktie, Carver, upon his arrival at Union Station, was rebuffed by a waiting porter who, when Carver asked him to help him with his bags and direct him to Congress, replied: "Sorry, Pop, I ain't got time for you now. I'm expecting an important colored scientist coming from Alabama." Patiently Carver hefted his own bags to a taxi which took him to Capitol Hill.

Though the committee had accorded him no more than ten minutes to testify, when he began his presentations and took from his bag face powders, petroleum substitutes, shampoos, creosote, vinegar, woodstains, and other samples of the countless creations concocted in his laboratories, the Vice President of the United States, testy "Cactus Jack" Garner from Texas, overruled protocol and told Carver he could have as much time as he liked because his demonstration was the best that he had ever seen presented to a Senate committee.

In half a lifetime of research Carver, though he created fortunes for thousands, rarely took out a patent on any of his ideas. When practical-minded industrialists and politicians reminded him of the money he might have made had he only afforded himself this protection, he replied simply: "God did not charge me or you for making peanuts. Why should I profit from their products?" Like Bose, Carver believed that the fruit of his mind, however valuable, should be granted free of charge to mankind.

Thomas A. Edison told his associates that "Carver is worth a fortune" and backed up his statement by offering to employ the black chemist at an astronomically high salary. Carver turned down the offer. Henry Ford, who thought Carver "the greatest scientist living," tried to get him to come to his River Rouge establishment, with an equal lack of success.

Because of the strangely unaccountable source from which his magic with plant products sprang, his methods continued to be as wholly inscrutable as Burbank's to scientists and to the general public. Visitors finding Carver puttering at his workbench amid a confusing clutter of molds, soils, plants, and insects were baffled by the utter and, to many of them, meaningless simplicity of his replies to their persistent pleas for him to reveal his secrets.

To one puzzled interlocutor he said: "The secrets are in the plants. To elicit them you have to love them enough."

"But why do so few people have your power?" the man persisted. "Who besides you can do these things?"

"Everyone can," said Carver, "if only they believe it." Tapping a large Bible on a table, he added, "The secrets are all here. In God's promises. These promises are real, as real as, and more infinitely solid and substantial than, this table which the materialist so thoroughly believes in."

In a celebrated public lecture, Carver related how he had been able to call forth from the low mountains of Alabama hundreds of natural colors from clays and other earths, including a rare pigment of deep blue which amazed Egyptologists, who saw rediscovered in it the blue color found in the tomb of Tutankhamen, as bright and fresh after so many centuries as it was when it had been first applied.

When Carver was eighty or thereabouts—his exact date of birth never having been established since no records were kept for slave children—he addressed a meeting of chemists in New York as World War II was erupting in Europe.

"The ideal chemist of the future," said Carver, "will not be satisfied with humdrum day-to-day analysis, but is one who dares to think and work with an independence not permissible heretofore, unfolding before our eyes a veritable mystic maze of new and useful products from material almost or quite beneath our feet and now considered of little or no value."

Not long before Carver's death a visitor to his laboratory saw him reach out his long sensitive fingers to a little flower on his workbench. "When I touch that flower," he said rapturously, "I am touching infinity. It existed long before there were human beings on this earth and will continue to exist for millions of years to come. Through the flower, I talk to the Infinite, which is only a silent force. This is not a physical contact. It is not in the earthquake, wind or fire. It is in the invisible world. It is that still small voice that calls up the fairies."

He suddenly stopped and after a moment of reflection smiled at his visitor. "Many people know this instinctively," he said, "and none better than Tennyson when he wrote:

"Flower in the crannied wall,
I pluck you out of the crannies,
I hold you here, root and all, in my hand,
Little flower—but *if* I could understand
What you are, root and all, and all in all,
I should know what God and man is."

8

Nature As Psyche

PATRICK MILBURN

A new perspective on nature is emerging, one arising chiefly out of developments in depth psychology and critical philosophy, though also driven to a degree by the "observer problem" in quantum physics. This new perspective seeks to retain the benefits of the technical thought of the last three centuries, but to place it in a wider frame of reference which will allow a richer and more adequate understanding of the relationship between *subjectivity* and *objectivity*. The bright success of technical and economic analysis has been accompanied by a shadow—the loss of a felt-sense of the aliveness of the world. An awareness of the esthetic quality of nature, let alone a moral sensibility, has been difficult to sustain due to the prestige afforded the "value free" objectivistic framework. From a critical perspective, the confidence placed in this objective stance has been unwarranted, but the wave of technical and economic success it has engendered has, for the most part, overwhelmed all criticism.

A shift to a new frame of reference has, however, been prepared by a gradually rising dissatisfaction with the quality of life produced by the success of the technical mind-set—a widespread feeling of emptiness, moral dissatisfaction and meaninglessness arising in the very midst of our lives. At present this is often expressed in environmental metaphors of pollution and the loss of natural environments, but it seems that the popular force sustaining these abstract concerns must arise from deeper wellsprings than those the media command. The likely source of each of these metaphors is the felt loss of soul from the world.

This loss could perhaps not have been forestalled unless Western society had been graced with more creative and understanding leadership at key turning points in its history. The loss arose chiefly out of a generalization of the powerful technical and objectifying frame of reference from its valid application in research and development to use as a model for the world in general. In the parlance of phenomenology, a *regional* ontology—a "theory of being" used by a particular discipline, such as technical science—has come to serve as a popular *general* ontology—a "theory of being" for reality as a whole.

While this essay has the tentative character of a "work in progress," it calls attention to developments that open the way for a recovery of our awareness of the "aliveness" and value of all reality, for a recovery of the soul of the world. The central figure in this cultural transformation is James Hillman, a leader in archetypal psychology. His *Re-Vision of Psychology* stands at the center of an emerging awareness of our need for an angle of vision adequate to the whole of human reality. Other figures whose ideas are contributing to the re-valuation of objectivism are the French philosopher Jacques Maritain and his modernization of Thomism; the Japanese comparative philosopher Toshihiko Izutsu; the French phenomenologist Maurice Merleau-Ponty; the American critical philosopher Lawrence Hatab; and, very important, the Japanese philosopher Kitaro Nishida. There are others, of course. Whole fields, most notably the history and philosophy of science, are also preparing the way for a shift in the meta-phors that govern our perception. The impact of this work on our lives is first and foremost transforming our perception—widening it out so that we once again become open to the soul of the world and to our presence in the world as an expression of this intrinsic dimension of reality.

The Idea of Subjectivity

James Hillman has charted the transformation of the concepts of *subject* and *object* from the late medieval period, through Descartes and the birth of the modern epoch, on to the present. This great transformation has led to the withdrawal of sub-jectivity from the world—to our being governed by metaphors which prevent us from seeing the subjective qualities of objects and to the gradual recognition of human beings as the only *real* "subjects." All attribution of subjective qualities to the things of the world is currently regarded as "projection" and as "giving meaning" to a world which is not "really" there. Manifold demands for the radical separation of subject and object, most of all in technology and psychiatry has withdrawn all meaning-giving into the individual mind. The world has been radically depersonalized. The core of this style of analysis and perception, as Hillman has pointed out, is *experience* as the criterion for a subject:

> Of course things are dead, said the old psychology, because they do not "experience" [feelings, memories, intentions] . . . . Because things do not *experience*, they have no subjectivity, no interiority, no depth. When psychic reality is equated with experience, then ego becomes necessary to psychological logic. We have to invent an interior witness, an experiencer at the center of subjectivity—and we cannot do otherwise.[1]

The modern conceptualization of the subject as experiencer represented a departure from the Scholastic concept, but one that was prepared by the development of thought, especially that of Thomas Aquinas. However, the Scholastic model had another resource which Jacques Maritain in his reinterpretation of Thomas has brought to view.[2] The Thomistic model regarded the world as formed entirely of "subjects" (subsistants), whose role was "to pour forth their being as actions," where action includes all forms of manifestation. Objects, in this schema, were the appearances of subjects to perceiving minds. Thus, all beings were subject-objects—subjects expressing themselves through appearances-actions, and objects for other subjectivities. Persons were regarded as the "most perfect" subjects, and with this ideal of perfection, the way was prepared for the modern shift in the way subjects were conceived, away from "pouring forth their being as action" to "experiencing." With this shift the world became "objectivized," and the only subject became the spectator consciousness of human beings. The core of the medieval idea may, however, be regarded as a useful resource in rethinking our relationship to the world.

Hillman is suggesting that each thing has a subjective reality which one can read on its surface, in its gestures. Thus, he is interpreting each thing as engaging in "self-expression." This is not so different from Aquinas regarding all things as subjects, and subjects as "pouring forth their being as actions." Hillman's suggestion may be regarded as a return to a great turning point in late medieval philosophy and, with that, an opportunity to shift the meaning of subject more towards its creative medieval intent. "Pouring forth being as action" may appropriately be understood as a form of self-expression and expressiveness:

> With things returned again to soul . . . then their interiority and depth . . . depend not on their experiencing themselves or on their

self-motivation but upon self-witness of another sort. An object bears witness to itself *in the image that it offers*, and its depth lies in the complexities of this image.

Subjectivity here is freed from literalization in reflexive experience. . . . Instead, each object a subject, and its self-reflection is its self-display, its radiance.[3]

Hillman uses words very similar to those of the medieval synthesis; each thing is a subject, pouring forth its reality, its radiance, in self-display. With this shift away from the modern understanding, we realize that we have disregarded the "subjective" qualities of things under the prevailing fashion of understanding subjects and objects. Hillman's perspective urges us to look at all the things around us with new interest, seeing them as subject-objects expressing themselves in appearance and action.

Hillman's angle of vision leads us into a figure-ground change and prompts us to look for the emotional quality and meaning of an event in the appearance of subject-objects and in the physiognomy of situations, rather than only within individuals. The "field concept of emotion and meaning," as developed by Gestalt psychology and existential phenomenology, is the scientific equivalent of becoming open to the *anima mundi*, the soul of the world.[4] As Hillman emphasizes, an appearance or image "bears the gift of significance; it is fecund with implications; or in Gestalt language, an image has pregnancy."[5]

The Imaginal Qualities of Landscapes

The modern view of meaning as occurring only within human beings has led us to ignore the imaginal and expressive qualities of landscapes, animals, and plants. This, together with the concommittant loss of a "moral sense of nature" has been the chief manifestation of the depersonalization that has followed from the objectivistic model of reality. If we now shift our perception of the world, looking in a new way to see the imaginal quality of things and landscapes as subject-objects, as active images "pregnant with their own significance," we will find that we require both a richer vocabulary and much practice to cultivate the skills which can enable us to discern the living character of reality. The change involves looking with a different gaze, an "animal eye," as Hillman says, scenting out the meanings there before us in mountains, forests, and even city streets. It is a different style of perception, an openness to the inherent richness of things. Most of all, it is patience and a caring interest in things that can open our eye and mind to this face of the world.

We have spoken of things in this new perspective as "subject-objects," pregnant with significance. Things seen in this way come to seem as though they are persons ready to speak. This feature of sensitive perception is its essential characteristic, a spontaneous personifying—not as a thought or judgment, but as a strongly felt sense that things are "about to speak," or that they are speaking to us silently. Even if the notion of indwelling minds is dismissed, there is still, in the perception of the character of things, a dramatic sense of latent "personages" embodied there. If one does not rush to explain this away, or to shake off the touch of the uncanny that this experience can evoke, one comes to an appreciation of such statements of the ancients as "all things are full of gods."

It is, however, very important to avoid rushing to the conclusion that there are "gods" or "minds" in things, for example, and to stay with the living reality at hand. While it is likely that the notions of ancient and traditional cultures about gods were at least partly in reference to experiences of this sort, it is possible that the full sense of this experience of "latent" personages in things will turn out to have a different significance. At the least, this kind of experience directs us to an awareness of the world as *a field of personification*.[6] The simple practice of being attentive to the gesture-like and mood-like quality of things leads into a kind of Gestalt closure on these patterns into wholes that have the character of persons. It is most effective to spend some time every day walking around just attending to the qualities of places and things, suspending inner dialogue enough so that one can really notice both the surface and the depth in appearances. Then, it is valuable to take time to describe these qualities as carefully as possible in a journal. Fleetingly at first, but then more and more often, one begins to notice the latent personages behind the masks and within the gestures. This practice might be called a "re-personalization of the world." This practice is important, for without it one will easily dismiss the force of these experiences as "merely projection" or "illusion." Once one has gathered a large number of such experiences that speak to us in ways of which we have no expectation, the only option left for the standard model is to assume that we are projecting some very deep part of our unconscious. Finally, at some point, it dawns in our awareness that what we have been calling the unconscious permeates all reality and is speaking to us in the manner of our dreams.

The Issue of Truth and Error

Before we proceed further with our exploration of the *anima mundi*, the soul of the world, we must speak to the issue of truth and error, objectivity and subjectivity. Lawrence Hatab, in his book *Myth and Philosophy: A Contest of Truths*, has explored the changed situation surrounding the issue of objectivity as it has emerged from contemporary critical philosophy and related studies in the social sciences.

It has been common for several generations to speak of what is *objective* as true and of what is *subjective* as merely personal and of no general validity. The history and philosophy of science have now made clear to everyone who takes an interest in it that the objectivity of the sciences is not so clear-cut as was once believed. Hanson and others have emphasized the "theory laden" quality of observation in science; people see the kinds of things they are looking for. More serious for the common sense idea of objectivity is the fact that scientists often disagree over the apparent "meaning" of their observations. Different schools of thought contend over evidence until consensus is reached, a consensus which may undergo transformation within a decade with the appearance of new and often unanticipated evidence.

Another major issue has been the "value free" character of science. The social and environmental impacts of technological processes have raised a host of issues about the values inherent, at least in the *application* of knowledge. More fundamental has been the disclosure by research in the sociology of science that science itself operates within a value context of rigorous honesty and of search for the actual character of reality. Departure from these norms raises periodic storms of scandal within the scientific community. Science grows in a context of values and is given meaning by values shared by the research community.

The crucial issue has been that different persons may have different perceptions of value as well as different perceptions of the facts. This led the ancient Greeks to prefer mathematics over "mere opinion." Developments in critical philosophy and phenomenology offer resources for dealing with this problem that were not available even at the founding of modern philosophy in the sixteenth century. As Hatab makes clear,

> No one who *practices* science or *holds* ethical values or *responds* to beauty or *engages* in philosophical inquiry ever perceives such activity to be a subjective projection upon a neutral or unknowable world. The direction is decidedly *from* the world, no matter how much the activity requires the participation of the subject.[7]

The critical solution to these problems may be called *contextualism*. Persons and worlds are shaping one another, but the world consists of a manifold of "worlds"—contexts—whether one considers the question ethically, scientifically, or esthetically. The growth of ethical, artistic, and scientific traditions occurs in communities engaged with particular perspectives on the world, particular contexts that disclose value or meaning in distinctive ways. At all times in the scientific area, as in the ethical and artistic areas, there will be both majority consensus views and dissent. In spite of the lack of absolute truth or objectivity and the presence of dissenting views, ethical, artistic, and scientific understanding does continue to undergo gradual development. It is important for those accustomed to referring casually to "objective judgments" or to "mere subjectivity" to understand that the issue is not as simple as that. The unfoldment of knowledge as well as of ethical and artistic understanding takes a more complex path than was believed in the past. As Hatab points out,

> I think that historical and phenomenological analysis forbids the idea that *any* form of knowledge involves (or can involve) total agreement.[8]
>
> . . . agreement cannot be the only mark of truth. What we say must also be in some way a response to the world and have some degree of coherence.[9]

Among other marks of truth, Hatab suggests *appropriateness* in our inquiry and in the response of the world; *reliability* and continuity, even if these are not absolute; *workability*, permitting us to engage the world and the world permitting our engagement; and *sense*, giving coherence to particulars.[10]

Such contextualism is pluralistic and permits the coexistence of different modes of disclosure. It recognizes that there are value and esthetic components to the practice of science, a recognition now gaining such general recognition as to be obvious to most persons. This is, then, a more complex picture than we have been accustomed to, and a more realistic one. Moreover, the inherent pluralism of this understanding requires that each form of knowledge or value be seen as arising in its own *subject-object context* and as an opening on the world that is shaped by values and interests which disclose one particular face of reality.

In such a contextualistic matrix it is no longer necessary to dismiss a framework like Hillman's as "merely subjective" or as "projection." Rather, such a view can be seen to represent one "face" of reality, one mode of disclosure within which great riches may be uncovered.

At the same time, contextual pluralism creates its own critique of the "value-free" standpoint and depersonalization of the world of modern objectivism. This viewpoint, for all its claims to complete generality, is itself context-bound, arising from particular values and interests and disclosing particular kinds of truth. It does not represent the whole picture or do justice to the whole of experienced reality, and *it does not need to*. The growth of critical philosophy allows for multiple contexts—many openings on the world with diverse forms of understanding. Awareness of the multi-contextual character of experience and knowledge enables us to be more aware of the complex nature of experiential reality.

Contexts and the Deeper Issues of Subjectivity

The idea that knowledge is contextual allows us to situate Hillman's ideas in several important ways. On the one hand the view of the world as imaginal and personified may be seen as arising in a particular experiential context; it shows us a particular "face" of the world. Then, too, it offers us a new sense of subjectivity and objectivity that is exciting, interesting, and worthy of exploration. Moreover, the felt-sense of latent personages in natural and artificial things cannot but evoke a sense of "thou" in each of them felt to be deserving of our respect. In this, the view of the world as formed of "subjects" or of "subject-objects" offers a contextual and experiential basis for a moral sense of nature and for the design and use of things and landscapes. Further, the imaginal and personifying sense of reality, especially when seen contextually, does not make the claims to general truth that the objectivist position had to make at the beginning of the modern period. Pluralism of contexts reintroduces the observer into the activity and seeks to identify the value and object character of all enterprises. Contextualism, thus, is an overview of fields of study and activity that shows each of them to have *a subjective and an objective component.* Contexts, as we have been using the term, are themselves subject-objects of a distinct kind.

Finally, implicit in this view is the understanding that all human activity is going on within an ultimate reality about which little can be said, and so is in a way mysterious. Contextual analysis discloses human experience and human history to be an adventure in the face of a complex ultimate reality.

The Relation of Self and World

These perspectives allow us to return to the question of subject and object with more room to maneuver, more room to explore the options implicit in the personifying mode of engaging with the world. It is important that three openings on the relation of self and world be explored. These may be referred to as (1) the field structure of Ultimate Reality, (2) the intertwining—the chiasm, and (3) the basho of pure experience.

The Field Structure of Ultimate Reality. Toshihiko Izutsu has introduced a useful formula for thinking about fundamental modes of perception in the Zen experience:

> ... the basic formula $s->o$, or *i see this*, which is designed to describe schematically the epistemological relation between the perceiving subject and the object perceived, conceals in reality a far more complex mechanism than appears at first sight. For, according to the typically Buddhist analysis, at the back of s there is a concealed $(S->)$; at the back of o there is also $(S->)$. And the whole thing ... is ultimately to be reduced to the very simple, all-pervading and all-comprehensive act of SEE ... (which is in Zen understanding none other than the Absolute or ultimate reality).[11]

Izutsu pursues this way of describing the ultimate character of subjectivity and objectivity by emphasizing that "subject" and "object" are abstractions that result when we articulate the non-articulated (undivided) Field "into an active and a passive sphere, and establish the former as an independently subsistent entity."[12] Zen aims at witnessing the originally non-articulated Field articulating itself freely, of its own accord, into subject and object. In this experience, subject and object, as well as either the subject or the object, may be experienced as the focus or concretization of the whole Field:

. . . if the total Field in its original state of non-articulation is to be represented by the formula: *SEE*, the same total Field in its articulated state may be formulated as: *I SEE THIS*. . . . This last formula must remain the same, whether the whole Field actualizes itself as the subject or as the object. Thus, in this particular context, the subject or I means *I(= I SEE THIS)*. Likewise the object of this means *(I SEE THIS=) THIS*.[13]

The Field, in other words, is of such a mobile and flexible nature that if emphasis is laid on the "subjective" side, the whole thing turns into the Subject, while if on the contrary emphasis is laid on the "objective" side, the whole thing turns into the object. . . . If the emphasis is evenly diffused all over the Field, there is the Subject, there is the Object, and the world is seen as a vast, limitless Unity of a multiplicity of separate things. And, whichever of these forms it may assume, the Field always remains in its original state, that of I SEE THIS.[14]

Izutsu's provocative and insightful approach to the Zen experience offers us an analogy for understanding how, in the experience of archetypal psychology, things that in the objectivistic standpoint are regarded only as "objects" may, in a more fluid form of experiencing, be felt as subjects, objects, or as subject-objects. The Field character of ultimate reality may be an issue. So, rather than literalizing the appearance of "persons" or "gods," or even "objectivity" in stones or trees or human beings, we would do well to consider that such experiences may represent an experience of the total Field actualizing itself as subject, object, or as subject-object.

In another metaphor, one might speak of the personages appearing in stones, trees, or landforms as "angels" or *persona* (in the sense of masks) of the ultimate Field. Either way, both the total Field and the things within the Field take on the quality of subject-objects capable of a certain amount of shape-shifting or reversal depending on the style of attention. When perceived in one mode, the things appear as objects; in another mode, they appear as the "masks" of personages or as the declarations of "gods" or "angels."

The experience of Nature as psyche may arise from moments of opening ourselves to the Field character of ultimate reality so that the Field and the things of the Field may appear as subjects, objects, or as subject-objects.

The Intertwining—The Chiasm. The French phenomenologist Maurice Merleau-Ponty sought through several of his books to identify a more productive understanding of the relationship between subject and object than prevails in the objectivism that has dominated the modern period. His essay "The Inter-twining—The Chiasm" in *The Visible and the Invisible* represents one of his most interesting approaches to this important problem.

Merleau-Ponty's critical reflections on seeing and touching—one hand touching the other while watching both—led him to discover an opening to a new depth of the relationship of subject and object:

> We say therefore that our body is a being of two leaves, from one side a thing among things and otherwise what sees them and touches them; we say, because it is evident, that it unites these two properties within itself, and its double belongingness to the order of the "object" and to the order of the "subject" reveals to us quite unexpected relations between the two orders.[15]

> Where are we to put the limit between the body and the world[?] . . . My body as a visible thing is contained within the full spectacle. But my seeing body subtends this visible body, and all the visible with it. There is reciprocal insertion and intertwining of one in the other.[16]

> . . . the seer is caught up in what he sees . . . the vision he exercizes he also undergoes from the things, such that, as many painters have said, I feel myself looked at by the things. . . . The seer and the visible reciprocate one another and we no longer know which sees and which is seen.[17]

At once we will notice a similarity to Izutsu's portrayal of the Zen experience, the Field shifting so that "we are *seeing* the mountains and the mountains are *seeing* us." This *seeing* constitutes a very fundamental aspect of this experience. Like Izutsu's SEE, Merleau-Ponty's *seeing* is close to the common ground from which both subjectivity and objectivity arise.

In a related version of this understanding, the great scholar of Zen Buddhism D. T. Suzuki said, "Seeing . . . is Acting."[18] Such statements may be understood at one level through the common observation that "seeing" and "being seen" are partly experienced as "touching" and "being touched." In some situations, our gaze may go beyond "touching" to "moving" others—persons and animals—or impelling them to move. Similarly, being "seen" by others may impel *us* to move or to act. Not only persons have this effect. Merleau-Ponty notes that things and places "beckon" to us. All of these, I suggest, are related experiences of the Field shifting between subject and object. These reflections also open us to the possibility that all things are either subject-objects in themselves or carriers of the subjectivity-objectivity of the Field.

Merleau-Ponty continues his exploration as follows:

> . . . it is not *I* who sees; not *he* who sees, because an anonymous
> visibility inhabits both of us, a vision in general, in virtue of
> that primordial property . . . radiating everywhere and forever,
> being and individual, of being also a dimension and a universal.[19]

> By virtue of this mediation through reversal, this chiasm, there
> is not simply a For-Oneself/For-the-Other antithesis, there is
> Being as containing all that, first as sensible being, then as being
> without restriction.[20]

Reflective engagement with ourselves and things as subject-objects encountering subject-objects opens our awareness to experiences of being "seen" by things, being "beckoned" by things, and of our responding almost anonymously, as members of a Field. The things, as images, as faces, seem to embody a form of intentionality, to have an interest in us, to hold an interest for us, to bear a message for us. We can experience ourselves as "recognized," even as "known" by the things. In the expression of Martin Buber, things display a "thou-ness" as a kind of radiance. All persons have had these experiences. They should not be ignored or disregarded. They offer an opening onto the ultimate character of reality as simultaneously subjective and objective.

The Basho of Pure Experience. One of the most interesting philosophers of the twentieth century is Kitaro Nishida, a member of the Kyoto School. His encounter with the Western philosophical tradition, from Plato and Aristotle to Leibnitz, Kant, and Husserl, remains a model of intercivilizational dialogue.[21] Coming to terms with the implications of the Western tradition of thought, Nishida developed a remarkable synthesis of logic, ontology (theory of being), and epistemology (theory of knowing) that is most fundamentally a concrete existential phenomenology in the form of a logic. My discussion is indebted to the discussion of his work by David Dilworth, Robert Schinzinger, and Robert Wargo.

Nishida is one of those philosophers who understand reality to be "an inseparably interwoven unity of subjective and objective elements, as a unity of subject and object."[22] Nishida in fact defines reality as the "self-unification" of subject and object, while action remains the center of his concept of "concrete reality." Within this framework, Nishida developed a critique of Aristotle's logic of objects and Kant's logic of subjects (the preconditions of experience). He argued that our experience cannot be adequately understood through the concepts of objectivism alone and devised a kind of phenomenology, a critical reflection to display the preconditions for understanding objects as a series of "envelopes" or "places" called in Japanese *bashos*. Descending gradually deeper into the structure of experience from the cognitive level—the level of objects—Nishida discloses the structure of "concrete experience" to be made of three bashos: (1) an aesthetic-feeling-value basho enfolding the objective, (2) a basho of expressiveness-action-intention enfolding the feeling and cognitive bashos, and finally, (3) a place where there is no longer a difference between the experience of subject and object, the basho of pure experience. This last "enveloping place" is the domain of the "contradictory identity" of subject and object as a lived experience. Nishida's concepts have multiple, parallel meanings. Thus, "To be *known* is to be in a basho; similarly to *be* in any sense is to be a thing of a certain sort, this also means to be in a basho "[emphasis added].[23]

Now, while the basic intent of the system of basho is the analysis of conscious awareness "within the self," a use of these descriptions can also be made from Hillman's perspective. Thus, in modern culture we may be most aware initially of the cognitive and objective character of the things around us. If we begin a reflection in the spirit of Nishida, we find that an envelope of feelings and values enfolds the objective qualities of a thing. As we search deeper through the qualities of feelings and value, the domain of intention comes to awareness. This, I suggest, is what we discern when what Hillman calls *personification* occurs. The esthetic-feeling-value domain deepens out into a sense of the intending/acting presence of the thing that stands before us. When confronted with this "envelope," we have the experience of the object having a message for us, of urging us in particular directions, on occasion even seeming to demand that something be undertaken. Of course, to experience this "volitional" level of a thing, we must "bracket" or disengage the ready explanation that this is all projection (at least for a while) and hover while discerning the quality of the subject-object before us.

When we experience the subjective qualities of things in these ways as feeling-tone in the object and as personification— a sense of the volitional-intending-acting dimension of the object—we encounter the structure of "concrete reality" itself, a version of what Jung would have called the "objective psyche."

Using a slightly different description of these levels, the cognitive basho is the level of purely objective appearances. Reflecting on the preconditions and requirements for this cognitive-objectivity, we discern that it is "enfolded" by a field of concerns and interests, feelings that are essentially different from and even contradictory to the viewpoint of cognitive-objectivity. This envelope may be termed the basho of feeling and esthetic "objectivity." Deeper than that, one encounters another envelope, another discontinuity, and one experiences the sense of action-intention that enfolds the realm of esthetic-objectivity. This basho of action-intention, I suggest, is the envelope, the phenomenological level, of experiencing the personification of the thing before us, encountering its beckoning or demand, or being moved to action ourselves. This basho may be called a basho of expressive-objectivity. Each of these bashos represents a subject-object field, though the type of "object" shifts as the reflective disengagement continues from one envelope to the next. At the deepest and most concrete level, the domain of pure experience comes to view—the most complete domain of contradictory-affirmation beyond which lie no further envelopes.

I suggest that Nishida's matrix of envelopes, the bashos, indicate the structure of subjectivity-objectivity in general, and that the system of bashos are those which we find reflected in the experiences described by Hillman, Izutsu, and Merleau-Ponty. The analysis of the envelopes of the bashos may be taken to apply to the encounter with "gods" and "angels" in Hillman's archetypal psychology, the Field structure of reality in Izutsu's description of the Zen experience, and the contradictory-affirmation described in the experiences of Merleau-Ponty. This also suggests that the subject-object character of all reality displays the nesting of bashos described by Nishida. The important implication is that the ultimate character of reality includes and transcends the character of persons and is not less than them.

Nature As Psyche

The discussion to this point should have made clear that what we understand when we view "nature as psyche" is that nature is more than objective, more even than beautiful; it is a Field of subjective-objective unities, and human beings are an integral part and an integral expression of this reality.

Nishida's metaphor of "concrete logics" deserves to be developed in further detail to sketch the envelopes of subjectivity and objectivity throughout nature. One of the problems for our understanding nature consistently as formed of subjective-objective fields and entities is the vast period of the past which astronomy and geology have opened to us when there were no living things, no minds. This has seemed to most to demonstrate that matter preceeds mind, and, therefore, that mind and life are ultimately derivative. Of course, concealed in the objectivistic models of early phases of the earth and the primordial universe are the enfolding conditions of intelligibility, the bashos of the ancient worlds. Our reflections should make us more aware of the presence of subjective determinations surrounding and informing all aspects of reality. *To be*, in Nishida's concrete logics, is to be in a basho and in a system of bashos. This offers us a general subject-object framework for understanding all reality.

More important, it offers a model of subjectivity-objectivity for understanding all of nature, all of the universe, as a psychophysical reality. As in a kind of cosmological accounting, the other side of the entry system always needs to be filled in; the subjective dimensions of the universe need to be indicated. The spectator consciousness, the observer, and the subjective structures of Izutsu's Field of Ultimate Reality should always appear in the final accounting. At a minimum this will make us more aware of our presence as part of the scene, part of the SEEING.

In a cosmology that takes account of the observer and the subjective conditions of objectivity in general, the origin of organisms and the appearance of persons would appear less of a problem. Indeed, if Nishida's concrete logics were developed, they might well be found to include much of the mathematics and logic of genetic and intelligent systems. The emergence of symbiotic systems throughout evolution would seem likely derivatives of a matrix logic whose terms are subject-objects.

More important even than a general cosmology is a frame of reference in which to live our lives. As the Czech philosopher Erazim Kohak observed:

> In a nature . . . from which the dimensions most crucial to lived experience, those of value and meaning, have been intentionally bracketed out as "subjective" there is no more room for a moral subject.[24]

104

This indicates much of the flaw of generalized objectivism: it has no consistent basis for upholding the respectful treatment of others, other living things, and the landscapes in which we dwell. Recognizing a complex matrix of bashos which underlie the experience of persons and personification can have a profound effect on our attitude toward reality:

> This is the fundamental sense of speaking of reality as personal: recognizing it as Thou and our relationship to it as profoundly and fundamentally a moral relation, governed by the rule of respect.[25]

Kohak concludes with a call for, "a different viable strategy— that of a purposive repersonalization of our lives and our life-world."[26]

Shifting our frame of reference from the purely objective to its enveloping Nishidan realms of the esthetic and the expressive-intentional, we can see that the whole of reality is a Field that is latently alive and personal, filled with gesture and meaning and deserving of respect. The awareness of things as embodiments of the Field of ultimate reality will disclose all to be subject-objects, attuned to us as we are to them.

Notes

1. James Hillman, "Anima Mundi, The Return of The Soul To The World," *Spring*, 1982, 78.
2. Jacques Maritain, *Existence and the Existent*, trans. G. B. Phelan (New York: Doubleday, 1957), 72-74.
3. Hillman, "Anima Mundi," 78.
4. James Hillman, *Emotion*, (London: 1962), Routledge & Kegan Paul, Chapter 11, "Emotion and Situation" and Chapter 12, "Emotions and the Subject-Object Relation."
5. James Hillman, "Egalitarian Typologies versus the Perception of the Unique," *Spring*, 1980, 37.
6. James Hillman, *Re-Visioning Psychology*. (New York: Harper, 1977), 16-17; 33; 36.
7. Lawrence J. Hatab, *Myth and Philosophy, A Contest of Truths*, (La Salle: Open Court, 1990), 310.
8. Hatab, 323.
9. Hatab, 324.
10. Hatab, ibid.
11. Toshihiko Izutsu, *Toward a Philosophy of Zen Buddhism*, (Boulder, CO: Prajna Press, 1982), 26.

12. Izutsu, 46.
13. Izutsu, ibid.
14. Izutsu, 53-54.
15. Maurice Merleau-Ponty, *The Visible and The Invisible*, ed., C. Lefort, trans, A. Lingis (Evanston, IL: Northwestern University Press, 1968), 137.
16. Merleau-Ponty, 138.
17. Merleau-Ponty, 139.
18. D. T. Suzuki, *Zen and the Doctrine of No-Mind*, (London: Rider, 1970), 45.
19. Merleau-Ponty, 142.
20. Merleau-Ponty, 215.
21. Kitaro Nishida, *Last Writings: Nothingness and The Religious Worldview*, trans. with Introduction, David A. Dilworth, (Honolulu: University of Hawaii Press, 1987), 1-5.
22. Kitaro Nishida, *Intelligibility and The Philosophy of Nothingness*, trans. with Introduction, Robert Schinzinger (Honolulu: East-West Center Press, 1958), 50.
23. Robert J. J. Wargo, *The Logic of Basho and The Concept of Nothingness in The Philosophy of Nishida Kitaro*, (Ann Arbor, MI: University Microfilms International, 1972), 341.
24. Erazim Kohak, *The Embers and The Stars, A Philosophical Inquiry into The Moral Sense of Nature*, (Chicago: University of Chicago Press, 1984), 18.
25. Kohak, 128.
26. Kohak, 211.

9

What Is Life?—
Toward a New Paradigm

PAMELA KENT DEMERS

From my delightful years in high school biology I remember wanting to enter the fascinating world of the practicing biologist. The class not only studied in the classroom but added such marvelous learning experiences as hiking out to Ozette in Washington State for a closeup look at marine biology and a campout. Biology had always been to me nothing more or less than the absolute physical proof of the presence of God. The prose of philosopher Renée Weber exactly expresses what I felt about the grandeur of nature and its relation to the divine:

> All my life I have felt close to nature. Her presence was real to me long before I knew anything of the laws by which she works. . . .
> Looking back, I realize that since my earliest childhood I have sensed "something" in nature's background, and even in the foreground. The beautiful and lavish variety of the forms has been a source of real meaning to my life, and from the beginning I felt a kinship with nature's offspring—animals, plants, rocks, forests, water, earth, the sky, and even with remote stars and galaxies. . . . I simply awoke to the world with the conviction of my relatedness to these things. This feeling . . . has remained with me. . . . It is only much later that I learn the names for these feelings—the immanence and transcendence of a force in nature. . . .
> The pursuit of the source has shaped my life and my work.[1]

No accident or human intervention could have produced a physical universe of such perfection, which is recognizable if you are only willing to look for it.

In my high school years (the early 70s), molecular biology was beginning to become a popular concept to scientist and lay person alike. I remember learning about the double helix of DNA and its marvelously clever code and thinking that I had finally found the answer to where God the Creator was. I was seduced by the concept of the absolute beauty of form and function that DNA encompassed, and like many biologists and students before me, I thought that this meant that DNA was responsible for material life. I later learned the fallacy of DNA reductionism.

I entered college a very enthusiastic biology major and premed student. Then one day I attended a lecture in developmental biology which completely reorganized my thinking on biology, the meaning of life, and the Creator itself. I was instantly converted from being an "old biologist" to a "new biologist."

The essential point of the life-changing lecture was this: In developmental biology you start out with a sperm that fertilizes an egg, and then you have one cell with a complete complement of DNA. For development of any biological organism to begin, this one cell splits into two cells, the two into four, and so on. Each new cell from each split has *exactly* the same amount and configuration of DNA. But if each cell of an organism has exactly the same DNA, how does an organism develop different body parts, such as a head, arms, nose, legs?

That day the young professor on the fast-track to biological stardom posed several explanations of how this could happen. Then no biologist was sure of the mechanism of how you derive a complete organism from a fertilized egg with exactly the same DNA in each cell (and no one is yet). One of the hypotheses that the professor posited was of fields directing genes as they turn on and off inside the organism to cause development to occur. Rupert Sheldrake was later to expound the theory of fields in great detail.[2, 3]

However, perhaps the most startling revolution for me that day was that I could no longer believe the biological dictum "DNA to RNA to proteins" was the whole life story. There was suddenly more to God and life than DNA, and I had to become a "new biologist" in order to work out a new, more successful paradigm for myself. Although I had shown interest before this time, that day was the start of a much more exciting biological career. It was also the true beginning of my embracing mysticism.

I did not give up my search for the meaning of life in DNA and RNA easily, however. I spent several edifying years in laboratories studying molecular biology and genetics. The more I searched for an understanding of life there, the more I knew that much additional information was needed to understand how science and the divine are related.

What Is Life?

The question What is life? is one that the mythological trickster loves to pose to human beings. James Lovelock (who along with Lynn Margulis first proposed the complete theory of Gaia), when he searched the literature of all the life sciences for the answer to this question, found the following:

> I expected to discover somewhere in the scientific literature a comprehensive definition of life as a physical process, on which one could base the design of life-detection experiments, but I was surprised to find how little had been written about the nature of life itself. The present (mid '60s) interest in ecology and the application of systems analysis to biology had barely begun and there was still in those days the dusty academic air of the classroom about the life sciences. This seeming conspiracy of silence may have been due in part to the division of science into separate disciplines, with each specialist assuming that someone else had done the job.[4]

There is still no agreement about the meaning of the word *life*. Most biologists, when asked the question, will answer in some way especially related to their own field of study. Genetic theorists like Manfred Eigen and Richard Dawkins emphasize DNA and the self-replicating ability of organisms. General systems theorists such as Ludwig von Bertalanffy and Ilya Prigogine consider the self-organization of living things as the central feature of life (as do Francisco Varela and Humberto Maturana). These biologists see life as more like flames, waves, and whirlpools than like stones. Ethologists like Nikko Tinbergen and ecologists like James Lovelock see niche and organisms' interactions with each other and with the environment as key factors in identifying life. Some biologists have considered purpose as the central feature of life. For instance, phenomenologist Helmuth Plessner held directedness or the "telic" aspect of organisms as essential in the living world.

Each of these viewpoints addresses an important aspect of life. But none of them captures the ineffable sense of life that mystics speak of. Life in this sense is wider, more universal, than the life that can be studied in living things.

Even the life that distinguishes the living from the dead is ineffable. When you ask biologists where the life goes when an organism dies, I guarantee that they will fall silent or at best be able only to mumble platitudes. To find out scientifically what happens to the life of an organism when it dies, the first essential step is to examine the dead matter. You will find that the weight of the matter which still exists has not changed. However, the organism can no longer grow, move, repair, or maintain itself (it has lost its self-regulating ability). As Plessner noted, it has lost its plasticity or form, or its form within form, and its ability to take its place in the environment.[5]

We know intuitively that something seems to have left the organism, but by scientific criteria it does not appear to be physical. As Rupert Sheldrake, plant physiologist, points out, "Something leaves the body when it dies. And whatever it is, it is not made of ordinary matter; it is immaterial, made of subtle matter, or it is a kind of flow, like the flow of breath or like fire."[6]

Science today considers the vital force of life as energy. It is usually visible to us only in its transformed state—matter. The energy is drawn from the environment. Photosynthesis allows plants to turn light energy into chemical energy and matter. When animals digest food, they are really turning this matter into chemical energy for later use. When organisms die, the energy is cycled back to other organisms to be used over and over; energy is the ultimate recycled matter.

Dead organisms are no longer self-regulating or purposive— that special essence that seems to give purpose is no longer in the body. Organisms have lost that living center which, as Plessner put it, is not in space but in a core which transcends spatiality and at the same time controls the spatiality of the body. To us the body seems dead. But there are those who consider that matter itself has a degree of life, though imperceptible to us. According to a tribe of Amazonian Indians:

> The Ufaina believe in a vital force called *fufaka*, which is essentially masculine and which is present in all living beings. This vital force, whose source is the sun, is constantly recycled among plants, animals, men, and the Earth itself which is seen as feminine. Each group of beings, men, plants, animals, earth or water require a minimum amount of this vital force in order to live. When a being is born, the vital force enters it and the group to which the being belongs. The group is seen as borrowing the energy, and returns it to the stock. It is once again recycled. Similarly, when a living thing consumes another, for example when a deer eats a bush, a man eats a deer. . . . The consumer acquires the energy of the consumer, and it accumulates in its own body.[7]

If this vital force, like Sheldrake's "immaterial" and "subtle" something that makes a body alive, is the energy that is equivalent to all matter ($E=mc^2$), then indeed everything is alive, including those things we usually consider inanimate, such as rocks, water, and molecules.

Esoteric philosophy has long held that everything *is* alive. Helena Petrovna Blavatsky, in her source book of ancient wisdom *The Secret Doctrine*, confirms this view: "It has been stated before now that Occultism does not accept anything inorganic in the Kosmos. The expression employed by Science, 'inorganic substance,' means simply that the latent life slumbering in the molecules of so-called 'inert matter' is incognizable. ALL IS LIFE, and every atom of every mineral dust is a LIFE, though beyond our comprehension and perception, because it is outside the range of the laws known to those who reject Occultism."[8] In this view even the remains of a dead animal contain potential life force, though most of us are unable to perceive it. There is a life force that permeates everything in the universe, but it becomes obvious to us only when the organism is imbued with purpose and self-regulation, as is a living plant or a human being.

There are certainly those who would vehemently disagree with this interpretation of what in our world (and perhaps in the universe, too) can be considered as life. Lovelock mentioned in his definition of life, similar to Blavatsky's, that this sort of definition would also apply to flowing streams, to hurricanes, to flames, or possibly even to objects made by humans. However, Lovelock and Margulis, after much soul-searching, have come to observe that the boundary between life and what we consider inanimate (the fire, the flowing stream, rocks), which most of us intuitively believe not to be alive, may not be so easily drawn after all. They studied the complex interactions on our Gaian earth, the way plant becomes rock becomes gas becomes a part of plant again. They considered that matter and energy appear to be completely different yet completely interchangeable (Einstein's $E=mc^2$). They concluded that one can substitute living organisms and their inorganic environment for each other. This is tantamount to stating that at least all matter on earth is alive, and perhaps this includes all matter in the universe as well. According to Lovelock, "there is no clear distinction anywhere on the Earth's surface between living and nonliving matter. There is merely a hierarchy of intensity going from the 'material' environment of the rocks and the atmosphere to the living cells."[9]

Have we humans come close to discovering what is life and what is not life? One of the most important principles of the new biology is that life is *more* than physics, chemistry, DNA, RNA, proteins, enzymes, and heredity. But just what life is and what makes life "alive" has eluded us up to this point. The new biologist is profoundly interested in discovering the answer to this puzzle.

The fact that there actually is biological life on Earth, and perhaps elsewhere in the universe, is no accident, as many physicists and biologists would like to believe. Lovelock states, "If, for example, the sun's surface temperature were 500 degrees instead of 5000 degrees Centigrade and the earth were correspondingly closer, so that we received the same amount of warmth, there would be little difference in climate, but life would never have got going. Life needs energy potent enough to sever chemical bonds; mere warmth is not enough."[10] Blavatsky makes a similar statement in *The Secret Doctrine*: "It is the Sun-fluids or Emanations that impart all motion and awaken into life, in the solar system."[11]

We intuitively consider that electrons and atoms are not alive; however, as far as science is concerned, life is made up directly of these same electrons and atoms. Denying life in "nonliving" systems, like rocks or water, made up of these same atoms and electrons, begs the question of what exactly is life in a "living system." Perhaps the only way to begin to understand this conundrum is to return to pre-nineteenth century vitalism—all is alive unless proven otherwise.

Scientist Francisco Varela sides with those who see life as a continuum from the inorganic to the fully alive, with the impossibility of determining where life ends or begins: "But I want to join this syndicalist movement and become the speaker for the lymphocytes and the neurons, because they are just as alive as the little bacteria. For now it seems to me that we can look at life in all of its manifestations, at the cellular level, the immune level, the brain level, or the Gaian level, and notice that all of these tell us a little bit of what is going on with the organization of the living."[12]

A rock may be considered a form of "life" on earth since it is a participant in Gaia, in the entire chain of organics and inorganics that make up our home. But would a rock be "alive" on Mars, where it would not be a part of an interdependent biological system (since Mars is completely devoid of biological life)? According to Lovelock, you cannot have just a little life on a planet. Either you have a plentitude, such as on Earth, each part helping to support and providing a niche for every other part, or you have only the potential life of the inorganic universe.

In this view all matter participates, willingly or otherwise, in the "dance of Shiva," as Hinduism describes it, that we call life. Shiva embodies life in his eternal dance; he also embodies death, ever final, in the ring of fire that surrounds him. At any moment this ring of fire participates in the dance, and this part of the ring is embodied again with the vital principle. There is no dividing line between life and death in the domain of Shiva.

The New Biology

The new biology isn't really new at all. A better name for it might be the "true biology." Today, biology is experiencing a revolution just as physics did in the early to mid-twentieth century. The old biology that we learned in school is gradually being modified by startling discoveries that do not allow the old paradigm to exist anymore. It will continue to change and modify along with new discoveries as biologists finally open their minds to the fact that we no longer live in a Newtonian universe (in fact we never did—quantum reality has always been *the* reality though we did not know it). One day only the "true biology" will be recognized.

According to physicist Henry Margenau, "It is still widely believed that a complete knowledge of physics, chemistry, and biology will ultimately explain the phenomenon of life and account for consciousness and the mind. The latter are said to 'reduce' to the former when all the details are understood. Reductionism is a philosophy that affirms this view. Its simplest form is materialism, the doctrine asserting that all human experience is ultimately understandable in terms relating to physics of matter, more specifically the theories of quantum physics."[13]

Reductionism, especially in light of DNA and molecular biology, is a seductive concept. But reductionism is simply not true. A living organism is much, much more than the sum of its physical parts. As discussed, living things have a specific "something," a factor which distinguishes life from just molecules collected together randomly. When an organism has purpose, it has that life factor. But according to esoteric philosophy, even those random molecules are imbued with

113

life. They may simply have a purpose, a life force, that is more subtle than we humans are yet able to detect. But life can be prey to the trickster. Since the demarcation line between living and nonliving is not definite, we will never be able simply to reduce living organisms to the sum of their physical parts, as many physicists and biologists would like to do.

Before my conversion to new biology, I, too, was a reductionist. But, finally, I saw the following conundrum, pointed out by physicist Henry Margenau, and reductionism was no longer a viable philosophy of science for me: "For the biologists, every step down in size was a step toward increasingly simple and mechanical behavior. A cell is more mechanistic than a bacterium. But twentieth-century physics has shown that further reductions in size have an opposite effect. If we divide a DNA molecule into its component atoms, the atoms behave less mechanically than the molecule. If we divide an atom into nucleus and electrons, the electrons are less mechanical than the atom."[14] In other words, trying to reduce the biological to the supposedly more physical and mechanical physics backfires; you end up almost going around a circle—the closer you get to the ultimate physical particle, the more alive it becomes. Biology may actually be a more true, a more holistic science than physics. Physics is the numinous dance; biology is the dance of Shiva.

The Anthropic Principle

Perhaps one of the most startling aspects to be realized from the new physics is that the universe itself is evolving, along with everything in it: energy, fields, matter, ourselves. The corollary to the Big Bang theory is that the start of the universe instantly predetermines that it is evolutionary.

This fact is relevant to biology because physics and biology are inextricably linked, not through reducing biology to physics, but because physics, matter, energy, and biology are all parts of the same paradigm of matter. According to Sheldrake: "The universal spirit of the of the time was very different in the first few seconds after the Big Bang, than it was when galaxies began to form, and it was different again when planets came into being. The changing times permitted new forms of evolutionary creativity to occur, new forms and patterns of activity to be repeated, and these in turn changed the quality of time. Ultimately, the changing cosmic zeitgeist depends on the continuing growth of the universe, which gives a direction, an arrow of time, to the entire evolutionary process."[15] This direction inherent in the Big Bang naturally leads to the anthropic principle. Expressed colloquially, this is the idea that humanity, Gaia, and living creatures exist because of the Big Bang, and that the Big Bang occurred *in order* to produce Gaia and ultimately humanity.

In noncolloquial terms, the chance of the universe existing at all is extraordinarily minute and rests on many odd improbabilities. But probability for the universe to exist is much greater if we assume that the universe has a purpose: to evolve and to bring about life. Physics contains many oddities when it comes to cosmology; there are "strangely fortunate resonances" that allow for the synthesis of heavy elements in stars. Such cosmological oddities often make sense only if we assume the eventual production of life. The idea that everything tends to evolve toward life and ultimately humanity is called the strong anthropic principle. Many respected physicists, including Stephen Hawking, rebel strongly against this idea. Others including David Bohm, Paul Davies, and Freeman Dyson, embrace it equally strongly.

One interpretation of the strong anthropic principle is that there is only one possible universe, "designed" with the goal of generating and sustaining "observers." According to new biologists Stanciu and Augros: "The subordination of matter to life extends beyond the use that planets make of nonliving things. There is now abundant evidence from physics, chemistry, and cosmology that our universe, its history, and its material laws are uniquely suited to life in general. Physicist Paul Davies, for example, points out how the existence of Earth-like planets depends on the capacity of stars to explode as supernovae."[17]

Self-Organization

Coined by Francisco Varela and Humberto Maturana, the term *autopoiesis* embodies the self-organization and maintenance of living systems. It is the tendency toward self-organization and self-regulation, rather than random or competitive action, as the norm in living systems. Self-regulation was seen by physicist Edmund P. Sinnott as a hallmark of life: "This quality of directive self-regulation, whatever its final relation to chemical and physical processes may prove to be, is a uniquely biological phenomenon and an understanding of it, I believe, will prove a clue to the character of life itself."[18] According to Varela, "Life and cognition are inseparable things. The moment you have a living system in the sense of the cellular autopoietic, or perhaps Gaia-living-like system, you have cognition."[19] Sheldrake posits the idea of a morphogenetic field that interacts or may even be responsible for some of the aspects of autopoiesis. He feels that nature definitely seems to be self-organizing. This self-organization is based on fields—the field of gravity and others, including the morphogenetic field.[20]

The Many Faces of Gaia

The evolutionary, self-organizing new biology also throws light on the concept of the Earth itself being alive. As a living planet, the Earth has many guises—living organism, ordinary planet, goddess. It is a valid scientific hypothesis that we live on an organism that herself is alive, and it is also a bio-geochemical theory, to use a word coined by Lovelock.[21] Lawrence Joseph, student of the Gaia hypothesis, says, "Scientifically and theologically, the most practical question to ask about Gaia is not whether she is alive, but how alive is she?"[22] In line with the new biology, he goes on: "If there is an enduring theme to the science of Gaia, it is this seamless continuity of life and environment that to a vital extent all life forms adapt their surroundings to their needs and that, taken as a whole group, we biota are collectively responsible for the Earth's hospitable climate."[23] Gaia's evolution occurs in the weathering of rocks, the changing chemistry of the oceans, changes in the atmosphere, all of which make her survival more likely.[24] The organisms living on Gaia evolve right along with her and also cause her evolution as they alter the environment around them for their own needs. Gaia is emergent, which means that she is much more than the sum of her parts.[25]

Gaia, like all living things, can be considered as having self-organizing capacities. James Lovelock supports autopoiesis as a property of Gaia by acknowledging that "the development of the hypothesis that the entire range of living matter on Earth, from whales to viruses, and from oaks to algae, could be regarded as constituting a single living entity, capable of manipulating the Earth's atmosphere to suit its overall needs and endowed with faculties and powers far beyond those of its constituent parts."[26]

Some parts of Gaia, as of any living being, are more important to sustain the life of the organism than are other parts. Just as when an organism loses a limb or an eye, or perhaps seeing or hearing capacities, the life in the organism is not destroyed. Remove or seriously damage a vital organ, however, and the biological life force of the organism departs. Autopoiesis can only function properly if all of the vital organs of a system are in good health. This is certainly true of Gaia. Although Gaia is not yet fully comprehended, some of her vital organs are now being elucidated. These appear to be any spots on earth where there is a concentration of bacteria that are active within their surroundings, exchanging their byproducts with the earth or atmosphere (wetlands, certain coastal areas) or where oxygen transpiration is occurring at an extremely high rate (the rain forests of the world). For some reason, these seem to be the areas on earth that human beings are the most intent on quickly damaging, perhaps already beyond repair.

Still, Gaia has the remarkable ability to recover from the damage that humans have inflicted upon her. However, through carelessness and the pollution and fouling of our own nest, we may be seriously compromising the health of the human race. Most likely Gaia could survive quite healthily without human beings. However, if we destroy her fertile areas of bacteria, her life blood, her vital organs, we may end up not only destroying humanity but Gaia herself. We must take action to preserve the rainforests, the wetlands, and the coastlines of Gaia. If we fail to do so, we may commit the ultimate horror of destroying the nearly immortal Gaia who has been alive now for at least some three and a half to four and a half billion years.

Is Gaia conscious? If she is a living being, can we assume that she has some kind of awareness? Sheldrake thinks this may be possible:

> If Gaia is in some sense animate, then she must have something like a soul, an organizing principle with its own ends or purposes. But we need not assume that the earth is conscious just because she seems to be alive and purposive. She *may* be conscious, but if so, her consciousness is likely to be unimaginably different from our own, which is inevitably shaped by human culture and language. On the other hand, she may be entirely unconscious or she may be, like ourselves, be a creature of unconscious habit with some degree of consciousness some of the time.[27]

Interconnections

How do the organisms on our living planet interact? The idea of competition versus cooperation among organisms in their quest for survival on Gaia is hotly contested. According to Darwin's theories, all organisms constantly compete with each other, and only the most fit, toughest, meanest, hardiest survive (nature is "red in tooth and claw"). But more and more biologists are discovering that the organisms with the best chance of survival are those that behave symbiotically with other organisms, not competitively. These new biologists consider symbiosis, not competition, as the epitome of biological interactions. According to biologist Lewis Thomas, "Most of the associations between living things we know about are essentially cooperative ones. Symbiotic in one degree or another. . . we do not have solitary beings. Every creature is in some sense, connected to and dependent on the rest."[28] He proposes organismic unity: "A good case can be made for our nonexistence as entities. We are not made up, as we had always supposed, of successfully enriched packets of our own parts. We are shared, rented, occupied."[29]

An example of this sharing emerged from Lynn Margulis' and Ricardo Guerrero's studies of *Mixotricha paradoxa*, a supposedly single-celled organism that lives in the gut of the Australian termite. These researchers found that this organism is really composed of five separate organisms that work in concert to ensure that both Mixotricha and the termite (and the symbiants) survive happily and successfully in their niches in life. "So Mixotricha is an example of symbiosis in which organisms of completely different species, once separated, have come together and formed a completely different entity, a new entity with markedly different properties from the organism that composes it."[30]

Margulis and colleagues are working to demonstrate that all individual cells are complexes of organisms that have been symbiotically interacting for three and a half billion years. According to Margulis and Guerrero, the metaphysical summation of this organismal cooperation is that "in the arithmetic of life, One is always Many. Many often make one, and one when looked at more closely, can be seen to be composed of many."[31]

In this new view of evolution, the way an organism thrives is not by the Darwinian notion of destroying all of its competitors. According to Japanese biologist Kinji Imanishi, "I regard the biological nature we see not as the scene of survival competition, but as the scene of peaceful coexistence among species."[32] Organisms survive by finding and evolving their own niche, and then either altering the niche or altering themselves to enhance the ability to survive.

One way an organism may alter its niche is to encourage other organisms to interact closely within the niche. An example of three-way cooperation in an ecological niche is between an African honey bee, a bird, and a bushman. A species of bird in the Kalahari will purposely lead a bushman who has learned to follow its signs to a nest full of honey. The bushman will take some honey, but always leaves enough for the bees to survive nicely. Taking honey actually encourages the bees to increase foraging for food sources. It also allows growth and prevents overgrowth of the colony. When the nest has been disrupted by the bushman, the bird is able to share in the honey, too. Its dance as a honey guide is a beautiful dance of cooperation in which all the dancers benefit.

The theory of Gaia is the ultimate example of how cooperation and interconnection between organisms and their inorganic and organic environments proves to be best for the parts and for the whole. Gaia takes care of all of her creatures by regulating earth's very unusual atmosphere to be hospitable. She provides rainforests in the tropics that regulate the oxygen and carbon dioxide balance on the rest of the globe. She provides wetlands with innumerable bacteria that provide trace gases in the atmosphere that even organisms in the desert need to survive. She works like a living cell—materials on one part of Gaia are synthesized and transported to other places where they are needed.

It is hard to imagine that Gaia is the lone example of cooperation and interconnectedness in the universe. Rather, Gaia seems like a holographic image of the universe; she is both a complete picture of the wholeness of the cosmos and a part of that whole. According to esoteric philosophy, human beings, whom some believe are unique to Gaia, are also made in that image of wholeness and interconnectedness and are striving and evolving as biological and spiritual beings to reflect those principles.

Biology and Mysticism

Mysticism has a strong place in our own human evolutionary

development. So does a gnosis, or knowing, of biology—of the organization of the matter that we are made of during our incarnations. According to philosopher Renée Weber, "Simply stated, mysticism is the experience of oneness with reality. As I reflect on their essence, I perceive science and mysticism as two approaches to nature."[33] Over the years of my own biological journey with its mystical experiences, I have come to understand that we humans have incarnated into a physical body to experience life on earth for a reason. When we are willing to allow the two disciplines of mysticism and science to merge, to fuse into a greater whole, we will have a truer understanding of life, of Gaia, and of our part in the grand scheme of the universe.

As we look around us at the tremendous diversity of biological and nonbiological forms in the cosmos, it is sometimes hard for us to perceive the oneness that pervades them all. But as we learn more about the concept that life exists in all matter, even in that which we consciously perceive as dead; and that organisms benefit far more when they cooperate and share than when they fight; and that our planet is a fully functioning organism in its own right, we are beginning to tap into mysticism through science and to demonstrate that oneness pervades the universe. According to Blavatsky, the phenomena in nature are really "so many various differentiated aspects and transformations of that One."[34]

Unity of Life

The search in science for a unified field theory is the scientific equivalent to the mystical search for the unity of all life. As Fritjof Capra observed, "The Brahman of the Hindus, the Dharmakaya of the Buddhists, and the Tao of the Taoists can be seen perhaps as the ultimate unified field from which spring not only the phenomena studied in physics, but all other phenomena as well."[35] According to Hinduism, as in other religions, that ultimate field can be considered as life itself. "All things are said to be established in Life. Life . . . the same as Brahman."[36] In the view of the Vedas, ancient Indian texts, the cosmos is indeed alive, a single organism ensouled by Brahman, by God:

> The universe produced from the one undivided Atman by the on-rolling process of manifestation is a unified system, a mighty organism in which the inmost nucleus and pervading Spirit

and Self is the one abiding Being. . . .Every part, every particle in it is ensouled, inspirited by the All-aware All-feeling Being that is Atman. . . . The universe, with everything in it, is only an outward flow and a crystallized form of the unceasingly upwelling Joy of Brahman."[37]

The universe is ever evolving, and it develops new forms that demonstrate and personify the essential unity that exists everywhere. The earth, Gaia, humanity, and the universe are all part of the oneness that composes the universe. Sheldrake's statement echoes the theme of the above quotation from Hinduism:

The Cosmos is like a growing organism, forming new structures within itself as it develops. Part of the intuitive appeal of this story is that it tells us that everything is related. Everything has come from a common source: all galaxies, stars, and planets; all atoms; molecules, and crystals; all microbes, plants, and animals; all people on this planet. We ourselves are more or less related closely to everyone else, to all living organisms, and ultimately to everything that is or that ever has been. One of the great theories of traditional creation myths is the division of the primal unity into many parts, the emergence of the many from the one. The modern theory of cosmic evolution fulfills this mythic role.[38]

A wholistic understanding of biology and physics can be a path into the mystical aspects of the universe. Physicist David Bohm uses this method, proposing that *"meaning is a form of being.* In the very act of interpreting the universe, we are creating the universe. Through our meanings we change nature's being. Man's meaning-making capacity turns him into nature's partner, a participant in shaping her evolution. The word does not merely reflect the world, it also creates the world."[39] We are a creation of the universe and at the same time we create it. We influence the course of evolution. We are charged with ultimately understanding the universe and the oneness that pervades it. We are charged with mystically unifying our biological bodies, our Gaian Earth that is so much a part of us and we it, and our spirit—to fulfill the meaning of the universe.

Life pervades everything in the universe. Life is cooperative and interconnected. Life is evolutionary. Life is unitary. These are all concepts that the new biologist is beginning to hypothesize and to validate. These same ideas are part of the ancient mystical traditions. Biology is slowly beginning to catch up with the truths known to mystics through the ages.

121

Pamela Kent Demers

Open your eyes, your ears, and your intuition to the beautiful Gaian planet we live on. Everywhere around you there are whisperings of the new biology, of nature's inner life, just waiting to be perceived. Once you perceive them, your life in Gaia will be changed forever.

Notes

1. Renée Weber, ed., *Dialogues With Saints & Sages: The Search for Unity.* (London and New York: Routledge and Kegan Paul, 1986), p. 2.
2. Rupert Sheldrake, *A New Science of Life: The Hypothesis of Formative Causation* (Los Angeles: J. P. Tarcher, Inc., 1981).
3. Rupert Sheldrake, *The Presence of the Past: Morphic Resonance and the Habits of Nature* (New York: Random House, Times Books, 1988).
4. James E. Lovelock, *Gaia: A New Look at Life on Earth* (Oxford & New York: Oxford University Press, 1979), p. 3.
5. Marjorie Grene, *Approaches to Philosophical Biology,* (New York, Basic Books, 1968).
6. Rupert Sheldrake, *The Rebirth of Nature: The Greening of Science and God* (New York: Bantam, 1991), p. 98.
7. M. von Hildebrand, "An Amazonian Tribe's View of Cosmology," in Bunyard & Goldsmith, eds., *Gaia, the Thesis, the Mechanisms and the Implications* (Camelford, Cornwall: Wadebridge Ecological Centre, 1988).
8. Helena Petrovna Blavatsky, *The Secret Doctrine* (Los Angeles, CA: The Theosophy Company, 1925), Vol. II, pp. 248-249.
9. James Lovelock, *The Ages of Gaia: A Biography of Our Living Earth* (New York: W. W. Norton & Company, 1988), p. 40.
10. James Lovelock, *Gaia: A New Look at Life on Earth,* p. 5.
11. Helena Petrovna Blavatsky, *The Secret Doctrine,* Vol. III, p. 529.
12. Lawrence E. Joseph, *Gaia: The Growth of an Idea* (New York: St. Martin's Press, 1990), p. 227.
13. Henry Margenau, *The Miracle of Existence* (Woodbridge, Conn.: Ox Bow Press, 1984), p. 32.
14. Freeman Dyson, *Disturbing the Universe* (New York: Harper & Row, 1979), p. 248.
15. Rupert Sheldrake, *The Rebirth of Nature,* p. 73.
16. Robert Augros & George Stanciu, *The New Biology: Discovering the Wisdom of Nature* (Boston and London: New Science Library, 1987), p. 219.
17. Ibid., p. 218.
18. Edmund W. Sinnott, *Matter, Mind and Man* (London: Allen & Unwin, 1958), p. 38.
19. William Irwin Thompson, ed., *Gaia 2: Emergence, The New Science of Becoming* (Hudson, NY: Lindisfarne Press, 1991), p. 232.

20. Rupert Sheldrake, *The Rebirth of Nature*, p. 95.
21. Lawrence E. Joseph, *Gaia*, p. 248.
22. Ibid., p. 53.
23. Ibid., p. 245.
24. Rupert Sheldrake, *The Rebirth of Nature*, p. 154.
25. James E. Lovelock, *Gaia*, p. 33.
26. Ibid., *Gaia*, p. 9.
27. Rupert Sheldrake, *The Rebirth of Nature*, pp. 157-158.
28. Lewis Thomas, *The Lives of a Cell* (New York: Bantam, 1974), p. 6.
29. Ibid., p. 2.
30. William Irwin Thompson, ed., *Gaia 2:*, p. 52.
31. Ibid., p. 51.
32. Kinji Imanishi, quoted by Beverly Halstead, "Anti-Darwinism in Japan," *Nature* 317 (17 October 1985), 587.
33. Renée Weber, ed., *Dialogues with Saints & Sages*, p. 5.
34. Helena Petrovna Blavatsky, *The Secret Doctrine* (Adyar, India: The Theosophical Publishing House, 1978), 1:142.
35. Fritjof Capra, *The Tao of Physics*, (Berkeley: Shambhala, 1975), p. 211.
36. J. C. Chatterji, *The Wisdom of the Vedas*, (Wheaton, IL: The Theosophical Publishing House, 1992), p. 57.
37. Ibid., p. 85.
38. Rupert Sheldrake, *The Rebirth of Nature*, p. 24.
39. Renée Weber, ed., *Dialogues with Saints & Sages*, p. 18.

Part Three
Traditional Views of Nature as Alive

You should entreat trees and rocks
to preach the Dharma, and you
should ask rice fields and gardens
for the truth. Ask pillars for the
Dharma and learn from the hedges
and walls. Long ago the great god
Indra honored a wild fox as his
own master and sought the
Dharma from him, calling him
"Great Bodhisattva."
                              Eihei Dogen

*The current belief in nature as alive is less a new development than
a rediscovery and revitalization of a view with a long history. As
cultural historian Thomas Berry describes our return to old beliefs
about nature in the essay that follows, "We are returning to our
native place after a long absence, meeting once again with our kith
and kin in the earth community."*

*Seers, mystics, and spiritual practitioners from traditions as
widespread and diverse as the Native American, Celtic, Buddhist,
shamanic, and medieval Christian have long testified that the world
is inhabited by supersensible beings. Whether called the* Sidhe, *as they
are known to devotees of the Celtic fairy-faith; gnomes, salamanders,
and sylphs, as the medieval alchemist Paracelsus called them; or
Thunder and Mother Corn, as the Pawnees named two of their nature
deities, the living forces of nature have been worshipped and celebrated by spiritual traditions around the world and throughout history.*

*Moreoever, the similarities between these traditional beliefs far
outweigh the differences. As Joan Halifax points out in the essay
that follows, "Both tribal [Native American] cultures and Buddhist
tradition . . . use nature as a primary source of inspiration and understanding. Buddha had his Bo tree, deer park, and previous lifetimes
as animals. Shamans have their world trees and animal transformations
and familiars." Moreover, even the Western Neoplatonic tradition,
so influential in the European Renaissance, as Carolyn Merchant
points out below, was based on a belief in a cosmic world soul
immanent within nature, "vivifying it like a cosmic animal."*

*The essays in this section serve as a reminder of what we have
lost and of the deep learning we regain as we reanimate the physical
world of nature. The trees, rocks, rice fields, and gardens, can surely,
these essays attest, "preach the Dharma" and teach us "the truth."*

10

Returning to Our Native Place

THOMAS BERRY

We are returning to our native place after a long absence, meeting once again with our kin in the earth community. For too long we have been away somewhere, entranced with our industrial world of wires and wheels, concrete and steel, and our unending highways, where we race back and forth in continual frenzy.

The world of life, of spontaneity, the world of dawn and sunset and glittering stars in the dark night heavens, the world of wind and rain, of meadow flowers and flowing streams, of hickory and oak and maple and spruce and pineland forests, the world of desert sand and prairie grasses, and within all this the eagle and the hawk, the mockingbird and the chickadee, the deer and the wolf and the bear, the coyote, the raccoon, the whale and the seal, and the salmon returning upstream to spawn—all this, the wilderness world recently rediscovered with heightened emotional sensitivity, is an experience not far from that of Dante meeting Beatrice at the end of the *Purgatorio*, where she descends amid a cloud of blossoms. It was a long wait for Dante, so aware of his infidelities, yet struck anew and inwardly "pierced," as when, hardly out of his childhood, he had first seen Beatrice. The "ancient flame" was lit again in the depths of his being. In that meeting, Dante is describing not only a personal experience, but the experience of the entire human community at the moment of reconciliation with the divine after the long period of alienation and human wandering away from the true center.

Something of this feeling of intimacy we now experience as we recover our presence within the earth community. This is something more than working out a viable economy, something more than ecology, more even than Deep Ecology, is able to express. This is a sense of presence, a realization that the earth community is a wilderness community that will not be bargained with; nor will it simply be studied or examined or made an object of any kind; nor will it be domesticated or trivialized as a setting for vacation indulgence, except under duress and by oppressions which it cannot escape. When this does take place in an abusive way, a vengeance awaits the human, for when the other living species are violated so extensively, the human itself is imperiled.

If the earth does grow inhospitable toward human presence, it is primarily because we have lost our sense of courtesy toward the earth and its inhabitants, our sense of gratitude, our willingness to recognize the sacred character of habitat, our capacity for the awesome, for the numinous quality of every earthly reality. We have even forgotten our primordial capacity for language at the elementary level of song and dance, wherein we share our existence with the animals and with all natural phenomena. Witness how the Pueblo Indians of the Rio Grande enter into the eagle dance, the buffalo dance, and the deer dance; how the Navajo become intimate with the larger community through their dry-paintings and their chantway ceremonies; how the peoples of the Northwest express their identity through their totem animals; how the Hopi enter into communication with desert rattlesnakes in their ritual dances. This mutual presence finds expression also in poetry and in story form, especially in the trickster stories of the Plains Indians in which Coyote performs his never-ending magic. Such modes of presence to the living world we still carry deep within ourselves, beyond all the suppressions and even the antagonism imposed by our cultural traditions.

Even within our own Western traditions at our greater moments of expression, we find this presence, as in Hildegard of Bingen, Francis of Assisi, and even in the diurnal and seasonal liturgies. The dawn and evening liturgies, especially, give expression to the natural phenomena in their numinous qualities. Also, in the bestiaries of the medieval period, we find a special mode of drawing the animal world into the world of human converse. In their symbolisms and especially in the moral qualities associated with the various animals, we find a mutual revelatory experience. These animal stories have a playfulness about them, something of a common language, a capacity to care for each other. Yet these movements toward intensive sharing with the natural world were constantly turned aside by a spiritual aversion, even by a sense that humans were inherently cut off from any true sharing of life.

At best they were drawn into a human context in some subservient way, often in a derogatory way, as when we projected our own vicious qualities onto such animals as the wolf, the rat, the snake, the worm, and the insects. We seldom entered their wilderness world with true empathy.

The change has begun, however, in every phase of human activity, in all our professions and institutions. Greenpeace on the sea and Earth First! on the land are asserting our primary loyalties to the community of earth. The poetry of Gary Snyder communicates something of the "wild sacred" quality of the earth. In his music Paul Winter is responding to the cry of the wolf and the song of the whale. Roger Tory Peterson has brought us intimately into the world of the birds. Joy Adamson has entered into the world of the lions of Africa; Dian Fossey the social world of the gentle gorilla. John Lilly has been profoundly absorbed into the consciousness of the dolphin. Farley Mowat and Barry Lopez have come to an intimate understanding of the gray wolf of North America. Others have learned the dance language of the bees and the songs of the crickets.

What is fascinating about these intimate associations with various living forms of the earth is that we are establishing not only an acquaintance with the general life and emotions of the various species, but also an intimate rapport, even an affective relationship, with individual animals within their wilderness context. Personal names are given to individual whales. Indeed, individual wild animals are entering into history. This can be observed in the burial of Digit, the special gorilla friend of Dian Fossey's. Fossey's own death by human assault gives abundant evidence that if we are often imperiled in the wilderness context of the animals, we are also imperiled in the disturbed conditions of what we generally designate as civilized society.

Just now one of the significant historical roles of the primal people of the world is not simply to sustain their own traditions, but to call the entire civilized world back to a more authentic mode of being. Our only hope is in a renewal of those primordial experiences out of which the shaping of our more sublime human qualities could take place. While our own experiences can never again have the immediacy or the compelling quality that characterized this earlier period, we are experiencing a postcritical naiveté, a type of presence to the earth and all its inhabitants that includes, and also transcends, the scientific understanding that now is available to us from these long years of observation and reflection.

Fortunately we have in the native peoples of the North American continent what must surely be considered in the immediacy of its experience, in its emotional sensitivities, and in its modes of expressions, one of the most integral traditions of human intimacy with the earth, with the entire range of natural phenomena, and with the many living beings which constitute the life community. Even minimal contact with the native peoples of this continent is an exhilarating experience in itself, an experience that is heightened rather than diminished by the disintegrating period through which they themselves have passed. In their traditional mystique of the earth, they are emerging as one of our surest guides into a viable future.

Throughout their period of dissolution, when so many tribes have been extinguished, the surviving peoples have manifested what seems to be an indestructible psychic orientation toward the basic structure and functioning of the earth, despite all our efforts to impose on them our own aggressive attitude toward the natural world. In our postcritical naiveté we are now in a period when we become capable once again of experiencing the immediacy of life, the entrancing presence to the natural phenomena about us. It is quite interesting to realize that our scientific story of the universe is giving us a new appreciation for these earlier stories that come down to us through peoples who have continued their existence outside the constraints of our civilizations.

Presently we are returning to the primordial community of the universe, the earth, and all living beings. Each has its own voice, its role, its power over the whole. But, most important, each has its special symbolism. The excitement of life is in the numinous experience wherein we are given to each other in that larger celebration of existence in which all things attain their highest expression, for the universe, by definition, is a single gorgeous celebratory event.

The native peoples of this continent give to the human mode of being a unique expression that belongs among the great spiritual traditions of mankind. It is an observed fact in history that high religious traditions are often carried by peoples who are not as numerous, as powerful, or as advanced in science and technology as other peoples. Just as other traditions have their specific glories—as India has its awareness of divine transcendence, China its mystical humanism, and Europe its sense of a historical divine savior—so the Indian peoples of America have their own special form of nature mysticism. Awareness of a numinous presence throughout the entire cosmic order establishes among these peoples one of the most integral forms of spirituality known to us. The cosmic, human, and divine are present to one another in a way that is unique. It is difficult to find a word or expression for such a mode of experience. It might simply be called a nature mysticism. This is precisely the mystique that is of utmost necessity at the present time to reorient the consciousness of the present occupants of the North American continent toward a reverence for the earth, so urgent if the biosystems of the continent are to survive.

This numinous mode of consciousness has significance for the entire human community. Indeed, one of the primary instincts of the human community is to protect and foster such primordial experiences. These experiences, which generally present themselves as divine revelations, are irreplaceable. They provide the foundations upon which the cultural systems of the various peoples are established. They also determine the distinctive psychic structure of individual personalities within the culture. Together these revelations form the ultimate psychic support for the human venture itself.

The Indian peoples have become increasingly aware that they carry a primordial tradition of great significance for the entire human community. Because of their hurt in association with the dominant political powers of the continent, the Indians might well conceal the inner mysteries of their spiritual traditions lest they be trivialized by a secular society that destroys the inner meaning of everything it touches. But the reality is there; it is widely recognized. Its inner resplendence is finding its fitting modern expression and the wide influence it deserves.

11

A Poem and a Painting: Nature as Expressed in the Native American Tradition

DAVID P. McALLESTER

There is a profound qualitative difference in the concept of "closeness to nature" between the Euro-American tradition and that of the Native Americans. The former sees nature as object, to be controlled and used, however responsibly. The latter sees nature as family and deity, with whom one seeks to coexist on terms laid down by kinship and religion.

These differences are at the root of philosophies so unlike that the two cultures were unable to understand each other from the first contacts five hundred years ago. The cultural values, both existential and normative, were so basically different as to preclude real communication, a condition that persists today. Though the history of a certain accommodation over the years—including recent reverse missionizing by Native American teachers—is fascinating in itself, my intent here is to present examples of the spiritual and personal understanding of nature in Native American tradition.

This article discusses two ceremonial gestures from widely separate Native American communities. The first is a poem, a song text from the Thunder Ceremony of the Skiri Pawnees, a Plains people from Nebraska, later settled in Oklahoma. The other is a drypainting from the Mountainway Chant of the Navajos, desert dwellers whose reservation extends over twenty-five thousand square miles of Arizona, New Mexico and Utah. The Pawnee material was recorded in 1912-1920 by James R. Murie, himself a Pawnee, and published in 1981 and 1989.[1] The Navajo material was recorded in 1884 by Washington Matthews, an Army surgeon, and published in 1887.[2]

The Pawnee Thunder Ceremony

The ceremony takes place when spring is near and two small stars, called the Swimming Ducks, appear above the northeast horizon near the Milky Way. Their appearance, a certain position of the Pleiades, and the occurrence of sheet lightning in the skies are warnings that the people can soon expect the first big thunder, that starts in the west and rolls around the circuit of the heavens. The accompanying lightning is thought to be the force that charges quiescent nature with new life.

On hearing this thunder, the Evening Star Bundle[3] Priest is obliged to send immediately for the keepers of the four other principal ceremonial bundles. With the help of the other keepers, the Evening Star Bundle Priest renews the bundles' sacred power by reenacting, ceremonially, the original creation of the earth and humankind, according to the Pawnee creation myth.

The Myth. According to the myth, when Paruxti (Creator, Wonderful Being, Lightning) made his preliminary journey upon the earth bringing his giant Lightning sack of star people, he first took twenty-six steps toward the east; then he rested. He then continued his journey, resting at the thirtieth step. Thereafter on his journey, he rested at the end of every ten steps.

With each step, Paruxti took out of his sack another element in the origin and furnishing of the world. First came the earth, itself; then came growing things and the elements to nurture them; then homes for people and home furnishings, secular and ceremonial. The first twenty-six steps were for the woman's side of creation. The next thirty steps brought gifts for men, including clothing and weapons for hunting and warfare and the qualities necessary for these activities, symbolized by such powerful and resourceful creatures as the bear, mountain lion and wolf. The final gifts were ceremonial, such as the pipestem in the Thunder bundle.

The series of ten steps after these first fifty-six indicated to the people that they could "shorten their pathways" by using ceremonial songs.

Preparing the Place. The Thunder Ceremony starts with the preparation of a sacred place. A buffalo skull is marked on the forehead with red paint symbolizing the gardens of Lightning, Thunder, Cloud and Wind, the four deities who sang the world into existence. Red lines from the nose of the skull extend towards the gardens to represent the rays of the sun. The skull is placed at the west wall of the ceremonial lodge, facing east, and before it sit five priests, also facing east. In front of them is an altar made of mats placed on the ground and covered with a buffalo robe. Here the contents of the Evening Star Bundle are laid out. A sacred black stone pipe is placed in the center of the altar with its stem extending to the east. On either side of it are placed ears of corn, known as Female Seer Comes Through (Summer) and Female Seer Goes Through (Winter). The former is placed to the south of the pipe at this season, but the positions of the corn are reversed if the bundle is used in the winter.

The sacred ears of corn are the most important contents of the bundle. Also called "Mother Corn," they represent the first human beings placed on earth by the Morning Star. He laid down an ear of corn wrapped in a buffalo calf skin, which changed into a woman and a buffalo. Corn ceremonialism was the dominant theme in Pawnee religious life, though the buffalo hunt was also a major part of their economic and spiritual life.

Next to the corn on the altar, on either side, an owl skin is placed, and next to them, two hawk skins, representing warriors. To the east of the pipe, a line is drawn on the earth, leading to a circle. The line is called the "throat" or "mouth of knowledge," and the circle is the "wise sayings of the ancestors," representing the heart or inner life of humankind.

Still farther east, in the center of the lodge, is the fireplace, and east of that, the doorway, on either side of which sit the

South Errand Man and the North Errand Man. As the ritual of singing the earth into being is about to begin, the Evening Star Priest asks an Errand Man to go outside and find five gourd rattles to accompany the singing. No rattles are kept in the Evening Star Bundle. As soon as the rattles are brought in and the five priests are ready, the first song begins. Usually only the priests sing.

The First Song. The first two "steps" (verses) of the first song demonstrate how the song reflects the myth of the Thunder Ceremony.

> Verse 1. Above, this is what they said,
> Above, this is what they said,
> "The earth, it was taken out; yonder he is coming,
> Power, it was taken out; yonder he is coming."

> Verse 2. Above, this is what they said,
> Above, this is what they said,
> "The trees, they were taken out; yonder he is coming,
> Power, it was taken out; yonder he is coming."
> (repeat)

This song refers to the Four Powers: Lightning, Thunder, Cloud and Wind, as they sit in the western sky. They recreate the earth by singing about the first origin, when Paruxti came down with his great sack.

"Power" (*waaruksti'*) represents the vitalizing of the earth after it has been put in place by the power of Thunder and Lightning. This word begins the fourth line of all fifty-six verses or "steps" of the song. Each verse is sung twice. In the second verse, the first word of line three is changed to represent the second step and the second creative act of Paruxti's journey. "The trees" refers to vegetation being brought to cover the earth. The next two steps complete the four main acts in the creation of the world: "waters" are bestowed, representing rivers and lakes, and "seeds" are given, representing all useful plants, especially corn.

Other verses mention "Mother Corn," referring to the ears of corn in the Evening Star bundle (and every other sacred bundle of the Pawnees); some of the great richness of meaning in the concept of corn will be discussed below. "Bluebird," another part of a warrior's personal bundle, is the vehicle for carrying prayers to the sky. A bluebird skin might be tied

135

to the mouthpiece of a pipe or to the top of a warrior's head while he is on the warpath, so that his prayers will reach their destination. "Hawk" represents the highest rank. Its wings are thought of as a warclub. It also represents the Morningstar, the father of humankind.

"Colors" is the key word in another of the verses. Black, red, yellow and white are the colors mentioned specifically. They connote, among other things, the semi-cardinal directions, animals as metaphors of warrior qualities, sacred trees and the four main Star bundles of the Pawnees. The connections are most easily suggested in a chart:

black	elm	thunder	Southwest	Black Meteor Bundle
red	box elder	cloud	Southeast	Red Star Bundle
yellow	willow	lightning	Northwest	Yellow Star Bundle
white	cottonwood	wind	Northeast	White Star Bundle

The Ritual. The complete Thunder Ceremony takes several days and many songs, some of which are even longer than the one described above. The ceremony has six parts:

1. Creation of the world (which begins with the song above)
2. Smoke offerings to the heavens
3. Wonderful Being revitalizes the Earth
4. People go out over the Earth
5. The pipe is smoked
6. The feast

In the course of the first five rituals, thousands of lines of sacred poetry are sung. *The Creation of the world* alone contains 2,800 lines divided into five songs, but usually the later songs are abbreviated. Many different ritual acts take place during the ceremony. Offering sticks are prepared and placed around the lodge, dedicated to Star deities and other powers in the heavens; burnt offerings and tobacco offerings are made; the deities are sung down from the sky to the village and back again; the stages of a buffalo hunt are enacted; the participants in the ceremony are lustrated with the smoke of sweetgrass mixed with buffalo fat; children are blessed, and individuals wishing a new name have it bestowed.

After the feast, the contents of the bundle are rewrapped, and it is hung up again in the back of the lodge where it is kept. It is permissible for the priests of other major bundles to renew them concomitantly, but it is more usual for them all to be present for the ceremony for the Evening Star bundle and then to renew their own bundles shortly afterwards.

The deep integration of religious thought with the natural world is evident in every line of the poetry described above and in every act of the ritual that accompanies it. These and the ceremonial properties used relate humankind to stars, lightning, thunder, clouds and wind in the sky, and to all growing things on the earth. These heavenly bodies, elements, plants and animals are seen as intelligent, decision-making creative forces; Pawnee religion teaches the ways of living in harmony with these forces by giving and receiving vital and spiritual power.

The Navajo Mountainway Chant

The Mountainway is performed for an individual suffering from mental distress. Dreams indicating disharmony with mountain deities or visions of a diviner-diagnostician might provide the clue that this ceremony is needed. The Mountain-way Chant is one of several dozen, long and short in the Navajo repertory. None is calendrical, except that most of them should not be performed in the warm weather when thunder and snakes are active. These forces, frequently invoked in song, prayer, drypainting[4] and other ritual acts, are so potent that they should not be aroused.

The Myth. A Navajo family was wandering in the Carrizo Mountains looking for good hunting and a place to make their home. The elder son, disobeying his father, hunted too far to the south and was captured by the Utes. With the help of Owl Man and Talking God, he escaped, taking with him beautifully embroidered Ute bags and clothing.

Pursued by his captors, the elder son was hidden and given increasingly supernatural power by Talking God and other mountain deities, such as Bears, Weasels, Snakes, Holy Woman, Mountain Gods and Changing Bear Maidens. At one point, while being attacked by a tornado, he realized that his name had become "Reared Within the Mountains" and, by invoking his new name, he averted the danger.

On his journey, Reared Within the Mountains was taught how to make prayer offerings to the mountain deities to call for their aid in the future. He learned how to perform supernatural acts, such as swallowing sacred arrows, and he learned how to make drypaintings. When he reached his home, he instructed his family in the Mountainway ceremony. A proto-typical performance was done over him to protect him from the dangers inherent in the divine contacts he had made during his captivity and on his journey. In his changed state, Reared Within the Mountains could no longer live an ordinary life; "the Gods came to him in his dreams." On a hunting trip with his younger brother, he bade farewell to his human family and returned to the mountains to live with the gods.[5]

The Ceremony. In a nine-night[6] Mountainway ceremony, the first four nights and the related ritual acts on the following mornings are exorcistic (unraveling, sudatory, emetic), driving out harmful influences. They are also invitational; the prayer offerings are gifts to the deities to persuade them to come and lend their power to the ceremony. Offerings are deposited in a place where the deity will find them; a lightning offering might be placed by a lightning-struck tree, for example.

On the fifth day, offerings and prayers are made to Reared Within the Mountains, and the first great drypainting is pre-pared. It represents the visit of Reared Within the Mountains to the home of Long Frog, Watersnake and other water creatures, who taught him how to make the design. Each of the dry-paintings is sung into existence; songs for each part of it are sung as it is laid down.

When completed, the drypaintings are the locus of a ritual transfer of power. The one-sung-over sits on an appropriate figure on the painting. Pigments from the figure's feet are applied to the feet of the one-sung-over, a process repeated for the other parts of the body in a special ritual order. The human is thus identified with the deity, who has responded to the invitation of the prayer offerings and is present, em-bodied in the drypainting.

Metaphors of life are everywhere. Corn pollen, the life powder of the life-giving corn, is applied to the body of the one-sung-over, ending with the top of the head ("feather") and the tongue (speech, personal wind), after which a pinch of corn pollen is thrown out to the whole world. The prayer offering is a hollow reed painted to represent the deity to whom it is addressed. After valuables have been placed inside, the reed is given life by focusing a sun ray into its interior through a piece of rock crystal. Then the ray is held inside by a stopper of moist corn pollen sealing the open end. The ceremony is religious theater, an enormously extended magic spell, employing music, dance, poetry, graphic art and puppetry to create potent symbols from deep within Navajo culture.

As the fifth day merges into the sixth night, a mountain deity clad in spruce garments rushes at the one-sung-over, who is seated on the first drypainting. On the deity's fourth approach, the one-sung-over faints, is restored by the singer and then is given a ritual bath. From this point to the end of the ceremony, a drypainting is created each day, with rituals of identification performed each time. As more and more deities become present through graphic art and song, the feeling of power grows.

The ninth night rituals, like those of the fifth night, continue until dawn. Mountainway is the most spectacular of the Navajo ceremonials, with a dozen or more different kinds of dances, many of them showing supernatural prowess, such as the swallowing of plumed arrows and the magical growth, the blossoming and fruiting of a yucca plant. Many of these events were foretold in the myth and were brought to human-kind from the gods by Reared Within the Mountains.

The ceremony ends with dawn songs and the early departure of most of the attendees. The one-sung-over spends the next four days quietly in an individual retreat.

The Mountain God Drypainting. I have chosen the drypainting of the sixth day, given to Reared Within the Mountains by the Bear deities, as the example of Navajo religious art to be discussed in detail.

Every element in the Mountain God drypainting reveals the quality of the Navajo relationship with the natural world. The center represents water and fire. The black circle is often an actual bowl of water sunk into the ground. The bowl is covered with a film of powdered charcoal on which are laid down four sunrays in the four cardinal directions. Extending to the water are the white roots of the four sacred plants: corn in the southeast, beans in the southwest, squash in the northwest, and tobacco in the northeast. Mountain deities stand on sunrays in the cardinal directions; they represent the sacred mountains located in these directions, and their bodies are depicted in the directional colors. Each has an empty, proprietory hand extended toward the plant rendered in his color. From each right hand hangs a rattle made of dried buffalo skin and painted with a zigzag of lightning. The gods' forearms and lower legs are also painted with the same design. Also attached to each right hand is a "charm" and a basket,

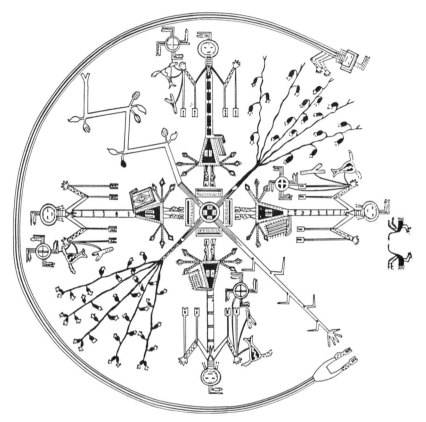

Mountain God Drypainting

which is often referred to as the possession or power of a deity in a drypainting.

The kilts of the deities are made of red sunlight, decorated at the corners with sunbeams. The sashes are highly decorated with individual designs and recall the clothing stolen from the Utes by Reared Within the Mountain when he made his escape. The feathers on the heads of the gods and the rainbow are bent to the right of the figure, showing that the whole design is in clockwise motion—"according to the Sun," the Navajos say. Each of the baskets is also turning sun-wise in a planetary rotation within the general orbit. These are graphic signs that the drypainting is a living entity, like the ceremony as a whole.

An encircling anthropomorphic rainbow protects the drypainting and the one-sung-over during the ritual that takes place on it. The rainbow is also a helper during the ceremony; when the singer is using a bowl of liquid medicine and needs to put it down, he places it on the outstretched hand of the rainbow. Most drypaintings with an open east side have guardians or protectors drawn outside the opening. In this case, the protectors are a pair of bluebirds who represent all small singing birds, symbols of peace and happiness.

Like the multiple metaphors in the Pawnee Thunder Ceremony, interconnections are everywhere in Navajo thinking. For example, the associations of color with natural phenomena are highly complex. The white deity and cornplant in the east and southeast of the drypainting also stand for the Mountain of the East, the lightnings that fasten it to the earth, its coverings of daylight and dawn, its jewel of white shell, the pigeon, spotted corn and white corn, and the sound symbol, thunder.

Other connotations of white and east are in the complex of meanings associated with White Shell Woman, one of the forms of Changing Woman. She is the daughter of Earth and Sky, deity of vegetation and symbol of renewal. She derives her name from her transformations from a young girl in the spring, through maturity in the summer and fall, to an old woman in the winter. In the spring, she is young again. She represents earth renewal, the cycle of vegetation and eternal life. Other names for her parents are Sạ'ah Naagháii and Bik'eh Hózhǫ (Living Again into Old Age and According to This Everywhere is Blessed).

The forearms and lower legs of the gods and of the rainbow are the same as the body paint of Reared Within the Mountains. As he journeyed in search of ever-increasing power, he came to the house of Dew, where Butterfly Girls bathed and decorated him so that he would have a suitable appearance when he came to Holy Woman. At this point in the story, he turned away the threatening tornado with his new name. After his visit with Holy Woman, he went on to the Mountain Gods and "realized that he looked just like them." These Mountain God arm and leg markings seem to be a talisman of the Mountainway. They are also worn by the plumed arrow dancers and the couriers who go out on the sixth day to invite deities, practitioners and others in the ceremony.

Pawnee and Navajo

The different functions served by the two ceremonies described here represent the differences in the perspectives of Pawnee and Navajo society. The former live in a federation of eleven close-knit village communities, each one under the tutelage of a particular Star deity, from whom the village's sacred bundle derived. The latter live in scattered individual households; a given locality has a sense of community based on kinship ties. Though both tribes cultivate corn, Pawnee agriculture is very old with affinities suggesting central American origins, while the Navajos were a nomadic hunting people who came to the Southwest from the north and took up farming relatively recently.

Pawnee ceremonialism is a calendrical series of celebrations of creation, designed to strengthen the community and revitalize the earth and its plants, animals and people. Navajo ceremonies are performed when an individual is in need; the extended family rallies to provide the means for restoring the afflicted person to harmony with the community and the surrounding natural world. In the former case, the underlying myth is of the creation of the community; in the latter it is of an individual who gets into difficulty, is saved by supernatural beings and learns from them a ceremony to help other individuals in the future.

The Pawnee ceremony is quiet, almost civic, reaffirming the Star-given unity of the villages. The Navajo ceremony is theatrical, combining music, dance, graphic arts, and the impersonation of deities in the reenactment of the myth. Though the Pawnees have doctors who cure the sick, this is a minor aspect of their religion, while it is the main focus in the case of the Navajos.

In spite of differences such as the above, there are deep similarities that suggest a general Native American view of relations to the natural world. In both Pawnee and Navajo thought, for example, spiritual power derives directly from nature, rather than from a human seer or prophet. Sun, stars, winds, earth, sky, birds, animals and other creatures, trees, corn and other plants are the teachers, the sources of information and help. The ceremonial arts are symbolic of these tutelary deities; the entire natural world is sacred. Earth and corn are both mother and deity to the Pawnees and Navajos and also to Native Americans generally, wherever corn can be grown.

The ceremonies are reenactments of myths, and the myths are explanations of the origins of the ceremonies. Though the Pawnees are starborn and the Navajos are born from the union of earth and sky, both see their origin as from the natural world around them, and both derive from this world the information on how life should be lived. In neither culture is there any great emphasis on an afterlife but rather a focus on the continuation of humankind as part of the great natural cycle of rebirth.

Notes

1. Murie, James R. *Ceremonies of the Pawnee,* ed. Douglas R. Parks (Lincoln: University of Nebraska Press, 1984). Originally published as Smithsonian Contributions to Anthropology, Number 27, 1981.
2. Matthews, Washington, "The Mountain Chant: A Navajo Ceremony," in *Fifth Annual Report of the Bureau of Ethnology,* Washington, Government Printing Office, 1887, 385-467.
3. *Bundle:* In many Native American religions, the sacred objects used in ritual are carefully wrapped, separately, and then gathered together in a sack or bundle. The bundle usually has a name and is cared for by a priest especially trained in its ritual. The bundle is thought to be a living entity whose proper care and use are essential to the welfare of the community.
4. These designs are commonly called "sandpaintings," but since other dry pigmented materials such as corn pollen, cornmeal, and charcoal, are used in addition to colored sand, "drypainting" is a more accurate term.
5. Matthews, ibid. 387-417.
6. The Navajos count the progression of a ceremony by nights, rather than by days. Though Matthews' account of Mountainway is the most detailed and carefully documented description we have, it is a composite of several partially witnessed performances. He does not give details of the first five nights, except in a general way. It is possible to guess at some of these details from my own field observations and from descriptions of related ceremonies as in Kluckhohn, Clyde, and Leland C. Wyman, *An Introduction to Navaho Chant Practice,* Memoires of the American Anthropological Association, No. 53, 1940.

12

The Third Body: Buddhism, Shamanism, and Deep Ecology

JOAN HALIFAX

In 1964, I lived in New York City and worked at Columbia University on a project that analyzed song and dance styles cross-culturally. Sitting in the archives at Columbia, I was convinced that the planet was still a place with many secrets, many places of refuge. I was aware that numerous indigenous cultures of the world had suffered profoundly, and some were no longer in existence. But naively, like most Americans, I did not know the extent to which tribal people's natural environments and life-ways had been and would continue to be tragically eroded, or in many instances, extinguished by the fear and greed of people in dominating nations.

In 1990, the world looks very small to me. There is a widening realization that human economies, as well as environmental systems, from the World Bank to Brazilian rainforests, are intimately interconnected, affecting all life on the planet. Time/space is compressed: in two days I can be in the heart of what is left of the Lacandon rainforest in southern Mexico. I can visit with the old shaman Chan Kin Viejo and listen to his words:

> What the people of the city do not realize . . . is that the roots of all living things are tied together. When a mighty tree is felled, a star falls from the sky. Before one chops down a mahogany, one should ask permission of the guardian of the forest, and one should ask permission of the guardian of the stars. . . . When the great trees are cut down, the rain ends, and the forest turns to weed and grass. . . . There is too much cold in the world now, and it has worked its way into the hearts of all living creatures and down into the roots of the grass and the trees. But I am not afraid. What saddens me is that I must live to see the felling of the trees and the drying up of the forests, so that all the animals die, one after the other, and only the snakes live and thrive in the thicket.[1]

These thickets are where we meet now, this boundary land between the past and the future. It is here that we may still find some of the old wisdom of tribal peoples, how they felt and feel about the earth; how our star and other stars lined out a choreography of hunting, gathering, planting, and praying; how the passing of the moons and the coming and going of plants and creatures shaped a living calendar; how prophecy projected the future, and myth instructed the present; how, for many peoples, one's relations did not end with bloodlines but with lifelines; how all was perceived as being alive, including a landscape full of power and song.

This essay is about the suffering and joy of understanding "the truth of things as they are," even in their changing. Hopefully, it is a place where the voices of tribal peoples can be heard and where some of what I have learned as a friend to the wilderness and to medicine people can be explored by others.

The title "The Third Body" refers in part to the contemporary encounter between Buddhism and tribal wisdom, especially shamanism. When two bodies meet each other in space and time, whether in human form or in the form of ideas or traditions, there always exists the possibility of a third body emerging. In my own academic and spiritual experience, the traditions of shamanism and Buddhism have been meeting over the past twenty-five years. The Third Body emerging from this union could be described as a nature philosophy, or deep ecology, with its notion of the ecological Self.

What is deep ecology? In the book *Thinking Like A Mountain*, co-author John Seed states that the philosophy of nature, called deep ecology,

> questions the fundamental premises and values of contemporary civilization. Our technological culture has co-opted and absorbed all other criticism, so that parts may be questioned but not the whole, while deep ecology as a fountain of revolutionary thought subjects the core of our social existence and our thinking to piercing scrutiny. Deep ecology recognizes that nothing short of a total revolution in consciousness will be of lasting use in preserving the life-support systems of our planet.[2]

It is this Third Body, or what ecophilosopher Arne Naess has called the ecological Self, that we are asked to consider. From one point of view, this body is Earth. From the third body's perspective, it can be known as an awareness realized beyond the boundary of an enclosed and disconnected self.

In what follows I want to explore five directions on a mandala or medicine wheel of deep ecology. These directions have been generated and will be looked at through the perspectives of Buddhism and traditions of tribal peoples. This is not an academic analysis of the relationship between Buddhist philosophy and the lifeways of indigenous peoples. It is a humble attempt to open up Western hearts and minds to how we might live on the Earth today and how we can see "the truth of Earth as it is."

The Living Earth

A growing number of biologists and ecologists have come to accept that the Earth, and all that is on it, is a living, inter-related system. But this has long been understood by tribal peoples in their own ways. Eco-biologically, this perspective sees the selfness of Earth not enclosed, but rather as an expression of nested systems interacting to yield life and change.

This view has been made accessible by James Lovelock in his "Gaia hypothesis." Lovelock states that

> the physical and chemical condition of the surface of the Earth, of the atmosphere, and of the oceans has been and is actively made fit and comfortable by the presence of life itself. This is in contrast to the conventional wisdom which held that life adapted to the planetary conditions as it and they evolved their separate ways.

Lovelock goes on to say, however, that life "has so far resisted all attempts at a formal physical definition."[3]

For tribal cultures, Earth is seen as a whole and living organism as well. It has been variously characterized as mother, father, lover, god, goddess, and extended family. Earth and its life forms and systems, including mountain and river, salmon and cedar, wind and storm, are consistently experienced as not only alive but also sentient, a great being with whom we can communicate and exchange energy.

At the heart of this understanding of Earth as a living being is an experience of holiness, of the numinous, of life as power, of life as sacred mystery. Anthropologists have used the Melanesian term *mana* to describe this unseen yet pervasive condition. Since R. H. Codrington's discovery of this Melanesian concept in the late nineteenth century, it has been found in many other tribal cultures. Western culture has no equivalent term and so our understanding of the concept is not exact.

Looking at the Buddhist perspective of beingness and sentience in relation to the tribal experience of mana or power might stretch our imaginations, but it is worth considering. According to Avatamsaka Buddhist philosophy, the world is an interconnected network of creatures and objects, all of which are necessary and illumined. All have Buddha nature. This potential for illumination extends to include all things in the web of life, since no creature or thing can exist in isolation. Seeing oneself as part of this great family of beings is a source of spirit energy which teaches us how to live respectfully with all beings.

A description of the Lakota equivalent to mana by a Prairie Osage may begin to assist us in making the relationship more transparent:

> All life is *wakan*. So also is everything which exhibits power, whether in action, as the winds and drifting clouds, or in passive endurance, as the boulder by the wayside. For even the commonest sticks and stones have a spiritual essence which must be reverenced as a manifestation of the all-pervading mysterious power that fills the universe.[4]

The Net of Relatedness

In contemporary Buddhism, the term *sangha* refers to the community that practices the Way together. I have often asked myself, where is the boundary of this community? From the perspective of some tribal peoples, sangha does not stop at the threshold of our species and next of kin. Community for many native peoples is regarded as including other species, plant and animal, as well as environmental features and unseen ancestors and spirits. Community is lived in and experienced as a whole system of interrelated types and species. Most importantly, this community is alive, all of it.

The boundary of community does not stop with the human realm. Community can include rocks and springs that have given birth to civilizing ancestors. The sacred eagle, bear, buffalo, and whale hold great power in the community, as can the local clowns—crow, raven, coyote, or jay. Ceremony then is a sacred time and space where interrelatedness, including the elements of earth, water, air, and fire, is remembered and celebrated.

The Stonepeople's Lodge, known to many as the sweat lodge, is a place where Lakota and other peoples of the Americas retreat for ceremonies of purification and self-transformation. In the tradition of the Lakota people, when entering the lodge, the words *mitakuye oyasin* are uttered. Translated, these words mean "all my relations," which is a prayer that this purification

147

is not just for the betterment of the individual but for the sake of all beings.

Entering the darkness of the Stonepeople's Lodge, crawling on one's knees through the low door into the womb of the lodge, to be cleansed by the four elements of earth, water, air, and fire, renews the experience of relatedness. One medicine man told me: "We go into that sacred Lodge to purify ourselves. We go in there to see just who we really are, and in the darkness, to see how we go on this Earth. We make ourselves really humble, like the littlest creature, and we pray to Spirit that we may be healed, that all may be healed. We see that we are not separate from anything. We are all in this together. And we always say all my relations." This prayer and its sentiment are quite similar to the Buddhist dedication of merit to all sentient beings, and to the bodhisattva vow, as well.

Earth's Language

The connection between language and the Earth as a living being is important for us to consider at this point since sentience seems to be related to communication. From the spirit of communication arises the sense of community, the recognition of relationship. Thus our identity expands to include not only the worlds of minerals, plants, animals, and elements, but also the world of the unseen, of the ancestors and spirits. All these are woven onto the loom of language. An example of this is the California Yokuts prayer:

> My words are tied in one
> with the great mountain
> with the great rocks
> with the great trees
> In one with my body and my heart.
> Will you all help me,
> with supernatural power,
> and you, day,
> and you, night!
> All of you see me
> One with the Earth.[5]

Recently, a Shoshone man explained to me that the language of his people came from the Earth. And among the Northern Ute tribe it is said that "the voice of the land is in our language." Through language, there develops a sense of companionship with those other species with whom language is shared. This is the "medicine" that Native Americans refer to—the experience of relatedness that allows the mystery to flow between seemingly unrelated entities. This language is not found in books, but lives in its speaking.

There are many examples of the role of sacred speaking in articulating our connection to the nonhuman realm. One of the richest collections which exemplifies this perspective was made by the poet Howard Norman, who gathered and translated a group of poems and stories told by the Swampy Cree of Canada. Many of the tellings open the listener-reader to a startling perspective of how the world lives in us. One Cree poemteller put it this way:

> I tell poems to a small pond first. I only tell them in summer. I throw a rock in. The circles go out from where it hits. Then I say, "Water, you stutter! Water, calm down!" Then I tell a poem to calm it down. Later I bring it to the people and tell it to them.

The language of culture and society creates the customary, making it possible for human beings to communicate with one another, but also shaping our ideas about this world and binding our perceptions to the past, the familiar, the socially acceptable. In ceremony, however, shamans can use language types that are altogether different from the language of everyday life, including the language of beasts, spirits, ancestors, elements, and environmental features; or the language body that is created by the communication between human and other that is a third language, unique to a particular encounter.

The second language body for the shaman opens when he or she communicates with another species from within the language of that particular species. The shaman can experience at least the temporary loss of the timespace of culture and enter the danger zone of the wild, a condition that is not infrequently characterized by shock, awe, and exultation. This total identification with another species allows the shaman to see the world from a completely different perspective, as well as to possibly develop the capacities of the being with whom he or she is communicating or has become identified.

Animals, natural objects and systems, and the world of spirits often mirror the human world. They can carry the thoughts and feelings of the social realm just as the language of society can have hidden within it the voices of rock and wind, creature and ancestor. A Dine man remembers the advice of his grandfather: "Know things in nature are like a person. Talk to tornados; talk to the thunder. They are your friends and will protect you."

The Cycle of Change

All that exists, according to Buddhist understanding, has no identity that is self-reliant and distinct or separate (*anatta*); existence is also characterized by suffering (*dukkha*) and impermanence (*anicca*). Later in this essay, we will briefly explore Buddha's First Noble Truth of suffering and the notion of impersonality or anatta. Here we want to look at the experience of change or anicca from the Buddhist and tribal perspectives, and explore how it relates to deep ecology.

Buddha, in his meditations, discovered that all phenomena, including visions, dreams, thoughts, emotions, physical sensations, and things of the physical world from the smallest insect to the greatest mountain—all were transitory in the long body of time. He saw that deep understanding and acceptance of the inevitability of change freed one from clinging to phenomena. Any attempt, any strategy to hold things in their fixed positions created disharmony and suffering. Eastern and tribal peoples have long understood that life is about mutuality and change, about arising, interacting, transforming, and passing away. Existence is not a still-life, like a painting hanging in a museum and gathering dust. It is, if nothing else, impermanent.

Children of the Dine people in the Four Corners area are reacquainted with their culture's wisdom about the Earth in the following lesson relating to the nature of the cyclic movement of transiency:

> Life moves in circles that have no end. Sun and rain bring plant life from the Earth. The plant life gives life to animals, to sheep and horses, prairie dogs and deer. They in turn give life to man and mountain lion, hawk and badger, flea and gnat. The buzzards and worms will also be fed, and in the end everything will go back to the ground to feed new plant life. . . . Nothing is wasted. Everything that is taken from the Earth is given back, so that all life on Earth is really part of one life. Even death brings new life.[6]

Various deities in the Dine pantheon personify the mystery of change, of death and rebirth. Among them are Spider Woman and Changing Woman. For tribal people, it is not so common or interesting to talk about philosophical concepts.

Rather, understanding flows into the lives of holy beings who continually remind forgetful humans of the nature of things.

In this world the cycle of life, the direct experience of death and rebirth, of decay and renewal, is embedded in the daily experience of a gatherer, hunter, and farmer. The flow of life is calculated in the turning of the season, with the rhythm of dry and wet, bloom and decay, wind and silence. Change in the social realm is also acknowledged. Like planting and harvesting ceremonies, maturation for the human being is celebrated in sacred rites that mark the transition from infancy to childhood, from childhood to childbearing, from adulthood to death. The slow transition into wisdom can also occur in the course of many ceremonies over time, as is the case for those Lakota adults who go on repeated quests for Spirit.

The power of change is more often celebrated than feared or resisted by tribal peoples. A change of status does not mean extinction. It heralds a transformation to another realm of being. The Eskimo woman Uvavnuk was struck by lightning. After that she became a shaman. She had been entered and taken by fire, and was no longer afraid of her past, or of living and dying. She had passed through the experience of the deepest form of change, a direct encounter with death. Arctic explorer Knud Rasmussen met her in the early 1920s. She gave him this poem:

> The great sea
> has set me adrift
> moving me
> as weed in a great river
> Earth and storm
> move me,
> have carried me away,
> 'til I am trembling with joy.[7]

What is being conveyed here is the experience of absolute change, when voluntary or spontaneous surrender is entered, like one entering completely a strange house or forest or temple. The very atmosphere is quickened by natural as well as mental forces. For a moment and forever, nothing is the same; everything is new.

One of the strongest places to learn about this changing body is in nature. Yet our fear of impermanence has driven us to attempt to fix that which always transforms, whether it is our minds or Earth. Our homes are architectural statements about our aversion to the change of seasons. Our automobiles are mechanical statements about our relationship to time, which we are fearful of losing. Our cosmetics and clothing attempt to hide our age. Our newspapers, radios, and televisions tell us about the weather, when we could know as much simply by stepping outside and looking up and around at how the sun, wind, and rain shape the day. We now try to buy our identities instead of deriving our identity from all that which is around us.

Even as we struggle and strive to create a still-life of our world and our lives, we create immeasurable suffering for earth and her creatures. Homes, schools, churches, and offices are built at the expense of forests, while our automobiles destroy the atmosphere. Cosmetics designed to cloak our aging are tested on animals, often torturing them in the process. The media distorts our imaginations and sensibilities, while our materialism and greed create hunger and want for millions of humans. All this because we cannot accept the simple fact of change.

The holy people of indigenous cultures have realized that entering the energy body of the Earth produces power and can bring forth a kind of wild harmony in the body of change. When the Potawatomi honor their sacred Man Bundle, they sing

Now we all move,
   we're moving with this Earth.
The Earth is moving along,
   the water is moving along
The grass is moving,
   the trees are moving,
   the whole Earth is moving.
So we all move along with the Earth,
   keeping time with the Earth.[8]

Entering the body of change freely breeds energy. This is the natural energy of rivers and oceans, of the wind and mountains. Buddhist teacher and friend Richard Baker-roshi once asked me why shamans seek power. In that moment I realized that seeking power for the medicine person is analogous to cultivating awareness for the Buddhist. If the shaman seeks the power of the eagle, he seeks the power to see; if she seeks the power of the bear, it is to dream awake. The power of the gander is to understand the three realms of past, present,

152

and future. The power of the wolf is to find the trackless way. The power of the buffalo, the bison, is that of wisdom and balance. All of these qualities are aspects of awareness.

These are the medicines or gifts that awaken when power is sought and won, when awareness is cultivated and activated. That they are called medicine in the parlance of tribal peoples of North America is interesting in that these qualities are used to heal others and are signs of a healed awareness, a mind that includes the cosmos, a mind that sees the numinous in ordinary things.

The Lakota visionary John Fire Lame Deer describes how silence cultivates the mind of medicine:

> The wicasa wakan loves the silence, wrapping it around himself like a blanket—a loud silence with a voice like thunder which tells him of many things. Such a man likes to be in a place where there is no sound but the humming of insects. He sits facing the West, asking for help. He talks to the plants and they answer him. He listens to the voices of the Wama Kaskan—all those who move upon the Earth, the animals. He is at one with them. From all living beings something flows into him all the time, and something flows from him. I don't know where or what, but it's there, I know.[9]

Silence is the context where communion and communication with the world is born. This silence has a voice. From it issues the many songs of Earth. These songs carry the energy that flows from nondual awareness. Entering freely the body of change breeds energy as one does in meditation or when in love. This energy is the natural power of river and ocean, wind and mountain. For the old medicine man Wolf Collar, this energy was sourced in wind, rain, hail, and stillness—atmospheric medicine which opened his mind ground.

Standing in a storm or the pounding surf, laying hands on the sick, or sitting peacefully in the midst of confusion, energy is moved and in the movement transformed. The challenge for shaman and meditators is to find balance in the current. When this equilibrium is realized, then harmony, beauty, and joy arise. This mindfield in Buddhism is called meditative stabilization, and in shamanism, shamanic equilibrium. It is at this point that clear awareness arises.

Seeing through the Eyes of Compassion

Ecologist Aldo Leopold, in *A Sand County Almanac* strongly

expressed his sense that the human being is a "plain citizen" of the larger biotic community, neither more nor less. At the philosophical core of deep ecology is biospecies equality, harmony with nature, recognition that the Earth's so-called resources for the human being are limited. It entails a human commitment to a responsible relationship with our co-species and the environment that supports all life, and a developed understanding not only of a global perspective but also of our own particular bioregion. These perspectives are realized not just through the accumulation of scientific facts, but through our direct experience with ourselves, each other, other species, and the environment we share.

Here again the encounter between shamanism and Buddhism has something to offer us. Both traditions are based in the experience of direct practice realization, of direct knowing, of intimacy and communion, of understanding through experience, of seeing through the eyes of compassion. Both traditions emphasize understanding suffering, exemplified by the initiation crisis of the shaman and by Buddha's First Noble Truth of the existential nature of suffering.

Suffering is approached in both traditions as a path or place where compassion can awaken. Shaman and bodhisattva are equally dedicated to help those in suffering. Both tribal cultures and Buddhist tradition also emphasize simplicity in lifeway. Both use nature as a primary source of inspiration and understanding. Buddha had his Bo Tree, deer park, and previous lifetimes as animals. Shamans have their world trees and animal transformations, and familiars. And both traditions stress interdependence, beingness, change, activation of energy, equilibrium *and* silence, solitude, and ceremony as a means for discovering all of the above.

We need now to look at the role of *ahimsa* or nonviolence in Buddhism and tribal cultures. Zen Master Thich Nhat Hanh has suggested that nonviolence can be called "awareness." The experience of awareness shows us who we are, and what we are doing. Obviously we cannot conclude that tribal peoples were consistently nonviolent. Social customs and territorial conditions gave rise to various forms of warfare in many cultures.

Nor was it usual for vegetarianism to be the order of the day. However, there was no end of respect accorded to salmon, deer, or buffalo who provided food, among other things. The old Lacandon medicine man Chan Kin Viejo offered respect not only to the plants and creatures of the rainforest but also to those who have destroyed the rainforest. This capacity to practice reconciliation by seeing through the eyes of another, whether creature, plant, environmental feature, or human is the basis for survival not only in the tribal world, but may have something to do with our common survival in the twenty-first century.

Can the wave and the ocean be separate? Can the tree and the leaf not be connected? Even if the leaf falls from the tree, it eventually becomes food for the tree. Ecologist Joanna Macy has compared this notion of interrelatedness to the Jeweled Net of Indra where each facet of every jewel reflects all the others,[10] or the web Grandmother Spider weaves that binds all things into a common destiny, or the modern-day bodhisattva networker whose role it is to reveal the connections that exist. One's true nature, from this perspective, is not separate from anyone or anything else's.

The shaman is one who is opened through suffering to see the suffering of others. Seeing through the eyes of compassion allows the shaman to heal with skill and sensitivity. It also informs an individual's relationship to the world that supports all life.

In Buddhism, the experience of loving kindness is expressed by the Pali term *metta*, which is derived from the term *mitta* ("friend"). Loving kindness means true friendliness.

This true friendliness toward Earth, this love and compassion for Earth, means freedom for Earth—and ourselves. In Carlos Castaneda's *Tales of Power*, Don Juan says

> Only if one loves this earth with unending passion can one release one's sadness. A warrior is always joyful because his love is unalterable and his beloved, the earth, bestows upon him inconceivable gifts. . . . Only the love for this splendorous being can give freedom to a warrior's spirit; and freedom is joy, efficiency, and abandon in the face of any odds.[11]

This third body, the ecological Self, feels and understands every part of itself. An Eskimo song rejoices:

> My whole body
>   is covered with eyes:
> Behold it!
> Be without fear!
>   I see all around.[12]

These "eyes that feel the world," this capacity for "seeing," for understanding deeply the nature of things as they are—exactly this, no more, no less—is the secret shape of the third body. It is this body that is becoming more and more visible during our era of Earth's suffering. And it is this body, if it is completely revealed to all, that will give birth to wholesome life in the twenty-first century.

Notes

1. Victor Perera and Robert Bruce, *The Last Lords of Palenque* (Berkeley: University of California Press, 1985), p. 86.
2. John Seed, Joanna Macy, Pat Fleming, and Arne Naess, *Thinking Like a Mountain: Towards a Council of All Beings* (Philadelphia: New Society Publishers, 1988), p. 9.
3. James E. Lovelock, *Gaia: A New Look at Life on Earth* (New York: Oxford University Press, 1979), p. 152.
4. Francis LeFlesche, "The Osage Tribe: Rite of the Chiefs, Sayings of Ancient Men," in *36th Annual Report of the Bureau of American Ethnology* (Washington, DC: Government Printing Office, 1921), p. 186.
5. From A. L. Kroeber, *Handbook of the Indians of California,* Vol. 2 (St. Clair Shores, Michigan: Scholarly Press, 1972), adapted by Nina Wise and Joan Halifax.
6. *Between Sacred Mountains* (Tucson: University of Arizona Press), pp. 28-29.
7. From Knud Rasmussen, adapted by Joan Halifax.
8. A. Skinner, *The Mascoutens and Prairie Potawatomi Indians* (Milwaukee: Bulletin of the Public Museum of the City of Milwaukee, Vol. VI, No. 1), p. 177.
9. John Lame Deer and Richard Erdoes, *Lame Deer, Seeker of Visions* (New York: Simon and Schuster, 1972), pp. 145-46.
10. See, e.g., Ken Jones' essay in *Dharma Gaia,* ed. Allan Hunt Badiner (Berkeley: Parallax Press, 1990).
11. Carlos Castaneda. See Jack Kornfield's title essay in *The Path of Compassion: Writings on Socially Engaged Buddhism* (Berkeley: Parallax Press, 1988).
12. E. M. Weyer, Jr., *The Eskimos: Their Environment and Folkways* (New Haven: Yale University Press), p. 401.

13

The Celtic Fairy-Faith: An Interview with George Russell (AE)

W. Y. EVANS-WENTZ

*Noted Oxford translator and researcher W. Y. Evans-Wentz inter-
viewed the Irish poet and mystic George Russell (AE) as part of
his investigation of the Celtic Fairy-Faith. In the interview, AE
testified to his visions of* Sidhe *(shee) beings in Ireland.*

Q.—Are all visions which you have had of the same character?

A.—'I have always made a distinction between pictures seen
in the memory of nature and visions of actual beings now
existing in the inner world. We can make the same distinction
in our world: I may close my eyes and see you as a vivid picture
in memory, or I may look at you with my physical eyes and
see your actual image. In seeing these beings of which I speak,
the physical eyes may be open or closed: mystical beings in
their own world and nature are never seen with the physical eyes.'

Otherworlds.—

Q.—By the inner world do you mean the Celtic Otherworld?

A.—'Yes; though there are many Otherworlds. The *Tir-na-nog*
of the ancient Irish, in which the races of the *Sidhe* exist, may
be described as a radiant archetype of this world, though this
definition does not at all express its psychic nature. In *Tir-na-nog*
one sees nothing save harmony and beautiful forms. There
are other worlds in which we can see horrible shapes.'

Classification of the 'Sidhe.'—

Q.—Do you in any way classify the *Sidhe* races to which
you refer?

A.—'The beings whom I call the *Sidhe,* I divide, as I have
seen them, into two great classes: those which are shining,
and those which are opalescent and seem lit up by a light
within themselves. The shining beings appear to be lower in
the hierarchies; the opalescent beings are more rarely seen,
and appear to hold the positions of great chiefs or princes
among the tribes of Dana.'

Conditions of Seership.—

Q.—Under what state or condition and where have you seen such beings?

A.—'I have seen them most frequently after being away from a city or town for a few days. The whole west coast of Ireland from Donegal to Kerry seems charged with a magical power, and I find it easiest to see while I am there. I have always found it comparatively easy to see visions while at ancient monuments like New Grange and Dowth, because I think such places are naturally charged with psychical forces, and were for that reason made use of long ago as sacred places. I usually find it possible to throw myself into the mood of seeing; but sometimes visions have forced themselves upon me.'

The Shining Beings.—

Q.—Can you describe the shining beings?

A.—'It is very difficult to give any intelligible description of them. The first time I saw them with great vividness I was lying on a hill-side alone in the west of Ireland, in County Sligo: I had been listening to music in the air, and to what seemed to be the sound of bells, and was trying to understand these aerial clashings in which wind seemed to break upon wind in an ever-changing musical silvery sound. Then the space before me grew luminous, and I began to see one beautiful being after another.'

The Opalescent Beings.—

Q.—Can you describe one of the opalescent beings?

A.—'The first of these I saw I remember very clearly, and the manner of its appearance: there was at first a dazzle of light, and then I saw that this came from the heart of a tall figure with a body apparently shaped out of half-transparent or opalescent air, and throughout the body ran a radiant, electrical fire, to which the heart seemed the centre. Around the head of this being and through its waving luminous hair, which was blown all about the body like living strands of gold, there appeared flaming wing-like auras. From the being itself light seemed to stream outwards in every direction; and the effect left on me after the vision was one of extraordinary lightness, joyousness, or ecstasy.

'At about this same period of my life I saw many of these great beings, and I then thought that I had visions of Aengus, Manannan, Lug, and other famous kings or princes among the

Tuatha De Danann; but since then I have seen so many beings of a similar character that I now no longer would attribute to any one of them personal identity with particular beings of legend; though I believe that they correspond in a general way to the Tuatha De Danann or ancient Irish gods.'

Stature of the 'Sidhe.'—

Q.—You speak of the opalescent beings as great beings; what stature do you assign to them, and to the shining beings?

A.—'The opalescent beings seem to be about fourteen feet in stature, though I do not know why I attribute to them such definite height, since I had nothing to compare them with; but I have always considered them as much taller than our race. The shining beings seem to be about our own stature or just a little taller. Peasant and other Irish seers do not usually speak of the *Sidhe* as being little, but as being tall: an old school-master in the West of Ireland described them to me from his own visions as tall beautiful people, and he used some Gaelic words, which I took as meaning that they were shining with every colour.'

The worlds of the 'Sidhe.'—

Q.—Do the two orders of *Sidhe* beings inhabit the same world?

A.—'The shining beings belong to the mid-world; while the opalescent beings belong to the heaven-world. There are three great worlds which we can see while we are still in the body: the earth-world, mid-world, and heaven-world.'

Nature of the 'Sidhe.'—

Q.—Do you consider the life and state of these *Sidhe* beings superior to the life and state of men?

A.—'I could never decide. One can say that they themselves are certainly more beautiful than men are, and that their worlds seem more beautiful than our world.

'Among the shining orders there does not seem to be any individualized life: thus if one of them raises his hands all raise their hands, and if one drinks from a fire-fountain all do; they seem to move and to have their real existence in a being higher than themselves, to which they are a kind of body. Theirs is, I think, a collective life, so unindividualized and so calm that I might have more varied thoughts in five hours than they would have in five years; and yet one feels an extraordinary purity and exaltation about their life. Beauty

159

of form with them has never been broken up by the passions which arise in the developed egotism of human beings. A hive of bees has been described as a single organism with disconnected cells; and some of these tribes of shining beings seem to be little more than one being manifesting itself in many beautiful forms. I speak this with reference to the shining beings only: I think that among the opalescent or *Sidhe* beings, in the heaven-world, there is an even closer spiritual unity, but also a greater individuality.'

Influence of the 'Sidhe' on Men.—

Q.—Do you consider any of these *Sidhe* beings inimical to humanity?

A.—'Certain kinds of the shining beings, whom I call wood beings, have never affected me with any evil influences I could recognize. But the water beings, also of the shining tribes, I always dread, because I felt whenever I came into contact with them a great drowsiness of mind and, I often thought, an actual drawing away of vitality.'

Water Beings Described.—

Q.—Can you describe one of these water beings?

A.—'In the world under the waters—under a lake in the West of Ireland in this case—I saw a blue and orange coloured king seated on a throne; and there seemed to be some fountain of mystical fire rising from under his throne, and he breathed this fire into himself as though it were his life. As I looked, I saw groups of pale beings, almost grey in colour, coming down one side of the throne by the fire-fountain. They placed their head and lips near the heart of the elemental king, and, then, as they touched him, they shot upwards, plumed and radiant, and passed on the other side, as though they had received a new life from this chief of their world.'

Wood Beings Described.—

Q.—Can you describe one of the wood beings?

A.—'The wood beings I have seen most often are of a shining silvery colour with a tinge of blue or pale violet, and with dark purple-coloured hair.'

Reproduction and Immortality of the 'Sidhe.'—

Q.—Do you consider the races of the *Sidhe* able to reproduce their kind; and are they immortal?

A.—'The higher kinds seem capable of breathing forth beings out of themselves, but I do not understand how they do so. I have seen some of them who contain elemental beings within themselves, and these they could send out and receive back within themselves again.

'The immortality ascribed to them by the ancient Irish is only a relative immortality, their space of life being much greater than ours. In time, however, I believe that they grow old and then pass into new bodies just as men do, but whether by birth or by the growth of a new body I cannot say, since I have no certain knowledge about this.'

Sex among the 'Sidhe.'—

Q.—Does sexual differentiation seem to prevail among the Sidhe races?

A.—'I have seen forms both male and female, and forms which did not suggest sex at all.'

'Sidhe' and Human Life.—

Q.—(1) Is it possible, as the ancient Irish thought, that certain of the higher *Sidhe* beings have entered or could enter our plane of life by submitting to human birth? (2) On the other hand, do you consider it possible for men in trance or at death to enter the *Sidhe* world?

A.—(1) 'I cannot say.' (2) 'Yes; both in trance and after death. I think any one who thought much of the *Sidhe* during his life and who saw them frequently and brooded on them would likely go to their world after death.'

Social Organization of the 'Sidhe.'—

Q.—You refer to chieftain-like or prince-like beings, and to a king among water beings; is there therefore definite social organization among the various *Sidhe* orders and races, and if so, what is its nature?

A.—'I cannot say about a definite social organization. I have seen beings who seemed to command others, and who were held in reverence. This implies an organization, but whether it is instinctive like that of a hive of bees, or consciously organized like human society, I cannot say.'

Lower 'Sidhe' as Nature Elementals.—

Q.—You speak of the water-being king as an elemental king; do you suggest thereby a resemblance between lower

Sidhe orders and what mediaeval mystics called elementals?

A.—'The lower orders of the *Sidhe* are, I think, the nature elementals of the mediaeval mystics.'

Nourishment of the Higher 'Sidhe.'—

Q.—The water beings as you have described them seem to be nourished and kept alive by something akin to electrical fluids; do the higher orders of the *Sidhe* seem to be similarly nourished?

A.—'They seemed to me to draw their life out of the Soul of the World.'

Collective Visions of 'Sidhe' Beings.—

Q.—Have you had visions of the various *Sidhe* beings in company with other persons?

A.—'I have had such visions on several occasions.'

And this statement has been confirmed to me by three participants in such collective visions, who separately at different times have seen in company with our witness the same vision at the same moment. On another occasion, on the Greenlands at Rosses Point, County Sligo, the same *Sidhe* being was seen by our present witness and a friend with him, also possessing the faculty of seership, at a time when the two percipients were some little distance apart, and they hurried to each other to describe the being, not knowing that the explanation was mutually unnecessary. I have talked with both percipients so much, and know them so intimately that I am fully able to state that as percipients they fulfil all necessary pathological conditions required by psychologists in order to make their evidence acceptable.

14

The World an Organism

CAROLYN MERCHANT

Organic Unity

Organic thought in the Renaissance had its roots in Greek concepts of the cosmos as an intelligent organism, which when revived and modified were assimilated into the consciousness of the fifteenth and sixteenth centuries. Three root traditions became the basis for later syncretic forms of organicism— Platonism, Aristotelianism, and Stoicism. Each of these organic traditions differed in important respects, so that when synthesized with other systems, such as Hermeticism, gnosticism, Neoplatonism, and Christianity, they produced a spectrum of Renaissance organismic philosophies.

Common to all was the premise that all parts of the cosmos were connected and interrelated in a living unity. From the "affinity of nature" resulted the bonding together of all things through mutual attraction or love. All parts of nature were mutually interdependent and each reflected changes in the rest of the cosmos. The common knitting of the world's parts implied not only mutual nourishment and growth but also mutual suffering. "When one part suffers, the rest also suffer with it," wrote Giambattista della Porta (1535-1615).[1] Or as Paracelsus expressed the idea, "If anything suffers from the error of the elements other things grow uncertain too . . . and the defects and errors of the firmament can be observed by us, no less than the firmament observes our defects."[2]

Astrologer John Dee (1527-1628) presupposed a harmonious universe in which celestial rays from the stars and zodiacal signs interacted with each other to produce different effects in each natural object. The coalescence and unification of natural forces as they flowed into each body produced a unique effect in that object, dependent on both source and receptor.

The organic unity of the cosmos derived from its conception as a living animal. A vast organism, everywhere quick and vital, its body, soul, and spirit were held tightly together.

As Della Porta put it, "The whole world is knit and bound within itself: for the world is a living creature, everywhere both male and female, and the parts of it do couple together . . . by reason of their mutual love."[3]

All parts of this world, even the metals, contained life and were nourished by the earth and sun. Bernardino Telesio wrote that

> those things which are made in the depths of the earth, or those which derive or grow therefrom: the metals, the broken sulfuric, bituminous or nitrogenous rocks; and furthermore those sweet and gentle waters, as well as the plants and animals—if these were not made of earth by the sun, one cannot imagine of what else or by what other agent they could be made.[4]

His follower Campanella affirmed the vitality of the elements and the pervasive life and feeling of the entire cosmos:

> Now if animals have, as we all agree, what is called sense or feeling, and if it is true that sense and feeling do not come from nothing, then it seems to me that we must admit that sense and feeling belong to all elements which function as their cause, since it can be shown that what belongs to the effect belongs to the cause. Consider, then, the sky and earth and the whole world as containing animals in the way in which worms are sometimes contained in the human intestines—worms or men, if you please, who ignore the sense and feeling in other things because they consider it irrelevant with respect to their so called knowledge of entities.[5]

As the sixteenth century organic cosmos was transformed into the seventeenth century mechanistic universe, its life and vitality were sacrificed for a world filled with dead and passive matter. By examining variations in Renaissance philosophies of nature we can see the process by which some assumptions were transformed and retained while others were criticized and rejected.

Neoplatonic Natural Magic

Neoplatonic natural magic presupposed a hierarchical cosmic structure and assumed that earthly changes were influenced by the celestial heavens and could be produced artificially by the human manipulation of natural objects in which these influences inhered. It originated as an elite aristocratic form of the magical world view in the Florentine Platonic Academy in the late fifteenth century.

A revival of Neoplatonic philosophy and an interest in the writings of Hermes Trismegistus took place under the sponsorship of the wealthy Medici family, who had obtained an aristocratic status through the commercial manufacture and trade of wool and silken goods, banking operations, and mine management. The Florentine Academy, which they funded, was a private community of scholars pursuing (outside the university structure) studies of a hierarchical cosmos in which changes could be effected by the manipulation of natural objects. The academy supported Ficino and visiting Neoplatonic scholars such as Pico della Mirandola.[6]

Neoplatonic magic postulated a hierarchical universe that extended from the base matter of the earth upward to the divine intellect. It accepted the tripartite division of the macrocosmic world into body, soul, and spirit, the components of a living organism. The divine mind beyond the visible cosmos was the seat of the Platonic forms, the pure Ideas of which sensible corporeal objects were merely imperfect copies. The female soul of the world was everywhere present and, as in Plato's *Timaeus*, was the source of motion and activity in the macrocosm. It contained the celestial images of the divine Ideas. The world's body was its matter, the elements out of which corporeal objects were generated. Linking the celestial images in the world soul to the matter in the body was the world spirit. The *spiritus mundi* was the vehicle by which the influences of superior powers in the celestial realm could be brought down and joined to the inferior powers in the terrestrial region. As Agrippa put it,

> In the soul of the world there be as many seminal forms as ideas in the mind of God, by which forms she did in the heavens above the stars frame to herself shapes also, and stamped upon all these some properties. On these stars therefore, shapes and properties, all virtues of inferior species, as also their properties do depend; so that every species hath its celestial shape, or figure that is suitable to it, from which also proceeds a wonderful power of operating, which proper gift it receives from its own idea, through the seminal forms of the soul of the world.[7]

This Neoplatonic conceptual scheme was common to natural philosophers such as Ficino, Pico della Mirandola, Agrippa, Della Porta, and Thomas Vaughan. The hierarchical arrangement of the parts of the universe was a great chain linking inferiors to superiors: "For so inferiors are successively joined to their superiors, that there proceeds an influence

165

from their head, the first cause, as a certain string stretched out to the lowermost things of all, of which string if one end be touched the whole doth presently shake."[8]

Della Porta illustrated the role of the golden chain in the operations of the magus who "marries and couples together inferior things" by means of the powers they receive from their superiors:

> Seeing then the spirit cometh from God, and from the spirit cometh the soul, and the soul doth animate and quicken all other things in their order . . . so that the superior power cometh down even from the very first cause to these inferiors, driving her force into them, like as it were a cord platted together and stretched along from heaven to earth, in such sort as if either end of this cord be touched, it will wag the whole; therefore we may rightly call this knitting together of things *a chain* . . . wherein he feigneth, that all the gods and goddesses have made a golden chain, which they hanged above in heaven, and it reacheth down in the very earth.[9]

Thomas Vaughan, a seventeenth-century Neoplatonic alchemist, likewise held that the world's soul, spirit, and ethereal water were all connected together like the links of a chain. The attraction of the spirit for the soul moved the first link followed by the attraction of the water for the spirit. The soul thus became imprisoned in the liquid crystal of the waters.

> In every frame, there are three leading principles. The first is this soul, whereof we have spoken . . . already. The second is that which we have called the spirit of the world, and this spirit is "the medium whereby the soul is diffused through and moves its body." The third is a certain oleous, ethereal water. This is the menstruum and matrix of the world, for in it all things are framed and preserved.[10]

At the basis of Neoplatonic hierarchical magic, therefore, was a causal chain linking elemental and celestial objects and making it possible for bodies above the terrestrial sphere to affect and alter those on earth.

In the Neoplatonic scheme, the cosmic world soul was the source of life and activity in the natural world. The soul was immanent within nature, vivifying it like a cosmic animal. Matter was distinct from both the world's soul and its spirit. Agrippa held that the soul was the source of the world's power, while matter was inactive: "Now seeing the soul is the first thing that is moveable and as they say, is moved of itself; but the body or the matter, is of itself unable and unfit for motion and doth degenerate from the soul."[11]

Likewise, for Thomas Vaughan, the principle of motion was the soul of the world, trapped by matter and struggling for freedom. He considered the Aristotelian notion of a substantial form too limiting and absurd to be the source of motive power. Motion was caused by a principle internal to the macrocosmic world, the *anima mundi*. But like the other Neoplatonists, Vaughan considered matter to be "merely passive and furnished with no motive faculty at all."[12]

Although the ultimate source of activity in the Neoplatonic world picture was the *anima mundi*, which was connected to earthly objects by the *spiritus mundi*, changes in particular natural objects were induced through occult properties. The natural magician drew a distinction between *elementary* qualities, the properties of matter, and *occult* properties, those derived from the stars and infused into natural objects by the *spiritus*. These occult virtues were more powerful than elementary virtues because they contained more form and less materiality. The occult properties had the power to "generate their like," to make the objects "like and suitable to" themselves.[13] Since an excess of occult virtue in any object could generate a like quality in another, plants or animals containing strong virtues could be utilized to produce the desired property. For example,

> Any animal that is barren causeth another to be barren, and of the animal especially the generative parts . . . if at any time we would promote love, let us seek some animal which is most loving, of which kind are pigeons, turtles, sparrows, swallows, wagtails and in these take those members or parts in which the vital virtue is most vigorous such as the heart, breast, and also like parts. . . . In like manner, to increase boldness, let us look for a lion, or a cock, and of these let us take the heart, eyes or forehead.

An occult property had the power not only to generate its like in another object, but also to "shun its contrary and drive it away out of its presence." These enmities or antipathies between occult properties could be used by the magus to effect cures and produce changes in natural objects. According to Della Porta, "Amongst all the secrets of nature, there is nothing but hath some hidden and special property; and moreover that by this their consent and disagreement, we may conjecture, and in trial so it will prove, that one of them may be used as a fit remedy against the harms of the other."[14]

For the Neoplatonists, therefore, the opposites, or sympathies and antipathies, were the properties of natural objects. They

167

were powers or forces within the material object, but distinct from it, deriving from the world soul in the celestial heavens and ultimately from the ideas in the divine mind. The tripartite distinction between matter, spirit, and soul was the foundation of the Neoplatonic hierarchical structure. Operating within this hierarchy, the magus could draw down the celestial powers to marry inferiors to superiors, and therefore to manipulate nature for individual benefit.

Condemned by the Catholic Church in the sixteenth century as heretical, natural magic was based on assumptions such as the manipulation of nature and the passivity of matter; these assumptions were ultimately assimilated into a mechanical framework founded on technological power over nature for the collective benefit of society. The Renaissance magus as an operator and arranger of natural objects became the basis of a new optimism that nature could be altered for human progress.

In the organic world view, the concept of nature as a living entity had limited the scale of power to individual needs and group benefits such as spiritual fulfillment, healing, the growing of crops, and the manufacture of tools. For the Neoplatonic magician, the upward gnostic ascent aimed at greater intellectual insight and spiritual regeneration. Knowledge and power could be obtained through a union with the understanding and intellect of God: "No one has such powers but he who has cohabited with the elements, vanquished nature, mounted higher than the heavens, elevating himself above the angels to the archetype itself, with whom he then becomes cooperator and can do all things."[15] But power obtained by such methods was restricted to each individual. It was an experience which could not be shared or transferred except through initiation.

Della Porta portrays the magician as nature's assistant in the cultivation of crops and breeding of animals, nature being the operator, the magician preparing the way:

> Wherefore as many of you as come to behold magick, must be persuaded that the works of magick are nothing else but the works of nature whose dutiful hand-maid magick is . . . as in husbandry it is nature that brings forth corn and herbs, but it is art that prepares and makes way for them. Hence it was that Antipho the poet said, *that we overcome those things by art wherein nature doth overcome us;* and Plotinus calls a magician such a one as works by the help of nature only, and not by the help of art.[16]

But although the magician is depicted here as nature's helpmate, the idea of altering and changing nature is also important to Della Porta's natural magic. Much of his book is devoted to the production of new plants, the generation of animals, and the changing of metals—how "an oak may be changed into a vine," how to generate "an apple compounded of a peach-apple and a nut-peach," and how to breed "new kinds of living creatures . . . of diverse beasts, by carnal copulation." He writes,

> Art, being as it were, nature's ape, even in her imitation of nature, effecteth greater matters than nature doth. Hence it is that a magician being furnished with art, as it were another nature, searching thoroughly into those works which nature doth accomplish by many secret means and close operations, doth work upon nature . . . and either hastens or hinders her work, making things ripe before or after their natural season, and so indeed makes nature to be his instrument.

Although Della Porta considered himself to be the humble servant of nature working within its seasons and growing periods, aping and emulating its organic processes in order to perfect and hasten them, such manipulations, when assimilated into the utilitarian framework of Francis Bacon, would become instead techniques for control. Mechanism removed the organic substratum and substituted a mechanical framework for the same operations. And although the mechanists, too, were limited by the laws of nature and operated within them, "commanding nature by obeying her," they were free of the ethical strictures associated with the view of nature as a living being.

The process of mechanizing the world picture removed the controls over environmental exploitation that were an inherent part of the organic view that nature was alive, sensitive, and responsive to human action. Mechanism took over from the magical tradition the concept of the manipulation of matter but divested it of life and vital action. The passivity of matter, externality of motion, and elimination of the female world soul altered the character of cosmology and its associated normative constraints. In the mechanical philosophy, the manipulation of nature ceased to be a matter of individual efforts and became associated with general collaborative social interests that sanctioned the expansion of commercial capitalism. Increasingly it benefited those persons and social classes in control of its development, rather than promoting universal progress for all. It was intimately connected to an empirical philosophy of

169

science and a concept of the human being as a designer of experiments who by wresting secrets from nature gained mastery over its operations.

Naturalism

Whereas natural magic tended to operate within a structure that conserved cosmic order in the form of hierarchy, the second organic variant, naturalism, laid greater stress on a concept of change that challenged the hierarchical structure of both nature and society. Renaissance naturalism, developing from within the Aristotelian framework, exposed it to a radical critique.[17] The ultimate terms of philosophical explanation were reduced to two—the material substratum and the dialectical opposition of contraries. Naturalism differed from Neoplatonism in that the contraries were principles of change rather than properties of matter. The lack of a distinction between the world soul and spirit broke down the Neoplatonic hierarchies, utilizing only one category to account for natural changes.

Naturalism differed from traditional Aristotelianism in that activity was not accounted for through the actualization of the potential by means of the form; instead, the contraries were the agents of change. They were active principles; matter was a passive principle that received specification through the activity of the opposites.

Telesio, in his book *De Rerum Natura (On the Nature of Things According to Their Own Proper Principles)* (1565), reduced the explanatory entities to two substances or natures, a corporeal material substratum and an incorporeal dialectical activity that produced individuation in matter. Throughout changes in individual objects, the same body and matter remained. Matter was dead and passive, completely uniform throughout and lacking the capacity to act or operate. Its function was to receive and conserve the activity of the incorporeal substance.[18]

The distinctive feature of Telesio's natural philosophy was to define activity as a dialectic, the conflict between contraries. Active agents "perpetually oppose one another; forever disturbing or destroying each other. They do not desire to be together, nor can they remain together in any way." The primary opposites were hot and cold, and from these followed the operations of the other opposites: density and rarity, darkness and whiteness, lightness and obscurity, mobility and immobility, bringing the "active natures into perpetual conflict."

The two fundamental active principles, hot and cold, appeared in corporeal garb as the sun and the earth, sensible manifestations of the opposites. The sun was "supreme heat, whiteness, light, and motion," the earth "supreme cold, darkness, and immobility." These principles also appeared in all things generated out of the earth and sun (or sky) in a reduced or diminished form. In generated objects, the opposites interpenetrated and caused change, while in the sun and earth they were primary, supreme, self-constituted, and independent. Each natural organism developed in accordance with its own nature, while its motion benefited and maintained the harmony of the whole.

Telesio's naturalism was an important formative influence on the early ideas of Campanella. Campanella asserted that the earth, the plants, and the metals were living beings with sense and feelings. Plants and animals derived their matter from the earth and their activity and motion from the sun. The sun was an "active, diffusive, and incorporeal power." Sense and feelings were characteristic of active causes. "That the sun and the earth feel is undeniable," he asserted.[19]

Following Telesio, Campanella argued that change occurred through the opposition of active contraries. "Hot and cold, I say, understood as active and wholly free of atomic passivity, are not born without active power." The modes of being were produced by the opposing actions of these dynamic causes. All things were produced from the matter of the earth and the activity of the sun, arising from the opposition of the two contraries heat and cold.

Campanella criticized the atomic theory of the ancient philosophers Democritus and Lucretius on the basis that the mingling of inert, passive, insentient particles could not give rise to beings with feelings and sensations. For the atomists, he observed, heat and cold were not active principles within matter, but were produced instead by mechanical coupling: "Heat is born from those atoms which are sharper, and cold from those which are obtuse, while the soul is born of the round ones."

The basic dynamic of the opposition of hot and cold was extended to a general theory of dialectical process in the philosophy of Giordano Bruno, who synthesized Neoplatonic and Stoic ideas. From an early Neoplatonist phase, he moved to the view, in his *Expulsion of the Triumphant Beast* (1584), that two universal substances, one corporeal and material, the other incorporeal and spiritual, explained change.[20] The soul and spirit of the Neoplatonists were fused into a single active substance, a world soul or inner principle of motion, while prime matter was its passive corporeal opposite. Matter was not created *ex nihilo*, nor could it return to nothingness; it was "ingenerable and incorruptible," "arrangeable and fashionable," and a divine mother of all things. The active substance, or universal spirit, did not mix by composition with matter, but had the power to hold matter intact, keep its parts united, and maintain its composition: "It is exactly like the helmsman on the ship, the father of the family at home, and an artisan who is not eternal but fabricates from within, tempers and preserves the edifice. . . . It winds the beam, weaves the cloth, interweaves the thread, restrains, tempers, gives order to and arranges and distributes the spirits. . . . " On the highest level, matter and spirit achieved an absolute unity as a single universal substance.

Change was the unification and opposition of contraries. An efficient formative principle within the universal spiritual substance acted to unite the contraries and to arrange discordant qualities in harmonies. And then, "necessitated by the principles of dissolution, abandoning its architecture [the efficient and formative principle] causes the ruin of the edifice by dissolving the contrary elements, breaking the union, removing the hypostatic composition."

Bruno's character of Sophia, ancient priestess of gnostic wisdom, puts forth his ideas on the unification and dissolution of contraries in *The Expulsion of the Triumphant Beast*. The transit between states defines the reality in change. One condition has meaning only in terms of its opposite. Pleasure becomes meaningful in terms of past boredom, walking in terms of previous sitting, satiety with respect to hunger: " 'Association with one food, however pleasing,' " says Sophia, " 'is finally the cause of nausea. . . . Motion from one contrary to the other through its intermediate points come[s] to satisfy [us]; and, finally we see such familiarity between one contrary and the other that the one agrees more with the other than like with like.' " Responding to Sophia, Bruno's Saulino pointed out that it is no small thing to have discovered the principle of the coincidence of contraries and that it is the magician who knows how to look for them. Everything comes "from contraries, through contraries, into contraries, to contraries. And where there is contrariety there is action and reaction, there is motion, there is diversity." Reality was thus defined in terms of activity and process. Cosmic unity was maintained through the coming together and dissolution of opposites. The source of activity in nature was the universal spirit, the immanent activity of God within nature.

Bruno's dialectic stressed the unity rather than the struggle of opposites, anticipating idealist rather than materialist dialectics.[21] He emphasized the harmony of the whole, pointing out that an organic whole is always more than the sum of its parts. His plurality of worlds within the infinite universe formed a living whole. "It is not reasonable," he wrote, "to believe that any part of the world is without soul life, sensation, and organic structure."[22] In his claim for the existence of innumerable other worlds, Bruno assigned no prime position to the human species and held that nature was everywhere uniform. "The ruler of our earth is not man, but the sun, with the life which breathes in common through the universe." In questioning the uniqueness of the earth-sun system, in emphasizing change, and in unifying the Neoplatonic soul and spirit into a single active principle, Bruno challenged the hierarchical conception of the cosmos.

In the final phase of his philosophy, Bruno focused on individual active substances or minimal units in nature. These soul-driven atoms or monads of different degrees applied not only to corpuscles of matter, but to planetary systems, the world soul, God, and the universe as a whole. The monads of one degree could include those of another degree within them, and all were parts of the same underlying substance.[23]

The distinctive feature of the naturalist philosophy was the dialectical process as the key to both the organic unity of nature and its immanent self-motion. Nature was a constantly growing, changing, and evolving organism. Naturalism thus postulated a more radical interpretation of change than Neoplatonism and more strongly reflected the breakup of the hierarchical social order and the movement to question the received authority of Aristotle.

Vitalism

The most radical analysis of activity in nature was put forward by Paracelsus and later refined by Jean Baptiste Van Helmont (1577-1644), his son Francis Mercury Van Helmont, and Anne Conway. In this theory, matter and spirit are unified into a single, active vital substance. Paracelsus' cosmos was infused by Neoplatonic, gnostic, Stoic, and Christian ideas, yet his philosophy of matter and activity was a monistic idealism. Here the term *vitalism* designates the unity of matter and spirit as a self-active entity, in which the spiritual kernel is considered the real substance and the material "cover" a mere phenomenon.

Paracelsus' theory of the four elements as active entities rather than passive substrata was expounded in his *Archidoxis* (published in 1570). Although the four elements might all exist in a given object, only one of them attained perfection as the "ruling power" of that object, growing yet remaining invisible within it. The other three were so imperfect as not to warrant being called *elements*, in the true sense of "active substances." The observed individual object was merely a cover for the real immanent active soul.[24]

The theory of the elements was elaborated in a treatise attributed to Paracelsus and published posthumously in 1564, entitled *The Philosophy Addressed to the Athenians*. Although some have questioned the authenticity of this treatise on purely textual grounds, the doctrine itself is regarded as genuine and was accepted as such by the generation following Paracelsus. Here the four elements were essentially spiritual self-active forces with a self-determining principle (*archeus*) guiding their unfolding lives through time. The observable sensible elements and material objects were merely gross manifestations of the subtle soul that was the element itself. By a cosmic separation, the elements were generated from the uncreated *mysterium magnum*—the great mystery or "first mother of all creatures"—and folded back into it at the end of created time.[25]

Each element formed a world of its own, and each of the four worlds developed and evolved independently of the others through a consensus of actions. The elements did not mix in composition, but existed simultaneously and independently in each individual object. The predominant element in the object determined the world to which it belonged and became its guiding kernel or soul.

Each element was a matrix or mother of one of the four worlds emanating from it. Thus, from water, a unique world was created: fish of all forms and kinds; fleshy animals; marine plants such as corals, trina, and citrones; marine monsters; the elementals (nymphs, sirens, dramas, lorinds, and nesder);

as an army surgeon, a position unacceptable to academic physicians. His life became a series of clashes with orthodox authorities and ruling officials. In city after city, he was able to cure princes and public officials pronounced incapable of recovery by the orthodox physicians. In each case, his success and fame procured him friends among the wealthy and influential town leaders. But soon his opinions and actions would alienate them and he would be forced to leave town secretly in order to escape arrest.[30]

Incensed by enslaving traditions and moved by the poverty and misery of the people, he identified with the peasants as he moved from spas to mines to towns attracting crowds and healing the sick. Often he refused to take money from the poor and sick, while at the same time he was again and again cheated by the rich. His violent reactions against these injustices would then make it necessary for him to leave the town.

Paracelsus' medical and chemical contributions became a stimulus to numerous sixteenth- and seventeenth-century followers working toward a new empirical methodology advocating the direct study of nature itself, instead of the books of the ancient Greeks. But his philosophy of the activity of nature became affiliated with revolutionary pantheistic and political ideas that surfaced in later neo-Paracelsist movements.

The animistic concept of nature as a divine, self-active organism came to be associated with atheistical and radical libertarian ideas. Social chaos, peasant uprisings, and rebellions could be fed by the assumption that individuals could understand the nature of the world for themselves and could manipulate its spirits by magic.[31] A widespread use of popular magic to control these spirits existed at all levels of society, but particularly among the lower classes. The raising of spirits, the construction of magical apparatus, the manufacture of talismans and charms, the preparation of love potions, the exorcism of demons, fortune telling, and hunts for treasures, lost relatives, and lovers were operations directed or performed by the village wizard. Every European village had its popular healers, sorcerers, and magicians, whose magical procedures had resulted from years of transmitting verbal recipes and cures handed down from medieval and ancient times. Articulation of the presuppositions of magical theory may be attributed to the natural magic tradition, but the practice of magic itself was an ancient folk tradition.

The natural philosophy of Jean Baptiste Van Helmont, the

seventeenth-century follower of Paracelsus, likewise emphasized the activity of matter. He called the dynamic principle the *archeus*, the organizer of specificity within matter. It originated ultimately from the divine light and organized the living developing seeds of matter—the *semina*. Van Helmont transformed Paracelsus' four elements into a plurality of seeds each containing its own inner activity: "In the whole order of natural things nothing of new doth arise which may not take its beginning out of the seed, and nothing to be made which may not be made out of the necessity of the seed."[32]

He strongly took issue with Aristotle's doctrine of the four causes and held that two causes "joined or knit together" were sufficient to explain nature. The two unified principles were the efficient cause, or *archeus* (the chief workman), and the material cause, or plurality of seeds. "Wherefore, after a diligent searching, I have not found any dependence of a natural body but only on two causes, on the matter and the efficient, to wit, inward ones." The two were joined into a single unit, the generating seed. The efficient cause was the inward agent of the *semina*—the moving principle or immanent active principle in the material seed.

Thus Aristotle erred in stating that "the thing generating cannot be a part of the thing generated." For Van Helmont, the inward agent was the generative principle; nothing new arose in nature that did not begin from the efficient power in the material seed.

The inward agent was also called the *chief* or *master workman*. In vegetables, it was a juice; in metals, it was thicker and homogeneous with the material; in other things, it was an "air." It was the inward spiritual kernel of the seed through which the seed developed and grew to full fruitfulness. "The *archeus*, the workman and governor of generation, doth clothe himself . . . with a bodily clothing . . . and begins to transform matter according to the perfect act of his own image."

The formal cause postulated by Aristotle, said Van Helmont, was not really a cause but an effect, the end of generation. For Aristotle, the more perfectly the form was attained, the more actuality the object had achieved. For Van Helmont, the actuality or activity was the inner agent within the matter. Form and matter could not be separated from one another. Secondly, the efficient or moving cause could not be external to matter, but must be within it. Thirdly, the final or teleological cause, which contained the "instructions of things to be done," could not be external to nature nor should it be considered distinct from the efficient cause, the *archeus*. But, although the efficient seminal cause was postulated to be within nature, Van Helmont admitted that external occasional causes could function as outward awakeners. These outward agents operated according to art.

Matter and the efficient cause were therefore sufficient as explanatory entitles fused together into one unit. "Every natural definition is to be fetched . . . from the conjoining of both causes, because both together do finish the whole essence of the thing."

The activity within each particle of matter meant that activity and process were primary in the order of things. Within the matter of the world, there existed an inherent spontaneity, and within each individual being an inner-directedness determined its destiny.

These ideas were set within a vitalistic philosophical framework which presupposed that nature was active, filled with God, and therefore good. Gerrard Winstanley wrote, "To know the secrets of nature is to know the works of God . . . how the spirit or power of wisdom and life, causing motion or growth, dwells within and governs both the several bodies of the stars and planets in the heavens above; and the several bodies of the earth below, as grass, plants, fishes, beasts, birds, and mankind." An early Ranter belief held that "every creature is God, every creature that hath life and breath being an efflux from God, and shall return into God again, be swallowed up in him as a drop is in the ocean." Jacob Bauthumley, a Ranter writing in 1650, agreed that "God is in everyone and every living thing, man and beast, fish and fowl, and every green thing, from the highest cedar to the ivy on the wall. . . . God is in this dog, this tobacco pipe, he is me and I am him." Richard Coppin, whose *Divine Teachings* (1649) influenced Ranter beliefs, held that "God is all in one and so is in everyone."

The sects pushed their radical ideas even further by undermining the basis for the patriarchal family. For the Familists, members of the Family of Love, a pantheistic sect emphasizing tenderness and quiet sympathy, founded in 1580, marriage was changed from a sacrament to a contract, and divorce became simply a matter of dissolution before the congregation. The Diggers advocated marriage based solely on love regardless of station or property. The Ranters challenged monogamy and believed that wives could be held in common. At Ranter and Quaker meetings, stripping to nakedness in church as a symbol of resurrection was not uncommon, and sexual freedom for both men and women was broached.[33]

Through membership in the new sects, women enjoyed significantly more religious freedom than in either the Church of England or the Catholic Church. The Puritans had elevated the female to helpmeet in the family, assigned her the task of instructing the family in religious matters, and argued for an end to wife beating, though women were still considered subordinate partners in the marriage relationship. In the sects, however, equality before God was stressed; women could be admitted to membership without their husbands and were free to preach, prophesy, and participate in governance. In many congregations, women outnumbered men, and in London women preaching on Sundays became common. Those women who joined the new religious sects were undoubtedly attracted by the freedoms and equalities found there.[34] (Such freedoms assumed by women were especially pronounced in Quakerism, a sect that claimed the allegiance of Francis Mercury Van Helmont and Anne Conway, who continued the vitalistic philosophy of the fusion of spirit and matter.) After the Restoration of 1660, with the reassertion of Anglican authority, Paracelsian and pantheistic ideas were denounced and refuted.

Similarly, in seventeenth-century France, Robert Fludd (1574-1637), a follower of Paracelsus and the naturalists, became identified with the "Rosicrucian scare" (a neo-Paracelsist movement), resulting in an examination and denunciation of his entire philosophy by the mechanists—Marin Mersenne, Pierre Gassendi, and René Descartes. France in the 1620s-40s and England in the 1650s-80s were at the center of the mechanical reconstruction of the cosmos. In both countries, ideas associated with the organic world view and with animistic and pantheistic philosophies were severely criticized.

Fludd's philosophy presented a synthesis of ideas from the preceding Neoplatonic, naturalist, and vitalist traditions. In his Neoplatonic hierarchical cosmos, founded on the microcosm-macrocosm analogy, God infused the world with his eternal spirit, which was housed in the sun and transmitted through the angels in the four corners of the world to the winds. The winds, in turn, representing the contrary principles of hot and cold, acted through a dialectical process of contraction and expansion, conveying activity to the clouds and air. The two contrary active principles, heat and cold, produced the opposites observed in nature. The hot winds caused dilation, mollification, rarefaction, volatility, and transparency; cold winds produced contraction, hardening, condensation, fixation, and opacity. Matter for Fludd was passive; not the source of activity, it was made active through the indirect operation of the winds. The angelical winds were "endued with most essential internal agents" and had "an essential and inward act, form, and principle." The clouds likewise moved through the internal agency of the spirit and represented its vehicle. God's activity in the world was the ultimate source of these dialectical tensions between contraries and the basis of cosmic unity and animate life.[35]

From the spectrum of Renaissance organicist philosophies outlined above, the mechanists would appropriate and transform presuppositions at the conservative or hierarchical end while denouncing those associated with the more radical religious and political perspectives. The rejection and removal of organic and animistic features and the substitution of mechanically describable components would become the most significant and far-reaching effect of the Scientific Revolution.

The breakup of the old order in western Europe was not only a period of challenge—a time when a broad spectrum of new ideas found articulation—but also a period of uncertainty and anxiety. Fear that nature would interdict her own laws, that the cosmic frame would crumble, and that chaos and anarchy would rule lay just beneath the sheen of apparent order. Fostered by the competitive practices of the new commercialism and reinforced by the religious wars of the Reformation period and the growing stress on individualism and the senses over the authority of the ancients, the perception of disintegration increased. The ecological deterioration of the earth, changing images of the cosmic organism, and a sense of disorder within the soul of nature reflected an underlying realization that the old system was dying.

Notes

1. Giovanni Battista della Porta, *Magiae Naturalis* (Naples, 1558). English trans.: G. B. della Porta, *Natural Magic*, facsimile edition, ed. Derek J. Price (New York: Basic Books, 1957; first published 1658), p. 13.

2. Theophrast von Hohenheim Paracelsus, "Philosophia ad Atheniensis," in *Sämtliche Werke*, eds. Karl Sudhoff and Wilhelm Matthiessen (Munich: Barth, 1922-1933), Abt. I, vol. 13, p. 409. Eng. trans.: Paracelsus, "The Philosophy Addressed to the Athenians," in *The Hermetic and Alchemical Writings* ed. and trans. Arthur E. Waite (London: Elliott, 1894), vol. 2, p. 268; Peter J. French, *John Dee: The World of an Elizabethan Magus* (London: Routledge & Kegan Paul, 1972), p. 93.

3. Della Porta, 1658 facsimile, p. 14.

4. Bernardino Telesio, *De Rerum Natura Iuxta Propia Principia* (Naples, 1587; first-published 1565). Quotations from excerpts trans. by Arturo B. Fallico and Herman Shapiro in *Renaissance Philosophy*, vol. I, *The Italian Philosophers* (New York: Modern Library, 1967), p. 309.

5. Tommaso Campanella, *De Sensu Rerum et Magia* (written 1591) (Frankfurt, 1629). Quotations from excerpts trans. Fallico and Shapiro, p. 340.

6. Gene A. Brucker, *Renaissance Florence* (New York: Wiley, 1969), pp. 68-78, 87, 124, 228-9; Frances A. Yates, *Giordano Bruno and the Hermetic Tradition* (New York: Vintage, 1964), Chaps. 2-5. Yates stresses the synthesis of Neoplatonism and Hermeticism in the natural magic tradition. The Hermetic texts are collected in the *Corpus Hermeticum*, ed. A. D. Nock and trans. A.-J. Festugière, 4 vols. (Paris, 1945-54). On Renaissance Neoplatonism and Hermeticism see A.-J. Festugière, *La Révélation d'Hermès Trismégiste*, 4 vols. (Paris, 1950-54); Paul Oskar Kristeller, *The Philosophy of Marsilio Ficino*, trans. Virginia Conant (New York: Columbia University Press, 1943); P. O. Kristeller, *Renaissance Thought: The Classic, Scholastic, and Humanist Strains* (New York: Harper & Row, 1961); Frances Yates, "The Hermetic Tradition in Renaissance Science," in Charles Singer, ed. *Art, Science, and History in the Renaissance* (Baltimore, Md.: Johns Hopkins University Press, 1968), pp. 255-74.

7. Henry Cornelius Agrippa, *De Occulta Philosophia Libri Tres* (Antwerp, 1531). English trans.: Agrippa, *Natural Magic*, trans. Willis F. Whitehead (reprint ed., New York: Weiser, 1971; first published, 1651), pp. 62-63.

8. *Ibid.*, p. 120.

9. Della Porta, 1658 facsimile, p. 8.

10. Thomas Vaughan (Eugenius Philalethes), *Works*, ed., A. E. Waite, (New York: University Books, 1968), p. 79.

11. Agrippa, trans. Whitehead, p. 69. See also Charles G. Nauert, *Agrippa and the Crisis of Renaissance Thought* (Urbana: University of Illinois Press, 1965), p. 267. Also useful is C. G. Nauert, "Magic and Scepticism in Agrippa's Thought," *Journal of the History of Ideas* 18 (1957): 161-82.

12. Vaughan, p. 78.

13. Agrippa, trans. Whitehead, quotations in order, on pp. 70, 71, 72, 78.

14. Della Porta, 1658 facsimile, p. 8.

15. Agrippa, *De Occulta Philosophia*, Bk. II, quoted in Yates, *Bruno*, p. 136.

16. Della Porta, 1658 facsimile, quotations in order on pp. 2, 33, 63, 64, 73.

17. On the critique of Aristotle, see Walter Pagel, "The Reaction to Aristotle in Seventeenth Century Biological Thought," in E. Ashworth Underwood, ed., *Science, Medicine and History* (London: Oxford University Press, 1953), vol. 1, pp. 489-509. On the divergence between the traditional scholastic Aristotelian approach and the criticisms of the Italian naturalists, Telesio, Bruno, and Campanella, see Charles Schmitt, "Towards a Reassessment of Renaissance Aristotelianism," *History of Science* 11 (1973): 159-73, esp. p. 164. On Telesio's reaction against Aristotle see Allen Debus, *The Chemical Dream of the Renaissance* (Cambridge, England: Heffer, 1968), pp. 8-13, 24-25. On the complex subject of Aristotelianism and its influence in the late Renaissance, see Neal Ward Gilbert, "Renaissance Aristotelianism and its Fate: Some Observations and Problems," in John P. Anton, ed., *Naturalism and Historical Understanding, Essays on the Philosophy of John Herman Randall, Jr.* (Albany, N.Y.: State University of New York Press, 1967), pp. 42-52; Charles Schmitt, *Critical Survey and Bibliography of Studies on Renaissance Aristotelianism, 1958-1969* (Padua: Editrice Antenore, 1971), and C. Schmitt "John Case on Art and Nature," *Annals of Science* 33 (1976): 543-59; John Herman Randall, Jr., *The School of Padua and the Emergence of Modern Science* (Padua: Editrice Antenore, 1961); Edward F. Cranz, *A Bibliography of Aristotle Editions, 1501-1600* (Baden Baden: Koerner, 1971).

18. Bernardino Telesio, *De Rerum Natura*, trans. Fallico and Shapiro, quotations in order on pp. 316, 318, 315, 319, 312. On Telesio's life and thought, see F. Fiorentino, *Bernardino Telesio*, 2 vols. (Florence, 1872-1874). Useful commentaries on Telesio include Neil Van Deusen, "The Place of Telesio in the History of Philosophy," *Philosophical Review* 44 (1935): 317-34 and N. Van Deusen, *Telesio: First of the Moderns* (New York, 1930). That the concept of the dialectic was fundamental to Renaissance magical and organic philosophies I owe to discussions with David Kubrin and his *How Sir Isaac Newton Helped Restore Law 'n' Order to the West* (San Francisco: Kubrin, 1972).

19. Tommaso Campanella, *De Sensu Rerum et Magia*, trans. Fallico and Shapiro, quotations on pp. 341-42, 345. Campanella's philosophy of nature was also developed in his *Philosophia Sensibus Demonstrata* (Naples, 1591). See also T. Campanella, . . . *Epilogo Magno* (Rome: Reale Accademia d'Italia, 1939). Relevant commentaries on Campanella's life and thought include Leon Blanchet, *Campanella* (Paris: Alcan, 1920); Bernardo M. Bonansea, *Tommaso Campanella* (Washington, D.C.: Catholic University of America Press, 1969); Luigi Amabile, *Fra Tommaso Campanella*, 3 vols. (Naples: Morano, 1882).

20. Giordano Bruno, *Spaccio de la Bestia Trionfante* (Paris, 1584). English trans. *The Expulsion of the Triumphant Beast*, trans. and ed. Arthur D.

Imerti (New Brunswick, N.J.: Rutgers University Press, 1964), quotations on pp. 75-76, 90, 91. See also Yates, *Bruno,* Chaps. 11-20; Paul Henri Michel, *The Cosmology of Giordano Bruno,* trans. R. E. W. Maddison (Ithaca, N.Y.: Cornell University Press, 1973), pp. 111-112; Edward Gosselin and Lawrence Lerner, "Galileo and the Long Shadow of Bruno," *Archives Internationales d'Histoire des Sciences,* 25 (December 1975), pp. 223-46; E. Gosselin and L. Lerner "Giordano Bruno," *Scientific American* 228 (1973): 84-94; Antoinette Mann Paterson, *The Infinite Worlds of Giordano Bruno* (Springfield, Ill.: Thomas, 1970); Dorothy Singer, *Giordano Bruno: His Life and Thought* (New York: Schumann, 1950); Robert Westman, "Magical Reform and Astronomical Reform: The Yates Thesis Reconsidered," in R. Westman and J. E. McGuire, *Hermeticism and the Scientific Revolution* (Los Angeles: University of California Press, 1977), pp. 3-91; Hélène Védrine, *La Conception de la Nature chez Giordano Bruno* (Paris: Vrin, 1967).

21. Irving Louis Horowitz, *The Renaissance Philosophy of Giordano Bruno* (New York: Ross, 1952), p. 29, 31, 37-38, 41,27.

22. Quotes in Horowitz, p. 27.

23. Giordano Bruno, *De Monade, Numero et Figura,* written ca. 1590 (Frankfurt, 1614); also in *Opere Latine,* ed. F. Fiorentino and others, 3 vols. (Naples, 1897-1901), vols. 1-2, pp. 323-473. For a discussion see Harold Höffding, *A History of Modern Philosophy,* trans. B. E. Meyer (London: Macmillan, 1915), vol. 1, pp. 130, 138-39.

24. Paracelsus, "Archidoxi," (first published 1570), in *Sämtliche Werke,* B. Aschner, ed. (Jena: Fischer, 1930), vol. 3, pp. 1-87. See esp. pp. 9, 10, 12, 13. English trans.: Paracelsus, *His Archidoxis Comprised in Ten Books Disclosing the Genuine Way of Making Quintessences, Arcanums, Magisteries, Elixers, etc.* trans. J. H. Oxon (London, 1660). Relevant commentaries on the philosophy of Paracelsus include Kurt Goldammer, *Paracelsus: Natur und Offenbarung* (Hanover: Oppermann, 1953); Walter Pagel, "Paracelsus and the Neoplatonic and Gnostic Tradition," *Ambix* 8 (1960): 125-66; W. Pagel, "Paracelsus: Traditionalism and Medieval Sources," in Lloyd G. Stevenson and Robert P. Multhauf, eds., *Medicine, Science, and Culture* (Baltimore, Md.: Johns Hopkins University Press, 1968), pp. 57-64; Oswei Temkin, "The Elusiveness of Paracelsus," *Bulletin of the History of Medicine* 26 (1952): 201-17. On Paracelsus' theory of matter and the elements, see W. Pagel, *Paracelsus* (Basel: Karger, 1958), pp. 38, 82-95, and W. Pagel, "The Prime Matter of Paracelsus," *Ambix* 9 (October, 1961): 117-35.

25. Paracelsus, "Philosophia ad Athenienses," Sudhoff, ed., *Sämtliche Werke,* Abt. I, vol. 13, pp. 389-423. The following discussion is based on pp. 390, 410-11, 403, 407, 395-96, 398. Two English translations exist: Paracelsus, *Three Books of Philosophy Written to the Athenians in Philosophy Reformed and Improved,* trans. H. Pinnell (London, 1657), and Paracelsus "The Philosophy Addressed to the Athenians," in Waite, ed., *Hermetic and Alchemical Writings,* vol. 2, pp. 247-81. On the question of authenticity, see Pagel,

Paracelsus, pp. 89-91, notes 237-38 and W. Pagel, "Recent Paracelsian Studies," *History of Science* 12 (1974): 200-11. Allen Debus treats the text as if it were Paracelsus' own in his book *The Chemical Philosophy: Paracelsian Science and Medicine in the Sixteenth and Seventeenth Centuries,* 2 vols. (New York: Science History Publications, 1977), vol. 1, pp. 55-57.

26. Paracelsus, "Philosophia ad Athenienses," ed. Sudhoff, vol. 13, p. 406; trans. Waite, vol. 2, p. 266.

27. Paracelsus, "Philosophia ad Athenienses," ed. Sudhoff, vol. 13, p. 409; trans. Waite, vol. 2, p. 269.

28. Owen Hannaway, *The Chemists and the Word: The Didactic Origins of Chemistry* (Baltimore, Md.: Johns Hopkins University Press, 1975), pp. 26, 30-31, 32. See also D. P. Walker, "The Astral Body in Renaissance Medicine," *Journal of the Warburg and Courtald Institutes* 21 (1958): 119-33; W. Pagel, *Paracelsus,* pp. 122-23.

29. Paracelsus, "Credo," *Selected Writings,* ed. Jolande Jacobi (Princeton, N.J.: Princeton University Press, 1951), pp. 5, 109.

30. Pagel, *Paracelsus,* pp. 5-30, esp. 17, 23; Jacobi, ed., p. 4; Waite, ed., vol. 1, p. 20.

31. On Paracelsus' influence in chemistry and medicine, see Allen Debus, *The Chemical Philosophy;* A. Debus, *The English Paracelsians* (New York: Watts, 1965) and A. Debus, *The Chemical Dream of the Renaissance* (Cambridge, England: Heffer, 1968). On the political ideas associated with Paracelsianism, see P. M. Rattansi, "Paracelsus and the Puritan Revolution," *Ambix* 11 (1963): 24-32. On popular magic, see Keith Thomas, *Religion and the Decline of Magic* (New York: Scribner's, 1971), pp. 228-29.

32. Johann Baptista Van Helmont, *Works,* trans. J. Chandler (London: Lodowick, Lloyd, 1664), quotations on pp. 32, 30, 29, 32, 35, 29, 30. On Van Helmont's philosophy, see W. Pagel, "The Religious and Philosophical Aspects of Van Helmont's Science and Medicine," *Supplements to the Bulletin of the History of Medicine,* no. 2 (1944), p. 20; W. Pagel "The Spectre of Van Helmont," in Mikulas Teich and Robert Young, eds., *Changing Perspectives: Essays in Honor of Joseph Needham* (London: Heineman, 1973), pp. 100-109; Debus, *Chemical Philosophy,* vol. 2, pp. 295-344.

33. Hill, pp. 251-52, 254, 256-57.

34. Keith Thomas, "Women in the Civil War Sects," *Past and Present,* no. 13 (April 1958); 42-62, see pp. 44-45, 47, 50-51.

35. Robert Fludd, *Philosophia Moysaica* (Govdae: Rammazenius, 1638); Eng. trans.: R. Fludd, *Mosaicall Philosophy* (London, 1659), pp. 59-60, 79-80, 91-92. See also, Allen G. Debus, *The English Paracelsians* (New York: Watts, 1965), pp. 105 ff.; A. Debus, *Chemical Philosophy,* vol. 1, pp. 205-93; W. Pagel, "Religious Motives in the Medical Biology of the XVIIth Century," *Bulletin of the Institute of the History of Medicine* [Johns Hopkins University] 3 (February 1935): 270; Kubrin, *How Sir Isaac Newton Helped,* p. 15.

15
The Elements and Their Inhabitants

MANLY PALMER HALL

For the most comprehensive and lucid exposition of occult pneumatology (the branch of philosophy dealing with spiritual substances) extant, mankind is indebted to Philippus Aureolus Paracelsus (Theophrastus Bombastus von Hohenheim), prince of alchemists and Hermetic philosophers and true possessor of the *Royal Secret* (the Philosopher's Stone and the Elixir of Life). Paracelsus believed that each of the four primary elements known to the ancients (earth, fire, air, and water) consisted of a subtle, vaporous principle and a gross corporeal substance.

Air is, therefore, twofold in nature—tangible atmosphere and an intangible, volatile substratum which may be termed *spiritual air*. Fire is visible and invisible, discernible and indiscernible—a spiritual, ethereal flame manifesting through a material, substantial flame. Carrying the analogy further, water consists of a dense fluid and a potential essence of a fluidic nature. Earth has likewise two essential parts—the lower being fixed, terreous, immobile; the higher, rarefied, mobile, and virtual. The general term *elements* has been applied to the lower, or physical, phases of these four primary principles, and the name *elemental essences* to their corresponding invisible, spiritual constitutions. Minerals, plants, animals, and men live in a world composed of the gross side of these four elements, and from various combinations of them construct their living organisms.

Henry Drummond in *Natural Law in the Spiritual World*, describes this process as follows: "If we analyse this material point at which all life starts, we shall find it to consist of a clear structureless, jelly-like substance resembling albumen or white of egg. It is made of Carbon, Hydrogen, Oxygen and Nitrogen. Its name is protoplasm. And it is not only the structural unit with which all living bodies start in life, but with which they are subsequently built up. 'Protoplasm,' says Huxley, 'simple or nucleated, is the formal basis of all life. It is the clay of the Potter.' "

The *water* element of the ancient philosophers has been

metamorphosed into the hydrogen of modern science; the *air* has become oxygen; the *fire*, nitrogen; the *earth*, carbon.

Just as visible Nature is populated by an infinite number of living creatures, so according to Paracelsus, the invisible, spiritual counterpart of visible Nature (composed of the tenuous principles of the visible elements) is inhabited by a host of peculiar beings, to whom he has given the name *elementals*, and which have later been termed the Nature spirits. Paracelsus divided these people of the elements into four distinct groups, which he called *gnomes, undines, sylphs,* and *salamanders.* He taught that they were really living entities, many resembling human beings in shape, and inhabiting worlds of their own, unknown to man because his undeveloped senses were incapable of functioning beyond the limitations of the grosser elements.

The civilizations of Greece, Rome, Egypt, China, and India believed implicitly in satyrs, sprites, and goblins. They peopled the sea with mermaids, the rivers and fountains with nymphs, the air with fairies, the fire with Lares and Penates, and the earth with fauns, dryads, and hamadryads. These Nature spirits were held in the highest esteem, and propitiatory offerings were made to them. Occasionally, as the result of atmospheric conditions or the peculiar sensitiveness of the devotee, they became visible. Many authors wrote concerning them in terms which signify that they had actually beheld these inhabitants of Nature's finer realms. A number of authorites are of the opinion that many of the gods worshiped by the pagans were elementals, for some of these *invisibles* were believed to be of commanding stature and magnificent deportment.

The Greeks gave the name *daemon* to some of these elementals, especially those of the higher orders, and worshiped them. Probably the most famous of these *daemons* is the mysterious spirit which instructed Socrates, and of whom the great philosopher spoke in the highest terms. Those who have devoted much study to the invisible constitution of man realize that it is quite probable the daemon of Socrates and the angel of Jakob Böhme were in reality not elementals, but the overshadowing divine natures of these philosophers themselves. In his notes to *Apuleius on the God of Socrates*, Thomas Taylor says:

"As the daemon of Socrates, therefore, was doubtless one of the highest order, as may be inferred from the intellectual superiority of Socrates to most other men, Apuleius is justified in calling this daemon a God. And that the daemon of Socrates indeed was divine, is evident from the testimony of Socrates himself in the First Alcibiades: for in the course of that dialogue he clearly says, 'I have long been of the opinion that the God did not as yet direct me to hold any conversation with you.' And in the Apology he most unequivocally evinces that this daemon is allotted a divine transcendency, considered as ranking in the order of daemons."

The idea once held, that the invisible elements surrounding and interpenetrating the earth were peopled with living, intelligent beings, may seem ridiculous to the prosaic mind of today. This doctrine, however, has found favor with some of the greatest intellects of the world. The sylphs of Facius Cardan, the philosopher of Milan; the salamander seen by Benvenuto Cellini; the pan of St. Anthony; and *le petit homme route* (the little red man, orgnome) of Napoleon Bonaparte, have found their places in the pages of history.

Literature has also perpetuated the concept of Nature spirits. The mischievous Puck of Shakespeare's *Midsummer Night's Dream*, the elementals of Alexander Pope's Rosicrucian poem, *The Rape of the Lock*; the mysterious creatures of Lord Lytton's *Zanoni*; James Barrie's immortal Tinker Bell; and the famous bowlers that Rip Van Winkle encountered in the Catskill Mountains, are well-known characters to students of literature. The folklore and mythology of all peoples abound in legends concerning these mysterious little figures who haunt old castles, guard treasures in the depths of the earth, and build their homes under the spreading protection of toadstools. Fairies are the delight of childhood, and most children give them up with reluctance. Not so very long ago the greatest minds of the world believed in the existence of fairies, and it is still an open question as to whether Plato, Socrates, and Iamblichus were wrong when they avowed their reality.

Paracelsus, when describing the substances which constitute the bodies of the elementals, divided flesh into two kinds, the first being that which we have all inherited through Adam. This is the visible, corporeal flesh. The second was that flesh which had not descended from Adam and, being more attenuated, was not subject to the limitations of the former. The bodies of the elementals were composed of this transubstantial flesh. Paracelsus stated that there is as much difference between the bodies of men and the bodies of the Nature spirits as there is between matter and spirit.

"Yet," he adds, "the Elementals are not spirits, because they have flesh, blood and bones; they live and propagate offspring; they eat and talk, act and sleep, etc., and consequently they cannot be properly called 'spirits.' They are beings occupying a place between men and spirits, resembling men and spirits, resembling men and women in their organization and form, and resembling spirits in the rapidity of their locomotion." (*Philosophia Occulta*, translated by Franz Hartmann.) Later the same author calls these creatures *composita*, inasmuch as the substance out of which they are composed seems to be a composite of spirit and matter. He uses color to explain the idea. Thus, the mixture of blue and red gives purple, a new color, resembling neither of the others yet composed of both. Such is the case with the Nature spirits; they resemble neither spiritual creatures nor material beings, yet are composed of the substance which we may call *spiritual matter*, or ether.

Paracelsus further adds that whereas man is composed of several natures (spirit, soul, mind, and body) combined in one unit, the elemental has but one *principle*, the ether out of which it is composed and in which it lives. The reader must remember that by *ether* is meant the spiritual essence of one of the four elements. There are as many ethers as there are elements and as many distinct families of Nature spirits as there are ethers. These families are completely isolated in their own ether and have no intercourse with the denizens of the other ethers; but, as man has within his own nature centers of consciousness sensitive to the impulses of *all* the four ethers, it is possible for any of the elemental kingdoms to communicate with him under proper conditions.

The Nature spirits cannot be destroyed by the grosser elements, such as material fire, earth, air, or water, for they function in a rate of vibration higher than that of earthy substances. Being composed of only one element or principle (the ether in which they function), they have no immortal spirit and at death merely disintegrate back into the element from which they were originally individualized. No individual consciousness is preserved after death, for there is no superior vehicle present to contain it. Being made of but one substance, there is no friction between vehicles: thus there is little wear or tear incurred by their bodily functions, and they therefore live to great age. Those composed of earth ether are the shortest lived; those composed of air ether, the longest. The average length of life is between three hundred and a thousand years. Paracelsus maintained that they live in conditions similar to our earth environments, and are somewhat subject to disease. These creatures are thought to be incapable of spiritual development, but most of them are of a high moral character.

Concerning the elemental ethers in which the Nature spirits exist, Paracelsus wrote: "They live in the four elements: the Nymphae in the element of water, the Sylphes in that of the air, the Pigmies in the earth, and the Salamanders in fire. They are also called Undinae, Sylvestres, Gnomi, Vulcani, etc. Each species moves only in the element to which it belongs, and neither of them can go out of its appropriate element, which is to them as the air is to us, or the water to fishes; and none of them can live in the element belonging to another class. To each elemental being the element in which it lives is transparent, invisible and respirable, as the atmosphere is to ourselves." (*Philosophia Occulta*, translated by Franz Hartmann.)

The reader should be careful not to confuse the Nature spirits with the true life waves evolving through the invisible worlds. While the elementals are composed of only one etheric (or atomic) essence, the angels, archangels, and other superior, transcendental entities have composite organisms, consisting of a spiritual nature and a chain of vehicles to express that nature not unlike those of men, but not including the physical body with its attendant limitations.

To the philosophy of Nature spirits is generally attributed an Eastern origin, probably Brahmanic; and Paracelsus secured his knowledge of them from Oriental sages with whom he came in contact during his lifetime of philosophical wanderings. The Egyptians and Greeks gleaned their information from the same source. The four main divisions of Nature spirits must now be considered separately, according to the teachings of Paracelsus and the Abbé de Villars and such scanty writings of other authors as are available.

The Gnomes

The elementals who dwell in that attenuated body of the earth which is called the terreous ether are grouped together under the general heading of *gnomes*. (The name is probably derived from the Greek *genomus*, meaning earth dweller. See *New English Dictionary*.)

Just as there are many types of human beings evolving

through the objective physical elements of Nature, so there are many types of gnomes evolving through the subjective ethereal body of Nature. These earth spirits work in an element so close in vibratory rate to the material earth that they have immense power over its rocks and flora, and also over the mineral elements in the animal and human kingdoms. Some, like the pygmies, work with the stones, gems, and metals, and are supposed to be the guardians of hidden treasures. They live in caves, far down in what the Scandinavians called the Land of the Nibelungen. In Wagner's wonderful opera cycle, *The Ring of the Nibelungen*, Alberich makes himself King of the Pygmies and forces these little creatures to gather for him the treasures concealed beneath the surface of the earth.

Besides the pygmies there are other gnomes, who are called tree and forest sprites. To this group belong the sylvestres, satyrs, pans, dryads, hamadryads, durdalis, elves, brownies, and little old men of the woods. Paracelsus states that the gnomes build houses of substances resembling in their con- stituencies alabaster, marble, and cement, but the true nature of these materials is unknown, having no counterpart in physical nature. Some families of gnomes gather in communities, while others are indigenous to the substances with and in which they work. For example, the hamadryads live and die with the plants or trees of which they are a part. Every shrub and flower is said to have its own Nature spirit, which often uses the physical body of the plant as its habitation. The ancient philosophers, recognizing the principle of intelligence mani- festing itself in every department of Nature alike, believed that the quality of natural selection exhibited by creatures not possessing organized mentalities expressed in reality the decisions of the Nature spirits themselves.

C. M. Gayley, in *The Classic Myths*, says: "It was a pleasing trait in the old paganism that it loved to trace in every operation of nature the agency of deity. The imagination of the Greeks peopled the regions of earth and sea with divinities, to whose agency it attributed the phenomena that our philosophy ascribes to the operation of natural law." Thus, in behalf of the plant it worked with, the elemental accepted and rejected food elements, deposited coloring matter therein, preserved and protected the seed, and performed many other beneficent offices. Each species was served by a different but appropriate type of Nature spirit. Those working with poisonous shrubs, for example, were offensive in their appearance. It is said the

Nature spirits of poison hemlock resemble closely tiny human skeletons, thinly covered with a semi-transparent flesh. They live in and through the hemlock, and if it be cut down remain with the broken shoots until both die, but while there is the slightest evidence of life in the shrub it shows the presence of the elemental guardian.

Great trees also have their Nature spirits, but these are much larger than the elementals of smaller plants. The labors of the pygmies include the cutting of the crystals in the rocks and the development of veins of ore. When the gnomes are laboring with animals or human beings, their work is confined to the tissues corresponding with their own natures. Hence they work with the bones, which belong to the mineral kingdom, and the ancients believed the reconstruction of broken members to be impossible without the cooperation of the elementals.

The gnomes are of various sizes—most of them much smaller than human beings, though some of them have the power of changing their stature at will. This is the result of the extreme mobility of the element in which they function. Concerning them the Abbé de Villars wrote: "The earth is filled well nigh to its center with Gnomes, people of slight stature, who are the guardians of treasures, minerals and precious stones. They are ingenious, friends of man, and easy to govern."

Not all authorites agree concerning the amiable disposition of the gnomes. Many state that they are of a tricky and malicious nature, difficult to manage, and treacherous. Writers agree, however, that when their confidence is won they are faithful and true. The philosophers and initiates of the ancient world were instructed concerning these mysterious little people and were taught how to communicate with them and gain their cooperation in undertakings of importance. The magi were always warned, however, never to betray the trust of the elementals, for if they did, the invisible creatures, working through the subjective nature of man, could cause them endless sorrow and probably ultimate destruction. So long as the mystic served others, the gnomes would serve him, but if he sought to use their aid selfishly to gain temporal power they would turn upon him with unrelenting fury. The same was true if he sought to deceive them.

The earth spirits meet at certain times of the year in great conclaves, as Shakespeare suggests in his *Midsummer Night's*

Dream, where the elementals all gather to rejoice in the beauty and harmony of Nature and the prospects of an excellent harvest. The gnomes are ruled over by a king, whom they greatly love and revere. His name is *Gob*; hence his subjects are often called *goblins.* Mediaeval mystics gave a corner of creation (one of the cardinal points) to each of the four kingdoms of Nature spirits, and because of their earthy character the gnomes were assigned to the North—the place recognized by the ancients as the source of darkness and death. One of the four main divisions of human disposition was also assigned to the gnomes, and because so many of them dwelt in the darkness of caves and the gloom of forests their temperature was said to be melancholy, gloomy, and despondent. By this it is not meant that they themselves are of such disposition, but rather that they have special control over elements of similar consistency.

The gnomes marry and have families, and the female gnomes are called *gnomides.* Some wear clothing woven of the element in which they live. In other instances their garments are part of themselves and grow with them, like the fur of animals. The gnomes are said to have insatiable appetites, and to spend a great part of the time eating, but they earn their food by diligent and conscientious labor. Most of them are of a miserly temperament, fond of storing things away in secret places. There is abundant evidence of the fact that small children often see the gnomes, inasmuch as their contact with the material side of Nature is not yet complete and they still function more or less consciously in the invisible worlds.

According to Paracelsus, "Man lives in the exterior elements and the Elementals live in the interior elements. The latter have dwellings and clothing, manners and customs, languages and governments of their own, in the same sense as the bees have their queens and herds of animals their leaders." (*Philosophia Occulta,* translated by Franz Hartmann.)

Paracelsus differs somewhat from the Greek mystics concerning the environmental limitations imposed on the Nature spirits. The Swiss philosopher constitutes them of subtle invisible ethers. According to this hypothesis they would be visible only at certain times and only to those *en rapport* with their ethereal vibrations. The Greeks, on the other hand, apparently believed that many Nature spirits had material constitutions capable of functioning in the physical world. Often the recollection of a dream is so vivid that, upon awakening, a person actually believes that he has passed through a physical experience. The difficulty of accurately judging as to the end of physical sight and the beginning of ethereal vision may account for these differences of opinion.

Even this explanation, however, does not satisfactorily account for the satyr which, according to St. Jerome, was captured alive during the reign of Constantine and exhibited to the people. It was of human form with the horns and feet of a goat. After its death it was preserved in salt and taken to the Emperor that he might testify to its reality. (It is within the bounds of probability that this curiosity was what modern science knows as a *monstrosity*.)

The Undines

As the gnomes were limited in their function to the elements of the earth, so the *undines* (a name given to the family of water elementals) function in the invisible, spiritual essence called humid (or liquid) ether. In its vibratory rate this is close to the element water, and so the undines are able to control, to a great degree, the course and function of this fluid in Nature. Beauty seems to be the keynote of the water spirits. Wherever we find them pictured in art or sculpture, they abound in symmetry and grace. Controlling the water element—which has always been a feminine symbol—it is natural that the water spirits should most often be symbolized as female.

There are many groups of undines. Some inhabit waterfalls, where they can be seen in the spray; others are indigenous to swiftly moving rivers; some have their habitat in dripping, oozing fens or marshes; while other groups dwell in clear mountain lakes. According to the philosophers of antiquity, every fountain had its nymph; every ocean wave its oceanid. The water spirits were known under such names as oreades, nereides, limoniades, naiades, water sprites, sea maids, mermaids, and potamides. Often the water nymphs derived their names from the streams, lakes, or seas in which they dwelt.

In describing them, the ancients agreed on certain salient features. In general, nearly all the undines closely resembled human beings in appearance and size, though the ones inhabiting small streams and fountains were of correspondingly lesser proportions. It was believed that these water spirits were occasionally capable of assuming the appearance of normal human beings and actually associating with men and women.

There are many legends about these spirits and their adoption by the families of fishermen, but in nearly every case the undines heard the call of the waters and returned to the realm of Neptune, the King of the Sea.

Practically nothing is known concerning the male undines. The water spirits did not establish homes in the same way that the gnomes did, but lived in coral caves under the ocean or among the reeds growing on the banks of rivers or the shores of lakes. Among the Celts there is a legend to the effect that Ireland was peopled, before the coming of its present inhabitants, by a strange race of semi-divine creatures; with the coming of the modern Celts they retired into the marshes and fens, where they remain even to this day. Diminutive undines lived under lily pads and in little houses of moss sprayed by waterfalls. The undines worked with the vital essences and liquids in plants, animals, and human beings, and were present in everything containing water. When seen, the undines generally resembled the goddesses of Greek statuary. They rose from the water draped in mist and could not exist very long apart from it.

There are many families of undines, each with its peculiar limitations. It is impossible to consider them here in detail. Their ruler, *Necksa*, they love and honor, and serve untiringly. Their temperament is said to be vital, and to them has been given as their throne the western corner of creation. They are rather emotional beings, friendly to human life and fond of serving mankind. They are sometimes pictured riding on dolphins or other great fish and seem to have a special love of flowers and plants, which they serve almost as devotedly and intelligently as the gnomes. Ancient poets have said that the songs of the undines were heard in the West Wind and that their lives were consecrated to the beautifying of the material earth.

The Salamanders

The third group of elementals is the salamanders, or spirits of fire, who live in that attenuated, spiritual ether which is the invisible fire element of Nature. Without them material fire cannot exist; a match cannot be struck nor will flint and steel give off their spark without the assistance of a salamander, who immediately appears (so the mediaeval mystics believed), evoked by friction. Man is unable to communicate successfully with the salamanders, owing to the fiery element in which they dwell, for everything is resolved to ashes that comes into their presence. By specially prepared compounds of herbs and perfumes the philosophers of the ancient world manufactured many kinds of incense. When incense was burned, the vapors which arose were especially suitable as a medium for the expression of these elementals, who, by borrowing the ethereal effluvium from the incense smoke, were able to make their presence felt.

The salamanders are as varied in their grouping and arrangement as either the undines or the gnomes. There are many families of them, differing in appearance, size, and dignity. Sometimes the salamanders were visible as small balls of light. Paracelsus says: "Salamanders have been seen in the shapes of fiery balls, or tongues of fire, running over the fields or peering in houses." (*Philosophia Occulta*, translated by Franz Hartmann.)

Mediaeval investigators of the Nature spirits were of the opinion that the most common form of salamander was lizard-like in shape, a foot or more in length, and visible as a glowing Urodela, twisting and crawling in the midst of the fire. Another group was described as huge flaming giants in flowing robes, protected with sheets of fiery armor. Certain mediaeval authorities, among them the Abbé de Villars, held that Zarathustra (Zoroaster) was the son of Vesta (believed to have been the wife of Noah) and the great salamander Oromasis. Hence, from that time onward, undying fires have been maintained upon the Persian altars in honor of Zarathustra's flaming father.

One most important subdivision of the salamanders was the Acthnici. These creatures appeared only as indistinct globes. They were supposed to float over water at night and occasionally to appear as forks of flame on the masts and riggings of ships (St. Elmo's fire). The salamanders were the strongest and most powerful of the elementals, and had as their ruler a magnificent flaming spirit called *Djin*, terrible and awe-inspiring in appearance. The salamanders were dangerous and the sages were warned to keep away from them, as the benefits derived from studying them were often not commensurate with the price paid. As the ancients associated heat with the South, this corner of creation was assigned to the salamanders as their throne, and they exerted special influence over all beings of fiery or tempestuous temperament. In both animals and men, the salamanders work through the emotional nature by means of the body heat, the liver, and the blood stream. Without their assistance there would be no warmth.

The Sylphs

While the sages said that the fourth class of elementals, or sylphs, lived in the element of air, they meant by this not the natural atmosphere of the earth, but the invisible, intangible, spiritual medium—an ethereal substance similar in composition to our atmosphere, but far more subtle. In the last discourse of Socrates, as preserved by Plato in his *Phaedo*, the condemned philosopher says:

"And upon the earth are animals and men, some in a middle region, others [elementals] dwelling about the air as we dwell about the sea; others in islands which the air flows round, near the continent; and in a word, the air is used by them as the water and the sea are by us, and the ether is to them what the air is to us. Moreover, the temperament of their seasons is such that they have no disease [Paracelsus disputes this], and live much longer than we do, and have sight and hearing and smell, and all the other senses, in far greater perfection, in the same degree that air is purer than water or the ether than air. Also they have temples and sacred places in which the gods really dwell, and they hear their voices and receive their answers, and are conscious of them and hold converse with them, and they see the sun, moon, and stars as they really are, and their other blessedness is of a piece with this." While the sylphs were believed to live among the clouds and in the surrounding air, their true home was upon the tops of mountains.

In his editorial notes to the *Occult Sciences* of Salverte, Anthony Todd Thomson says: "The Fayes and Fairies are evidently of Scandinavian origin, although the name of Fairy is supposed to be derived from, or rather [is] a modification of the Persian Peri, an imaginary benevolent being, whose province it was to guard men from the maledictions of evil spirits; but with more probability it may be referred to the Gothic Fagur, as the term Elves is from Alfa, the general appellation for the whole tribe. If this derivation of the name of Fairy be admitted, we may date the commencement of the popular belief in British Fairies to the period of the Danish conquest. They were supposed to be diminutive aerial beings, beautiful, lively, and beneficent in their intercourse with mortals, inhabiting a region called Fairy Land, Alf-heinner; commonly appearing on earth at intervals—when they left traces of their visits, in beautiful green-rings, where the dewy sward had been trodden in their moonlight dances."

To the sylphs the ancients gave the labor of modeling the snowflakes and gathering clouds. This latter they accomplished with the cooperation of the undines who supplied the moisture. The winds were their particular vehicle and the ancients referred to them as the spirits of the air. They are the highest of all the elementals, their native element being the highest in vibratory rate. They live hundreds of years, often attaining to a thousand years and never seeming to grow old. The leader of the sylphs is called *Paralda*, who is said to dwell on the highest mountain of the earth. The female sylphs were called *sylphids*.

It is believed that the sylphs, salamanders, and nymphs had much to do with the oracles of the ancients; that in fact they were the ones who spoke from the depths of the earth and from the air above.

The sylphs sometimes assume human form, but apparently for only short periods of time. Their size varies, but in the majority of cases they are no larger than human beings and often considerably smaller. It is said that the sylphs have accepted human beings into their communities and have permitted them to live there for a considerable period; in fact, Paracelsus wrote of such an incident, but of course it could not have occurred while the human stranger was in his physical body. By some, the Muses of the Greeks are be-lived to have been sylphs, for these spirits are said to gather around the mind of the dreamer, the poet, and the artist, and inspire him with their intimate knowledge of the beauties and workings of Nature. To the sylphs were given the eastern corner of creation. Their temperament is mirthful, changeable, and eccentric. The peculiar qualities common to men of genius are supposedly the result of the cooperation of sylphs, whose aid also brings with it the sylphic inconsistency. The sylphs labor with the gases of the human body and indirectly with the nervous system, where their inconstancy is again apparent. They have no fixed domicile, but wander about from place to place—elemental nomads, invisible but ever-present powers in the intelligent activity of the universe.

General Observations

Certain of the ancients, differing with Paracelsus, shared the opinion that the elemental kingdoms were capable of waging war upon one another, and they recognized in the battlings of the elements disagreements among these kingdoms of Nature spirits. When lightning struck a rock and splintered it, they believed that the salamanders were attacking the gnomes. As they could not attack one another on the plane of their own peculiar etheric essences, owing to the fact that there was no vibratory correspondence between the four ethers of which these kingdoms are composed, they had to attack through a common denominator, namely, the material substance of the physical universe over which they had a certain amount of power.

Wars were also fought within the groups themselves; one army of gnomes would attack another army, and civil war would be rife among them. Philosophers of long ago solved the problems of Nature's apparent inconsistencies by individualizing and personifying all its forces, crediting them with having temperaments not unlike the human and then expecting them to exhibit typical human inconsistencies. The four fixed signs of the zodiac were assigned to the four kingdoms of elementals. The gnomes were said to be of the nature of Taurus; the undines, of the nature of Scorpio; the salamanders exemplified the constitution of Leo; while the sylphs manipulated the emanations of Aquarius.

The Christian Church gathered all the elemental entities together under the title of *demon*. This is a misnomer with far-reaching consequences, for to the average mind the word *demon* means an evil thing, and the Nature spirits are essentially no more malevolent than are the minerals, plants, and animals. Many of the early Church Fathers asserted that they had met and debated with the elementals.

As already stated, the Nature spirits are without hope of immortality, although some philosophers have maintained that in isolated cases immortality was conferred upon them by adepts and initiates who understood certain subtle principles of the invisible worlds. As disintegration takes place in the physical world, so it takes place in the ethereal counterpart of physical substance. Under normal conditions at death, a Nature spirit is merely resolved back into the transparent primary essence from which it was originally individualized.

199

Whatever evolutionary growth is made is recorded solely in the consciousness of that primary essence, or element, and not in the temporarily individualized entity of the elemental. Being without man's compound organism and lacking his spiritual and intellectual vehicles, the Nature spirits are subhuman in their rational intelligence, but from their functions —limited to one element—has resulted a specialized type of intelligence far ahead of man in those lines of research peculiar to the element in which they exist.

The terms *incubus* and *succubus* have been applied indiscriminately by the Church Fathers to elementals. The incubus and succubus, however, are evil and unnatural creations, whereas *elementals* is a collective term for all the inhabitants of the four elemental essences. According to Paracelsus, the incubus and succubus (which are male and female respectively) are parasitical creatures subsisting upon the evil thoughts and emotions of the astral body. These terms are also applied to the superphysical organisms of sorcerers and black magicians. While these *larvae* are in no sense imaginary beings, they are, nevertheless, the offspring of the imagination. By the ancient sages they were recognized as the invisible cause of vice because they hover in the ethers surrounding the morally weak and continually incite them to excesses of a degrading nature. For this reason they frequent the atmosphere of the dope den, the dive, and the brothel, where they attach themselves to those unfortunates who have given themselves up to iniquity. By permitting his senses to become deadened through indulgence in habit-forming drugs or alcoholic stimulants, the individual becomes temporarily *en rapport* with these denizens of the astral plane. The *houris* seen by the hasheesh or opium addict and the lurid monsters which torment the victim of delirium tremens are examples of submundane beings, visible only to those whose evil practices are the magnet for their attraction.

Differing widely from the elementals and also the incubus and succubus is the vampire, which is defined by Paracelsus as the astral body of a person either living or dead (usually the latter state). The vampire seeks to prolong existence upon the physical plane by robbing the living of their vital energies and misappropriating such energies to its own ends.

In his *De Ente Spirituali* Paracelsus writes thus of these malignent beings: "A healthy and pure person cannot become obsessed by them, because such Larvae can only act upon men if the latter make room for them in their minds. A healthy mind is a castle that cannot be invaded without the will of its master; but if they are allowed to enter, they excite the passions of men and women, they create cravings in them, they produce bad thoughts which act injuriously upon the brain; they sharpen the animal intellect and suffocate the moral sense. Evil spirits obsess only those human beings in whom the animal nature is predominating. Minds that are illuminated by the spirit of truth cannot be possessed; only those who are habitually guided by their own lower impulses may become subjected to their influences." (See *Paracelsus*, by Franz Hartmann.)

A strange concept, and one somewhat at variance with the conventional, is that evolved by the Count de Gabalis concerning the *immaculate conception*, namely, that it represents the union of a human being with an elemental. Among the offspring of such unions he lists Hercules, Achilles, Aeneas, Theseus, Melchizedek, the divine Plato, Apollonius of Tyana, and Merlin the Magician.

Part Four
Encounters with Intelligences in Nature

Apprehend God in all things,
for God is in all things.
Every single creature is full of God
and is a book about God.
Every creature is a word of God.
If I spent enough time with the tiniest creature—
even a caterpillar—
I would never have to prepare a sermon. So full of God is every creature.

Meister Eckhart

Shamans and seers are not alone in the ability to perceive and interact with the natural world. As anthropologist James Swan explains, each of us can learn to use our parasenses to connect to the environment and its visible and invisible inhabitants:

When a world-famous geomancer says that we have one hundred senses to perceive the environment, instead of dismissing ninety-five of these as superstition, the Gaian scientist should assume an attitude of "let's see." Already we know that people can sense low level environmental fields, such as air ions and electromagnetic fields, which can influence health and consciousness. A wine taster can recognize extraordinary variety in wines by sniffing the corks of wine bottles while blindfolded. A good naturalist can do the same with plants and animals, as well as with stones, soil and water. An acupuncturist inserts needles into the human body to adjust a subtle life force energy called chi, whose existence modern science cannot confirm. Yet begrudgingly, science has admitted that acupuncture works. All around Gaia's skin, geomancers sense and manipulate this life energy too.

Such parasenses give mainline scientists fits, and yet there is considerable data, both anecdotal and from laboratory tests, documenting the existence of telepathy, clairvoyance, clairsentience and precognition. Trained sensitives score a significant number of direct hits, in which they describe the history of a place just by holding a bit of soil in their hands and reporting what impressions come to them. When I gave a group of Seattle sensitives some soil collected from the Michigan shrine where Jesuit explorer Father Marquette died, they each in turn described a feverish, exhausted man slipping into coma and being buried in the ground. Somehow the choice of the prefix clair- in clairvoyance seems not by chance at all.

When we learn to use our parasenses, our clarity of perception increases. Tribal cultures consider precognition to be an essential survival skill. While modern science scoffs at it, ask any good athlete or musician about precognition and intuition, and they'll readily report that if you haven't got them, chances are you're not very good.

16
Clairvoyance—What It Is

C. W. LEADBEATER

C. W. Leadbeater, a renowned clairvoyant and teacher in the first quarter of the century, saw clairvoyance as a natural ability latent in everyone. In this article he conveys the dramatically altered view of the world produced by such vision.

The article has been abridged and edited slightly to update and clarify a few passages. Masculine pronouns referring to humans in general have been changed to inclusive expressions, in accord with modern usage. The piece first appeared in The Theosophist, *October, 1903.*

Clairvoyance is in its origin a French word signifying simply "clear seeing," and is properly applied to a certain power or faculty possessed by some people which enables them to see more in various ways than others see, as I shall presently explain. For present purposes let us define it as the power to see realms of nature as yet unseen by the majority.

The first great point to comprehend clearly is that it is a perfectly *natural* power, really quite normal to humanity when it has evolved a little further, though abnormal to us at present because the majority have not yet developed it within themselves. It is only the few who have it as yet, but undoubtedly all the various faculties which are grouped under this head are the common property of humanity, and will be evolved in everyone as time goes on.

Most people are still in the position of being unable to see the wider world, and so they are very apt to say that it does not exist. That is not sensible, but it seems to be human nature. If there existed a community of blind people—people who had no idea of what was meant by sight, and had never even heard of such a faculty—how would they be likely to feel with regard to one who claimed that he could see? They would certainly deny that there could be any such faculty, and if he tried to prove it to them, though they might not be able to account upon their theories for all that he said to them, the one thing certain to their minds would be that there was some trickery somewhere, even though they could not quite see where it lay! That there might really be a power unknown to them would be the very last thing they would be likely to accept.

It is exactly the same with the world at large with regard to clairvoyance. There is a mighty unseen world all round us— many worlds in one, indeed; astral, mental and spiritual, each with its own inhabitants, though all are still part of this wonderful evolution in which we live. There are many now who are able to see this wider life, yet when they speak of it to others, when they try to show them how reasonable and natural it is, they are constantly met by the same accusation of imposition and trickery, even though it is quite obvious that they have nothing in the world to gain by making their assertions.

I wish therefore to make it clear from the commencement that there is no mystery with regard to clairvoyance—that, wonderful as its results may appear to the uninitiated, it is simply an extension of faculties which we already possess, and think that we understand. All impressions of any kind that we receive from without come to us by means of vibrations of one kind or another. Some are very rapid, as are those by which we see; others are comparatively slow, like those of sound. Out of all the enormous range of possible vibrations very few can affect our physical senses. Those within a certain range impress themselves upon our sense of sight; another small group which move much more slowly impress our sense of hearing; others, intermediate between the two extremes, may be appreciated by our sense of touch as heat-rays or rays of electrical action. But among and between all these, and far above those by which we can see, are myriads of others which produce no effect whatever upon any physical sense. Two whole octaves, as it were, of such vibrations exist just beyond those by which we see, and will impress the sensitive plate of a camera; but there are undoubtedly many other octaves far beyond these in turn which will not impress the camera.

You will observe that humans cannot possibly see anything which does not either emit or reflect that sort of light which they can grasp—which comes within the very small set of waves that happen to affect the eye. There may be very many objects in Nature which are capable of reflecting kinds of light which we cannot see; and from investigation of a different character we know that there are such objects, and that it is these which the clairvoyant sees. It is simply a question, therefore, of training oneself to become sensitive to a greater number of vibrations.

Now another fact that needs to be considered in this connection is that human beings vary considerably, though within relatively narrow limits, in their capacity of response even to the very few vibrations which are within reach of our physical senses. I am not referring to the keenness of sight or of hearing that enables one to see a fainter object or hear a slighter sound than another; it is not in the least a question of strength of vision, but of extent of susceptibility. This is a crucial point which anyone may test by taking a spectroscope and throwing by its means, or by any succession of prisms, a long spectrum upon a sheet of white paper, and then asking a number of people to mark upon the paper the extreme limits of the spectrum as it appears to them. Their powers of vision differ appreciably. Some will see the violet extending much farther than others; some will perhaps see less violet and more at the red end. A few may be found who can see farther than most at both ends, and these will almost certainly be what we call sensitive people—susceptible, in fact, to a greater range of vibrations than are most of the present day. There is just the same variety with regard to the sense of hearing; and those who can see and hear more than the rest are just so far on the way towards clairvoyance or clairaudience.

You will readily understand that to those possessing wider sight the world would look very different. Even the very slight extension which X rays give causes many objects which are opaque to our normal sight to become to a considerable extent transparent. Imagine how different everything would look to one who had by nature even that tiny fragement of clairvoyant power, and then imagine that multiplied a hundredfold, and you will begin to have a slight conception of what it is to be really clairvoyant. Yet that is not a new power, but simply a development of the sight we know. We have within ourselves etheric physical matter as well as the denser kind, and we may learn how to focus our consciousness in that, and so receive impressions through it as well as through our ordinary senses. A further extension of the same idea would bring the astral matter [fluid super physical matter associated with emotion] into action, and then further on we would be able to receive impressions through even mental matter. You will see that this idea of the possibility of extension is simple enough, though it is not so easy to imagine the full extent of the results which follow from it.

207

It is true that astral sight is not quite the same thing as the physical faculty, for it needs no special sense organ. In describing it we have to use the term *sight*, because that gives the nearest thought to the impression which we wish to convey; but in reality it is more a sort of cognition, which tells us much more than mere sight would tell. Those using astral sight do not need to turn their heads when they wish to see something behind them, for the vibration can be received by any part of the astral body.

Supposing that a person suddenly opens the inner sight. What more would he or she see than at present? Let us commence with the etheric sight only, for that is absolutely physical, though the majority have not yet achieved it. We have very little idea how partial our sight is in connection with this present physical plane without taking account of anything higher for the moment. There are seven conditions of physical matter, and our sight is able to distinguish only two of them, the solid and the liquid—for we can very rarely see a true gas, unless, like chlorine, it happens to have a strong color of its own. All round us is an immense amount of gaseous and etheric matter of the presence of which we are entirely unconscious, so that not only is there so very much that we do not see at all, but even that which we do see we see imperfectly. Every collocation of physical dense matter contains also much etheric matter, but it is only of the former part of it that we know anything, so defective is our vision.

What difference will etheric sight make in the appearance of one's surroundings? Perhaps what would first strike those developing that sight would be the comparative transparency of everything. Most matter is opaque to our ordinary sight, but to them it would be like a faint mist, through which they could see to a considerable distance. Then in looking at their friends they would see etheric bodies as well as the denser portion of the physical vehicles; and in this latter part they would be able to observe the structure of the internal organs, and so could diagnose some diseases—obviously a valuable faculty for the physician who is fortunte enough to acquire it.

Other creatures also would be seen—other inhabitants of our world which are not visible to ordinary sight, and so are not believed to exist by people of materialistic temperament. The folklore of all countries bears witness to the fact that there are spirits of the mountain and the stream, beings in the air and in the mines, called by many different names, such as fairies, elves, pixies, brownies, undines, sylphs, gnomes, good people and other titles. These are known to exist and occasionally seen by those whose work takes them far away from human haunts into lonely places, as does that of the shepherd or the mountaineer. This is not, as has been thought, a mere popular superstition, but has a foundation of fact behind it, as most popular superstitions have, when properly understood.

Another point that could hardly fail to strike newly developed clairvoyants is the presence of new colors about them—colors to which we can put no name, because they are entirely unlike any that we know. This is quite natural, for after all color is only a rate of vibration, and when one becomes sensitive to new rates of vibration new colors must follow.

For those who have developed astral senses as well as etheric, what would be the principal additions to their world? They would find it very different in several ways, not only in that they would see more, but in that the faculty itself is different. We have now passed beyond the mere development of the ordinary organ of sight and are dealing with a faculty which needs no organ—a sight which sees all sides of an object at once, and can see it as well behind as before. The only way in which you can thoroughly understand this sight is by regarding it as four-dimensional, and considering that it gives its possessor the same powers with respect to us as we have with respect to a two-dimensional being.

Another important point to bear in mind is the superior reality of this higher world which is thus opened to the sight of the student. This is difficult for us to understand because we have been so long accustomed to associating the idea of reality with what we can see and touch. We feel that when we can hold anything in our hands, then we know all about it, and cannot be deceived as to its reality. But this is just one of our many mistakes, for this very sense of touch is one of the most easily deceived of all. If you wish to test this for yourselves, take three bowls of water, one as hot as you can bear to touch, another tepid, and the third icy cold. Place them before you, and put your right hand into the hot water and your left hand into the cold water. Then, after allowing them to remain for a few minutes, put them both into the tepid water. You will find that at the very same moment your right hand will assure you that that water is uncomfortably cold, while your left hand will report it to the brain as almost too hot to bear. This is a trivial instance, but it does show you how little dependence can be placed upon the accuracy of the reports of the senses; it does teach us that merely to see or to feel anything is not sufficient for perfect knowledge of it. We know that we have constantly to correct one sense by another in order to obtain anything approaching accurate information.

If we look at a glass cube, we shall see the far side of it in perspective—that is, it will appear smaller than the near side. We know that it is not really so, that this is only an illusion due to our physical limitations. With astral sight we should see all the sides equal, as we know that they really are. Our physical sight does not in reality give us any measure of distance; it is only the brain that supplies that from its experience. You may see this at once in the case of the stars; none of us can tell by sight whether a star is large or small, for what appears a very large and brilliant star may seem so only because it is near us, and it may really be much smaller than others which seem insignificant because they are at a much greater distance. It is only by scientific methods entirely unconnected with apparent brightness that we are able to determine the relative size of some of the stars. The astral sight does give us much more real information, and as far as it goes it is reliable, so that we are in every way justified in speaking of this plane and its senses as more real than the physical world.

For those interested enough in this subject to begin to study clairvoyance as it is occasionally manifested among our fellows, they will very rarely find it fully developed. The experiences of the untrained clairvoyant—and it must be remembered that that class includes practically all the clairvoyants of Europe and America, with very, very few exceptions—will usually fall very far short of what I have attempted to describe. They will fall short in many different ways—in degree, in variety, in permanence and above all in precision. Sometimes a person has temporary flashes of a higher sight—sufficient, for example, to see some friend at the moment of his death. The same sort of temporary clairvoyance comes to some people in sickness, because after long illness the insistent physical faculties are usually somewhat weakened and subdued, and so it is possible for the astral faculties to enjoy unaccustomed freedom.

Whether interested people are trying to develop faculties within themselves or experimenting with others who already possess these abilities, they must understand what it is that is being seen. They must have in mind a broad outline of the possibilities, so that they may not be deceived or alarmed. By full and careful study, they will come to realize how perfectly natural clairvoyance is; they will comprehend its laws, and learn the necessity of submission to them.

17
Listener of the Wind

CHA-DAS-SKA-DUM or KENNETH COOPER

Thousands of years ago, my ancestors went up into the mountains and prayed for guidance. They bathed in the clear rushing mountain streams, made prayers to the sun and moon, the four directions, the earth and all her creatures, and showed their respect for the giant wise trees which grow in this land. On the wind, in the night, like a whisper, came the name "Cha-Das-Ska-Dum." Today I still carry this name, as well as Kenneth Cooper.

I am a member of the Lummi tribe, who have lived beside the friendly waters of Puget Sound for many, many years. There is a wisdom which speaks to men and women when they are alone in wild places. It comes from the spirit world, through the wind, from the big trees, up out of the ground, and from the mouths of birds. Each person seems to hear special voices. I hear stories on the wind that come from the Night Speaker, whose words echo off the walls of the mountains, waiting for the listener of the wind.

I was at the right place at the right time, and the Night Speaker came to me in the stillness of the night, when the stars become candles to light the way. I listened with my third ear. My heart heard these words, and I in turn have tried to put them on paper as best I can.

When I go to learn from the mountains, I fast so my mind will be clear and my heart will be open. When the voice comes, it's like the gentle sounds of an Indian flute, and the drum of my ancestors, which beats my soul. When all things are right, the mountains become my teacher. My soul becomes the land, and my mother and father become the earth and the sky. I listen, and the winds carry messages from the past to me. Songs dance across the mountain tops looking for the Listener of the Wind. The rattles of my ancestors stir my mind, making it become one with nature, and I see through the eyes of our old ones who knew how to look for and see only truth.

The sounds of thunder in the mountains are the sounds of my drum, waking people to what comes from within, the lightning. I sing the songs that I hear there. They let me walk on rainbows and take in all that surrounds me, which gives me better insight.

I have never been a writer, but these stories that I have been hearing from the mountains, the trees, and the waterfalls are so pretty and filled with spirit. My heart is laid down on this paper in hopes that you too can feel what the stories mean. These stories have told many things. They gave me forms to shape into making my ceremonial robe, my staff, and masks, which I carve from the red cedars, with their permission. Visions come too, sometimes. I want to share these with you, for when I speak, I become the Night Speaker. Although I may live far away from you, you can see me nearly every night when you look up at the moon. If you look there, you'll see the image of an Indian kneeling in prayer. This is me. I am the man in the moon.

Watching Things Grow

One day, not long ago, as I was sitting up on Mount Baker, beneath one of the precious Old Trees, I saw off in the distance a black spot coming towards me. At first I thought it was a raven, but as it came closer and closer to me I saw it was a Spirit Bird. Closer and closer it came, until it was hovering above me. Then in a loud voice it called to the Heavens and to Mother Earth, "Where is the one who wants to see things grow?"

"I am here," I cried out below.

The Spirit Bird came down and took my soul with him, and we flew off, higher and higher. I looked down and could see the Mother Earth. What a sight! With each beat of his wings my heart beat faster and faster, taking my breath away. Looking down on the Old Growth, those wise cedar trees who have seen and known my ancestors for so many lifetimes, I could see things in a different way and hear voices, the songs of Forefathers crying out, trying to reach the minds of our people. Some of what I heard goes:

"Come to the mountains, and we will show you the way of the past, and the future. We will show you the plants of healing, the plants to paint with, and a place meant only for you to sit and listen for your songs, your strength.

"We will let you look into nature, as it really is, not what you see it to be! Here you will learn how to be who you really

213

are. Making this journey will give you a high that nothing can compare to, for I can give you all the things that are needed to take care of you and yours.

"You were born to be a winner, and to win is to give, and then you must give what you get to win, for I will give you nothing but the best. Come to me. Come to the mountains and listen with your heart. Look with your heart. I will heal your mind and soul.

"The mind of modern man is like a sponge, absorbing all the trash and not filtering, only taking in more and more. When your soul is lost, as was that of the Animal People once in the Early Time, take from the Old Tree the Heart of his Heart and make the Spirit Poles known to us as the Tusketts. And, look for the souls of your beloved ones in your dreams, when you look in pools of water. If they have lost their bodies, then take from the Old Tree the inner wood and make your "Skga' de'lich," and look for their bodies, and bring them back together as one, or you will lose them to nature, as you did the Animal People.

"You will also need to cleanse your bodies and souls, for I am now a part of you, and you are a part of me. If we are in harmony, we will draw strength from each other, and walk as one. I will give you the songs you need to call spiritual beings, and to talk with nature. The Old Trees and I will always live in these mountains, only a short distance from where you live. Come to me, my Children, and I will teach you the songs of spirit power so you' can restore the conversations with all things which are longing for you to talk with them.

"Come and fast with me. Grow with me. I will not change you, but only make you strong and who you really are."

The Old Trees spoke:

"Don't cut us down. We can do much, much more than make boards to build. We are guides, and speak with the spirit of this place to let you know things that you will need to know. We are like members of your family, Old Trees, like wise elders, who need respect and love, and who give love and respect in return."

We go up into the mountains to fast, to pray, and take baths in the sacred mountain streams. We used to do this during the day, but there are so many people these days, that we usually go up into the mountains only at night, or in that time in the early morning when night and day walk in the same place in the sky. One day, not long ago, I had planned to go up into the mountains to pray, and listen, but I was so tired that I lay down and fell asleep. Almost as soon as my eyes closed, the "Night Walker" spirit was there, coming to take my soul with him.

We traveled off together, drifting higher and higher, until we came to a place far off in the mountains in a forest. Then I was standing there, as if in the flesh, and Night Walker was talking to me. His face became one with mine, and through his eyes I could see the mistakes I had made over the years, and the things I had missed out on. The Night Walker then said that with this wisdom, I would now be given another chance. Then voices spoke to me, voices out of the past, carrying the words of the Old Ones since the earliest beginnings of time. As each one finished, I said "thank you," and then another one began to speak, like whispers on the wind.

I felt more aware of myself than ever before, and then songs began to come, not just from the wind, but from the ancient past. They touched me so deeply and made me feel more and more alive. For each song, I gave thanks to the Creator. And this lasted all night long. As daylight began to return, I knew it was time to come back to my physical body.

As soon as I awoke, I went up into the woods to bathe. I stripped down and asked permission to enter the crystal clear mountain water by the waterfalls. On the wind, it came. I waded into the water, praying, as my soul was covered, thanking the Night Walker for allowing me to enter the spirit world with him. I went under four times, praying to each direction. As I came to the surface the fourth time, I asked permission to walk back on dry land, and it came from the Creator, through the Old Trees like a whispering wind.

Standing on shore, I looked toward the waterfalls and saw a cloudlike image drifting down toward me from the heavens. I closed my eyes and it enveloped me like a warm blanket. I could smell the aromas of the valley so clearly. A strange numbness came over me, like my outer skin had gone to sleep.

I opened my eyes, and I was wearing this cloud, a gray haze, sprinkled with the colors of the rainbow in it. It was the most beautiful robe I had ever seen. I looked to my right, and there was the most beautiful white drum, a rattler made from mountain goat horn, an eagle bone whistle, two clapper sticks carved like eagle feathers, and a blue-faced mask with long cedar hair. They were all laying on a pure white mountain goatskin.

At a glance I found I knew the tone of the drum, and its depth. Each instrument seemed to have a song it was singing, and then they came together as a group, with all songs becoming one.

I looked back at the rocks in the waterfalls, and there were written ancient legends. I didn't have to walk closer to see, as it seemed as though I could see through the water. The first story was about me and my people. It said how I had been preparing for this time. Then it said that these legends had been written here so the mountain water flowing over them would always wash over them and keep them pure.

I knelt down on the Mother Earth and reached to the heavens, offering prayers to the Creator for what was taking place. Then I looked above the falls and saw the animals of the area, all of them, looking down at me. A sense of love came to me.

Then the cloud started to lift, and as it lifted, I could still see the things on the white goatskin. Now the animals all seemed to merge and become one, looking at me with the same wise, loving eyes. I could see that the instruments before me were gifts from them.

Now the time had come to return to the body. The sights slipped away, but their feelings remained, and I felt a beautiful, deep sense of peace. I also could sense new energies and voices wanting to speak through me, and so I began to make the instruments, bringing the vision to life.

I know today that this vision is still with me, and I give thanks to the Creator and to my guardian spirit for allowing my soul to learn so much. And I give thanks for the love it gives me to share with other people. It should be very clear, as clear as the mountain water that falls over the rocks in that stream, why the Old Trees, the mountains and their sacred places are so valuable to my people.

The mountains call my name, "Cha-Das-Ska-Dum."

18

The Deva Consciousness

DOROTHY MACLEAN

My contact with the devas opened up in a natural way, rising organically from my life background. My two brothers and I were brought up by the most delightful and loving parents in a beautiful old house next to a wood in Canada. We had gardens of vegetables and flowers, but I was not especially attracted to cultivated plants. I loved wandering in the wild places.

I went to university with a lot of questions, but despite all the talk about the profundities of life, I found no satisfactory answers. Eventually I started paying attention to that voice within that had long been asking me to listen, and I began to write down the daily guidance I was receiving. During a period of spiritual training which was teaching me to place the will of this indwelling God first in my life, I met Peter and Eileen Caddy. Before moving to Findhorn, we worked together on the staff of the hotel where Peter was manager, putting this principle into action.

When I speak of God's will, I am aware that this might call up a stereotyped picture of an old gentleman somewhere out in the sky, making automatons of us by imposing an external will. This is not my meaning, but I do not know of another way in which to convey it. To me, God is an indwelling presence, the core of what I am and what everything is. God is life itself, speaking through all life. An God's will is the path we tread which develops the best for us and for all we encounter. *Let My will be a mystery for you to find in each moment,* my guidance told me. *Seek it within the little and the big. It includes all people and all things, all questions and all answers.*

Our first winter at Findhorn had been an especially harsh one for the area, with frequent gale-force winds adding to the snow and rain. But by early May, 1963, the first radishes and lettuce Peter had sown in the patio garden were coming up, and he was busy preparing another area for peas and beans and a few other vegetables. The spring weather was growing warm enough for us to sit outside on the patio during our daily time of quiet together. This was a delightful opportunity to experience God's presence in everything around me.

During that period of time, my guidance had been telling me to be open for new ideas and inspiration: *Be prepared, My child, and on the lookout for My promptings. Expect new ideas to come into your head. This is a further period of training for you and it entails many new things.* The guidance I received on the morning of May 8 was indeed the beginning of something new: *One of the jobs for you as My free child is to feel into the nature forces, such as the wind. Feel its essence and purpose for Me, and be positive and harmonize with that essence. It will not be as difficult as you immediately imagine because the beings of these forces will be glad to feel a friendly power. All forces are to be felt into, even the sun, the moon, the sea, the trees, the very grass. All are part of My life. All is one life. Play your part in making life one again, with My help.*

Well, I thought that was very nice, because as far as I was concerned, there was nothing I would like better than to sit in the sun and commune with nature. But when Peter saw this guidance, that's not how he understood it. "You can use that to help with the garden!" he said, feeling that direct contact with the nature forces might give him the answers he needed to his questions about the garden. Sure enough, the next day I was told in guidance, *Yes, you are to cooperate in the garden. Begin this by thinking about the nature spirits, the higher over-lighting nature spirits, and tune into them. That will be so unusual as to draw their interest here. They will be overjoyed to find some members of the human race eager for their help. That is the first step.*

By the higher nature spirits, I mean those such as the spirits of clouds, of rain, and of vegetables. The smaller individual nature spirits are under their jurisdiction. In the new world these realms will be quite open to humans—or I should say, humans will be open to them. Seek into the glorious realms of nature with sympathy and understanding, knowing that these beings are of the Light, willing to help, but suspicious of humans and on the lookout for the false, the snags. Keep with Me and they will find none, and you will all build towards the new.

I thought such instructions rather a tall order, taxing my credulity and certainly beyond my talents. I knew only a little about nature spirits and, although I was aware of the angelic hierarchy, I had not known that there were devas overlighting vegetables. I told Peter I couldn't do it and stalled for several weeks, despite his encouragement. However, instructions from the inner divinity—and Peter's promptings —are not lightly disregarded!

One evening in meditation I reached a powerful state of heightened consciousness, and I thought, now I'll contact one of those higher nature spirits. Since vegetables had been mentioned, I thought I might contact the spirit of some plant we were growing at Findhorn. I had always been fond of the garden pea which we had grown at home in Canada, and I could feel in sympathy in all ways with that plant. So I tried to focus on the essence of what the pea was to me and the love I felt for it. I got an immediate response in thought and feeling which I put into the following words: *I can speak to you, human. I am entirely directed by my work which is set out and molded and which I merely bring to fruition, yet you have come straight to my awareness. My work is clear before me—to bring the force fields into manifestation regardless of obstacles, and there are many in this man-infested world. While the vegetable kingdom holds no grudge against those it feeds, man takes what he can as a matter of course, giving no thanks. This makes us strangely hostile.*

What I would tell you is that as we forge ahead, never deviating from our course for one moment's thought, feeling or action, so could you. Humans generally seem not to know where they are going or why. If they did, what a powerhouse they would be. If they were on the straight course of what is to be done, we could cooperate with them! I have put across my meaning and bid you farewell.

When I showed this to Peter, he said, "Fine, now you can find out what to do about these tomatoes and what it is these lettuces might need. . . ." And I would take his questions to the deva of the species concerned and get straightforward practical advice.

At this point I might say that the term "deva" is a Sanskrit word meaning shining one. On the whole, I have chosen to use this word rather than the English equivalent, "angel," which calls up stereotyped images that are more of a barrier than a help in understanding the true nature of these beings.

It wasn't until nearly ten years later that I was introduced to some of the esoteric literature on devas. However, through my own contact with them we discovered that they are part of a whole hierarchy of beings, from the earthiest gnome to the highest archangel, and are a sister evolution to the human on earth. The devas hold the archetypal pattern and plan for all forms around us, and they direct the energy needed for materializing them. The physical bodies of minerals, vegetables, animals and humans are all energy brought into form through the work of the devic kingdom. Sometimes we call that work natural law, but it is the devas who carry out that law, cease-lessly and joyfully. The level of this hierarchy I was guided to contact was not that of the spirit of, say, a particular pea plant in our garden, but rather the overlighting intelligence, the soul essence, of all peas throughout the world.

While the devas might be considered the "architects" of plant forms, the nature spirits or elementals, such as gnomes and fairies, may be seen as the "craftsman," using the blueprint and energy channeled to them by the devas to build up the plant form. It was with these beings that R. Ogilvie Crombie established communication. When Roc joined our work at Findhorn, he helped to clarify and confirm certain undefined feelings I had had about the plant world. For instance, while I could not explain why I was upset when the gorse bushes were pruned in full blossom, Roc was able to clarify exactly what was wrong through his contact with the nature spirits.

Essentially, the devas are energy, they are life force. (We humans are as well, only in our own unique way.) I was told in guidance, *You are simply surrounded by life. You are a life force moving along with other life forces. As you recognize this, you open up and draw near to these others, becoming more and more one with them, working together for My purposes.*

The devas themselves have no particular form. But in attempting to establish communication and cooperation with humans, members of the devic realms have made themselves visible in a form intelligible to humans. These forms reflect their functions. For instance, a dwarf is usually depicted with a pickaxe, denoting our human interpretation of his work with the mineral world. Angels, on the other hand, are por-trayed with wings, and often as bearing something, such as a message of healing or mercy. As the devas have said, *We work in the formless worlds and are not bound or rigid in form as you are. We travel from realm to realm and are given wings to denote this movement. As we travel, our form changes, taking on the qualities of different realms. Therefore, you cannot pin us down to any one form. We deal directly with energy and that energy shapes us, is part of us, is us, until we breathe it out to where it is needed. We are limitless, free, and insubstantial.*

I have never seen any of these beings in a definite form, although sometimes I get an impression of a pattern, a shape or a color. Once when I had the image of the Red Cabbage Deva standing in front of many vague forms, I was told, *These forms are myself and those like me as we have been and as we shall be. Although we live in the moment and are always moving, yet is our past and present with us. We are close to the inner realms where all is living. I give you this picture so that you will not see me, or any of us, as merely one of a list of static forms but will connect us up more with life. Humans are so inclined to limit and depend upon their five senses to perceive the world that they forget that we are living, changing forces now, outside your sense of time.*

As we became more aware of the fact that everything around us is part of the same energy in different forms, we were opened up to an entirely new way of working in the garden. The devas said, *We realize it is easy for man to think of a plant as a thing, perhaps as living, but nevertheless a thing, for he cuts himself off from the vision that sees beyond the physical, just as he cuts himself off from his own inner being which is so vast.* Taking into account the inner being of plants, we began to realize that the garden must be known from within as well as from without, that it must grow spiritually as well as physically.

To a deva, the garden is not an assembly of various forms and colors but rather moving lines of energy. In describing our garden they said they could see the forces from below gradually being drawn up and blending with those coming down from them in great, swift waves. Within this field of energy, each plant was an individual whirlpool of activity. *We do not see things as you do, in their solid, outer materializations, but rather in their inner life-giving state. We deal with what is behind what you see or sense, but these are interconnected, like different octaves of the same melody. What we see is different forms of light.* Years later, when I read about Kirlian photography, which records the luminescence given off by matter, I felt this related to the subtler forces of which the devas speak.

The devas stressed the importance of our learning to see the true reality, as they do, so that we might with the power of our directed thought not only affirm the perfection of each plant but actually lift it to a higher level. *By thinking in terms of light, you add light to that already existing. Hence, you speed up growth and enhance beauty, you see truth and link up with God's perfection.* The intention of the devas in introducing us to their way of seeing was not to detract from the beauty of the world as seen by human eyes, but to enhance it by expanding our awareness into a broader and truer perception.

In time, we learned that thinking in this way was indeed a practical way of working in the garden. But at first, being wise teachers, the devas responded to what was most obviously vital to us at the moment—the actual physical needs of the garden, only gradually introducing us to this new perception. They gave us specific advice, for instance, on how far apart plants should be or where to place them. *We think that the land on the top there would be a good site for us, as long as it is not too windy*, the Globe Artichoke Deva advised. The Cabbage Deva suggested, *It would be better to thin out the plants now. Also taking off those lower leaves will be alright.* In springtime, the Blackcurrant Deva told us, *No, don't cut the plants back now. The root would not be strengthened if you did; it needs the leaves to make the process of life go through the plant.*

We used to gather sheep dung from a nearby field to make a liquid fertilizer. *Liquid manure is a great medium for certain ranges of forces, because liquid attracts and gathers in certain subtle forces which cannot enter into a more solid medium*, a deva informed us, and advised, *The strength is about right, although for certain plants it could be a little stronger.* I used to do regular rounds with the liquid manure, asking each vegetable deva whether or not the plants would like a dose that day. Sometimes the response was just a direct *Yes* or *No*, while at other times it was combined with a bit of general information. Asking the Tomato Deva about nutrients, I got, *You can give the plant liquid manure now. We will not let all the goodness of it be used for developing leaves. When there is cooperation between us like this, we can give instructions to the plant that it is the fruit which is to be developed.* The Carrot Deva told us, *The carrots are coming along nicely and could be missed when you put on another dose of liquid manure. You wonder why they are alright when the parsnips next to them are hungry. The carrots, through their special carrot quality, are able to convert energy from the radiations which parsnips do not tune into.*

The soil, of course, was one of the areas of our garden that received a great deal of attention. In transforming sand into soil, we were re-enacting the natural process of creation on our planet by drawing together the ingredients necessary to sustain life. The day following my first contact with the Pea Deva, I was told in guidance that we could ask questions about the soil from a certain being overlighting our geographical area. We were told that the magnetism of this angel and the magnetism of the land around us were linked and interacted. For want of a better name, we called this being the Landscape Angel. I got an initial impression of it with "hands" outstretched, passing energy into the ground. *You can see me juggling the life* forces into the garden and never ceasing the movement. We work in what you call mantras, in movements, which produce sound and make a pattern, working up to a certain pitch. By these moves, I am now putting a certain quality of life force into the garden. There are many irregularities in the composition of the soil and by adding these explosions of forces, they are being minimized. For about two years, we were given almost daily guidance from the Landscape Angel on how to build compost and enrich the soil. For instance, we were told, You have a real difficulty with that soil which does need more air but which would blow away if you loosened it. If possible, hoe it before a rain and loosen it before spreading compost on it.

The devas said, viewing it from the angle of energy, that the greatest physical contribution to the garden was the compost heap. We were given specific advice as to what ingredients to use, when to mix each individual heap, and when and where to spread the ripened mixture. For instance, the Landscape Angel told us, It would be good to turn the remainder of that first compost heap, but the other one is not quite ready for turning—a week or so, and then start building the others. We can tell by the degree of radiance that the one heap needs attention—it has dulled down. The others are still building up to the point where they should be moved.

Spreading compost throughout the garden brought the whole area into greater unity. It is a binding, uniting process, like the circulation of the blood in the body. Our ignorance in these areas is obvious to any gardener, but because of it we were able to accept the advice we received from the devas, see the successful results, and then open ourselves to what they had to teach us further about life.

However, working in cooperation with humans was pioneering for the devas as well, and so they could not always foresee what would happen in the garden. Our first season, the broad beans started out in an energetic flowering, but then the blossoms began falling off. When I asked the deva why this was happening, I received, To tell the truth, we threw ourselves fully into our cooperation with you and did not allow for the quality of the soil. The shot in the arm given us through your collaboration shot us ahead too fast! So we are balancing up this way. We have no regrets; it was well worth trying. They were always willing to experiment. I think this was sometimes done so that we would learn the true effects of certain actions and gardening practices.

In our garden, they did not feel limited, and they could see the creative power of humans, so they wanted to show what could be done with their cooperation. A wonderful example of this was our work with the Watercress Deva. Various gardening books were sharply divided on how to grow watercress. While one said it could not be done without running water, another said it could if grown in the shade, and yet a third advised growing it in the sun. Unsure of what to do, Peter asked me to contact the deva, who suggested that we experiment by growing half in the shade and half in the sun. This proved wise advice because, with daily watering, the plants in the sun grew quickly, providing us with watercress throughout the summer and then went to seed just as the plants in the shade were ready for picking in late summer and autumn.

It delighted the devas when Peter acted on their suggestions. While at the beginning of our contact they had seemed rather remote, our cooperation changed that, and they became friendly and even anxious to help. In fact, we were told that they were practically queueing up to experience this new contact with human life. They said that the few contacts made with Western man in the past had not usually been happy ones, except for those made by gardeners who truly loved plants. Contacts had also been made to bring about new plant forms, yet the horticultural experts who were responsible for these innovations had not always worked with the nature forces as equal partners but sometimes imposed their will on nature, making it respond to their designs. So although the devas welcomed our questions as a means to bring about understanding and true cooperation between us, what interested them most was the process by which a human—deaf, dumb and blind in their regions—was reaching out to know them and talk to them.

Both in the guidance Eileen received and in messages from the devas, we were told to grow as many varieties in our garden as possible. Besides producing a better balance in the soil, a large variety of plants focused the forces of more devas. That in turn attracted the great overlighting devas who could use the garden to serve a certain purpose on the planet. Peter was ordering vegetables and herbs we had not seen or heard of until the nursery catalogues brought them to our notice—plants with strange names like celeriac, salsify and scorzonera, kohlrabi and cardoon, soapwort and sweet cicely.

The herbs we ordered were sent to us by rail, beautifully packed in moss and cellophane and we carefully planted them out in our garden. As they grew, we discovered that sweet cicely was one of the commonest roadside "weeds" in the area!

As Peter brought each new plant into the garden, I welcomed the deva of its species. I found each had a unique feeling and quality. The Radish Deva, who has always been especially active in the garden at Findhorn, responded to my welcome with, *We swoop in again, delighted to spread ourselves. We are in a great hurry it seems to you. Our forces give the impression of eager beavers. We are that, but with hearts too!* The Angelica Deva on the other hand was a bit more hesitant: *We come in quietly, intent on our small world. To be asked to speak is unusual, to say the least, but you feel our influence and we hope that the particular quality with which you respond to us will be greatly strengthened here. Thus is our mission on Earth fulfilled.*

Most often the devas exhibited a quality of exuberance and vitality, as did the Marrow Deva: *We are delighted to be given so much space and should like to be able to throw great hefty marrows straight into your laps! But if we did that, we should not daily be making use of the available forces given us for growth through nature and man. The growing process is a great blessing in itself. It is creation, and perhaps it is difficult at times, but everything is used for that purpose and the greater good. We are glad to be a part of it, glad to grow for you.* When we decided to grow dandelions as a vegetable, the deva responded, *I am greatly honored to come into the garden by the front door! It does make a difference in the bond between us and man when we come at his desire instead of in spite of him, for with his aid the struggle is not so great and the plant can expand and do its best. Let us show what we can do in cooperation. Nevertheless, I hope to be greeting you from odd corners.* Cooperation indeed made a vast difference, because the dandelions we welcomed in grew to a relatively great size.

I find that I have to know something of a new plant before being able to contact the deva. Often I would read about the characteristics of a plant—or sometimes taste a bit of it. This was not always an enjoyable encounter! Sampling a wormwood leaf, I was quite taken aback by the strength of its flavor, and I can't say I would recommend the experience. The deva responded, *You are amazed that such a strong taste can be contained in such a little bit of leaf. Power is our nature—a little root can crack rocks. Power can be used for many purposes. You humans also have power. Yet power is a word which many people shy away from*

Dorothy Maclean

because in human hands it can be used for evil. Power is said to corrupt. We view it in another light entirely. We consider it the greatest gift of God because with it we can do more for God than without it. It is our joy to perfect that power in service. Because the herb devas concentrate all their energy in expressing one particular essence, the flavors of these plants are very distinct.

I found the herb devas especially amenable to contact with humans. *Plants such as us, the herbs, have long associations with humans and are thus ready to be leaders in the cooperation between our two worlds. We are part of human consciousness. You have discovered much about us and we can easily dance into your awareness. But remember, this is a new contact on a new level and not one from which you can compile dictionaries of long words about our abilities. I do not mean that we will not give you information about our use, but the contact comes when you rise to a level of joy and purity. You must respect us and love us as part of God's life before we can trust you with more secrets about ourselves. Plants are not here just for man's use, but when you learn that man's chief end is to glorify God and enjoy him forever, then we can be part of that enjoyment and glorification, each in our own way, in your consciousness.*

Each herb, we were told, embodied a particular quality or radiance. As we eat them that quality is enhanced in ourselves. Thus, the wider the range of herbs we eat, the more help they can give us. Gradually we became familiar with all those growing in our garden, mostly by eating them in various combinations in our daily salads.

When flowers were introduced into the garden, I found it easiest to contact each deva if the plant was in bloom, for at that time its essence was in fullest manifestation. With certain flowers I felt a natural closeness. The Mesembryanthemum Deva, in particular, felt just like a sister to me. Since the petals of this flower unfold only in the sun, this may be the link, because I, too, have a great love for the sun. With others, if I had difficulty feeling any unique characteristics, I sometimes even picked a bloom and kept it in my room for a while until I made its acquaintance. Straining for the contact only created a barrier. *What will come to you will come as on the wings of song, effortlessly,* the devas told me.

By springtime of our second year at Findhorn, the Landscape Angel told us that our garden was becoming more united and whole, and that as this took place, an angelic being, a sort of guardian angel for our area, was forming. I believe that any unit, whether it be a farm or a community, a couple or a nation, has an overlighting presence that in some way embodies the various levels of energy used within that unit. The Angel of Findhorn is a composite being, "born" from the substance of our thoughts and ideals, the radiations of the land, and the energies of the higher selves of not only the humans working on the land but of all the animals and plants there as well.

Each step of its development was described to us by the Landscape Angel. *The being forming here is a new type of deva. This is becoming increasingly apparent. It is gathering life from all of you in a unity with humankind hitherto unknown. You are in a sense part of its body. It will act as a bridge between you and others of my kingdom, and will help you in your work.*

At this point it is still nebulous. Although to you it may be slow in growing, it is phenomenally fast compared with others. You cannot feel this new creature yet; nor can we, but we sense it being brought about. Its eyes are still closed, so to speak, its reposeful hands still being defined. Its length is very great. Definite warmth directed to it will speed up the process and quicken its life.

A month later, when our garden had been further extended, the Landscape Angel said that the eyes of the new deva were open and that the head had some movement. However, it could not be fully formed until one complete round of plant growth— a year—had passed; otherwise it would not incorporate all the energies necessary for the garden.

When at last it was fully formed, the Findhorn Angel presented itself to us: *I take my stand with my brothers, tall and one in essence. Immensely vigorous and vital am I with a role that reaches to the four corners of the Earth and beyond. We all rejoice amongst ourselves in these realms that, with the help of all of you, has been born and grown to fulfillment one such as I, a prototype of cooperative activity. I have been planned from near the Godhead and given sustenance by both the deva and human worlds. Do not form a clear concept of me and keep me in limitation.*

Now I go from your consciousness, but I am in you and you are in me, different yet one. I am the spirit of a place, yet how much more. You are limited human beings, but you are gods in the making. We are one because we have all been given life.

Our cooperation with nature was not only affecting our human world, but the devic realms were also changing through it. The devas exist in the world of the One, without question carrying out the will of God. Because they allow the power to come through them unrestricted, they are, in a sense, more powerful than man. On the other hand, man, living in the world of opposites has freedom of choice and thus the power to create. Yet we are evolving towards each other, the devas into understanding how separation can enhance awareness and appreciation, and humans into participating once again in the consciousness of the unity of all life.

Expressing the new awareness brought about in their realms by contact with us, the devas said: *We have told you that we are one in essence, that we melt into one another at any time. Whereas that quality has not changed, to it has been added an ability to look at one another, as it were. This brings about a greater sharing, for it is easy to be one if you are not separate! Now our praises can ring higher and deeper, our wonder can mount, in this wider awareness of the forces of life.* For us humans, broader awareness comes by recognizing our oneness with all aspects of life. *You consider us beings of light and joy, which we are, but you seldom consider humans as beings of light, which you are. As you encompass all worlds, including ours, when you drop your burdens and become a creature of light, you are one with us.*

The primary impact on me of the deva world has been this necessity to rise to a higher state within myself in order to contact them. If I am depressed, angry, resentful or caught in some negative emotional state, I cannot enter the light and joyous atmosphere of their realms. *You cannot bring weights into our world, you cannot come to us unless you are free, child-like and light. If you choose, you can live your everyday life in the very same attitude which you bring to us. You know you have to drop your burdens to contact us and therefore you know you can do it. We say, why not do it all the time? It seems strange to keep on the old way when freedom is yours at any time you choose. You love the feel of our life; why not live in it more often?*

As I attune to the devas, I partake of their qualities. It is as if they sound a tuning fork that awakens a response within me—their joy and mine become one, and I find I am a joyous being. So every contact with the devas becomes an expansion of my own highest spirit.

I have been mainly speaking of the devas as spirits of nature. But they also embody qualities of the human spirit, such as perseverance, tolerance and courage. *One of our biggest roles in helping humans is to hold in absolute purity and perfection some quality, so that you may come and be steeped in it and carry its essence within to help you in life's ways.* The deva world has always been part of man's highest endeavors, his moments of inspiration and adoration, of wonder and enchantment. What the devas have said to me, wise men have expressed in many ways throughout the ages. This wisdom is the spirit within us calling to us through every part of life, within and without, whether in the song of an angel or the voice of a babbling brook.

While the kingdom of the devas exists as a life unto itself, they are also part of us. In fact, to the consciousness that is expanded enough, all things are within. *How can oneness be if you reach outside yourself for it? If God—who is all—is within, can you exclude us? Be sensible.* As our consciousness grows, we cannot help but be aware of the devas, for contacting them is basically the same as being in contact with our true selves.

All of us have experienced the devas in one way or another. In fact, they say that any contact with the plant world puts us in touch with their realms. When I first contacted the Rhubarb Deva, I was told: *We have met before. Whenever anyone contributes attention or feeling to a plant, a bit of that person's being mingles with a bit of our being, and the one world is fostered. You humans are therefore all very linked to us, but until you give recognition to these links, they are as nothing and remain undeveloped. The plants contribute to human food and give of themselves in this way. This also builds links, tangible ones. Although of the past, these links can be brought into the present by recalling them. This is one great use for memory, to recall the oneness of life.* To firmly establish these links, it is important to appreciate and enjoy the food we eat. *Our essence goes into your being much more readily when our flavor is enjoyed,* the Winter Savory Deva said. *That way you are open to our influence and let it spread through you.*

To contact the deva world, an interchange in word or thought is not necessary. Just as everyone responds to a person or a thing according to his or her own particular make-up and perhaps mood at the time, there are infinite levels of communication with the devas. Whenever we are in a state of joy, love, lightness, freedom, we are with the devas. When we are lifted out of ourselves, looking into the beauty of a flower or a sunset or the amazing shape of a shell, this is an experience of the deva world. *Consciousness of beauty brings you into oneness with any part of the universe,* they have said. My great love for being outdoors, in touch with the sun, the wind and rain was contact with the devic realms. But only when I had a conscious request from within to contact these beings, did I become aware of their existence.

Recognizing their world is most important. This had a tremendous effect on our garden. The devas told us, *Forces work through us into the soil, and extra strength is given them by your consciousness of them. Everything belongs to one world, but if each thing or life lives to itself, it cuts itself off from the one great teeming force field. If each opens out to the all, then currents flow through unhindered. So realize that your recognition of us opens up strength to us and to you, because it lets the forces flow naturally.*

Considerations we had hitherto thought impractical in the garden, the devas insisted were eminently practical. Our attitudes, thoughts and feelings had a great effect on the plants, they said. Knowing this had a great effect on us, as well, since we had to learn to be careful about how we felt, how we spoke and what we did around the garden. If we were not in a good state, it was best to go elsewhere. We began to realize the truth of what the devas were telling us: *Every creature, human or otherwise, reacts to and acts upon its environment (quite unwittingly sometimes) for all is one.*

The devas told us that since their purpose was to increase life, they couldn't tell us how to destroy the insects that were eating our plants. However, they said that by visualizing the plants as strong and healthy we could add to their life force and thus help them to withstand the attack. The power of such thought was clearly revealed to me one year when our gooseberry bushes were beset by a plague of caterpillars. Left alone, the insects would have completely stripped off all the young leaves. So I took it upon myself to help out by plucking the little creatures off each bush. This wasn't easy, considering my secret horror of caterpillars. Never before in my life had I even touched one. I would steel myself and spend hours on end collecting caterpillars into a jar, and then deposit them on top of the compost heap where the birds would eat them. It was the best solution I could think of.

One day in the middle of this task, I realized that I was so engrossed in the caterpillars that I had forgotten all about the gooseberry bushes themselves. During the rest of that round, I made a point of beaming out thoughts of love and health to the bushes. Next time I went on my rounds, I noticed that those bushes which had received love actually had far fewer caterpillars on them than those which I had not given specific attention to. It was an illuminating experience.

A further and more trying test of my faith in the power of thought came during our first year at Findhorn. Because of all the compost we were spreading around the garden, we were beginning to have great luscious earthworms—just what moles like. All around us was sand and gravel, so into our garden the moles came, rooting around in our patio and other areas, leaving the roots of the poor plants hanging in the air, unable to get water or sustenance. Peter came to me and said, "Moles—do something about them." Not knowing quite what to do, I decided I might try to use my inner contact.

Concentrating on the essence of a mole, I received the impression of a rather scary Great King Mole with a crown on his head sitting in an underground cavern. Feeling rather diffident, I began, "Well, we have a garden and you moles are upsetting it. Can't you do something about it?" I just presented the situation to him fairly, suggesting that they go to a neighboring area of land not being used for gardening. There was nothing more I could do. I gave him my promise that I would not harm him or any of the moles. He just sort of grunted and said, "Hmmmm," and I was left unsure whether this had helped at all. But for several weeks there was no sign of moles in the garden. Each time they reappeared, I repeated my plea to the Mole King. By the end of that season, they had all left the garden and didn't return.

However, several years later, when Findhorn was given the neighboring area of land, there they all were, just where we had asked them to go. By then I was no longer working in the garden, but I told the group of gardeners about my experience. Together, using the same technique, they contacted the moles and got an even swifter response than I had received by myself —and the garden remained mole free. This showed me that everyone can use that inner attunement to all aspects of life to work in cooperation with nature, rather than relying on destructive solutions.

Despite years of relating to the garden, I never developed into what I would call a real gardener. Therefore I cannot give a gardener's answers to gardening concerns; I can only give devic answers. Hopefully, as our consciousness expands into greater awareness, these will be the same.

In the Findhorn garden, we saw what the cooperation of humans and devas could bring about, each realm contributing a unique and vital energy. But the implications of such cooperation extend far beyond simply growing successful gardens. At a time when it appears that material solutions to ecological crises are not sufficient, perhaps the devas are offering us a real alternative on how to restore the upset balance of nature on our planet. *We know that if humanity could get the feel of our realms, life on Earth would be completely changed.* As wielders of energy, they are offering their help in making our world as light and joyful as theirs. But as they have told us again and again, we must play our part, using the power of our free will to direct the energy creatively, both within ourselves and in the world around us. Each one of us can consciously choose to function beyond our current limitations and use the energy he or she has for a larger purpose. And we can find joy and satisfaction in the growing awareness that each one's contribution is of importance, no matter how small it may seem.

The key to this transformation lies in recognizing that oneness of all life of which the devas continually remind us. *When you come to us we would not keep you, so to speak, but pass you on in consciousness to the One of whom we are ever conscious, who is our life and the light of the world.* This is the basic teaching of the devas, guiding each of us to our inner core, to the divinity within, from which we go out in harmony with all of life.

If we can thus transform our way of looking at life, our actions within our environment will be transformed. *Man drastically changes the face of the Earth as it suits him, without a thought that he is dealing with God's life, in various forms. To him it is just shifting matter around. But if he thought of everything in terms of light, all shining with the substance of God, he would not so carelessly alter the Earth.* As we begin to recognize God in every aspect of the world around us, that part of the world is redeemed, until ultimately the whole planet is redeemed.

We humans are supremely gifted. We can encompass the entire range of life on our planet, and it is our destiny to do so. We begin by becoming more and more of what we are, more of what the devas are. *We have often expressed to you our great joy as you turn to our kingdom, and we have come flocking with our power and bestowed much on your garden. We would pour down on you all, activating what you already have within, some characteristics of the angelic world: our abounding joy, our lightness, our vitality, our freedom, our flexibility. We could go on and on, for there is no end to God's gifts to his creation. In all this we are one, without separation. Let us extend that oneness to all levels, and let us do it here and now.*

The Messages

Every plant does have a unique ensouling presence. These

messages, however, have not been communicated by individual plants but rather by the overlighting intelligence and spirit— the deva—for each plant species. While the devas themselves are beyond form, yet are they responsible for the most precise and minute forms we behold in the plant kingdom, the wonderful exactness of each seed and leaf and blossom. This they do in joy and lightness, as the great servers of life.

The process by which I contact the devas is one of feeling into the essence of a plant and harmonizing my own self with it. The communication doesn't come to me as words, but as thoughts of inspiration, which I then express in words according to my own state of consciousness at the time. If I were to receive the same communication now, I probably would not word it in the same way, for my consciousness, as is only natural, has grown into a deeper understanding and awareness.

Because each garden is unique, the devas did not give general rules of action. As they told me, *Humans know most of these from the traditions of gardening. It is in the field of conscious-sharing that something new is to be learned.* Moreover, they wanted us to find out for ourselves what it is that we as humans are capable of doing. We have all knowledge within ourselves, they have said, and they would point us toward that.

To me, one of the most significant aspects of contact with the devas is simply that it helps to enlarge our viewpoint. If we treat everything as alive, intelligent and part of the One Life, our own life is greatly enriched. When we realize that we are in a sea of life with which we can communicate, there is bound to be cooperation between mankind and nature.

As we grow to understand that the key to contacting the devic realms is to seek within, to be what we truly are, we will discover that the devas are a part of our very selves.

19
Tree Spirits

DORA VAN GELDER

Leaving the more familiar home gardens with small plants and turning to the forest, we must note again that trees are very different from our usual ideas about them. They are living beings, just as we are, except that they possess a lesser degree of consciousness, and do not react to sensation as quickly and as keenly as we do. As mentioned before, within the tree there is a tree-spirit, from which it draws its life forces. There is no tree, however small, without its tree-spirit; the tree-spirit grows with the tree, and disappears with its death. This personality can emerge from the tree for a little distance when it so desires, usually assuming a form which is more or less human. When inside the tree, the form is much vaguer and practically invisible, for it really defines itself only when it projects itself outside. Most tree spirits look alike to the extent that they all seem to have a tall, brownish form which looks something like the first drawing a child makes of a human figure—square, slightly thick, and suggestive of a papoose, with little eyes and nose exactly as in a child's drawing, and hair also very like the few coarse lines drawn by a child, black and fiberous. This is, of course, a very general description of tree fairies. Different kinds of trees such as oaks, pines, birches, and so on have slightly different features typical of the species, and some trees seem to have a great deal more personality than others, just as human beings do. Certain trees are unique individuals, while others have nothing which particularly distinguishes them.

While they are inside the body of the tree, they do more work, in that they look after the tree and control its energies. It is analogous to the maintenance of a human body; the tree draws its chemical nutrients from the earth, water and air, and when these are right and plentiful the process goes well, and the tree spirit is happy. His happiness in turn reacts upon the chemical processes within the tree, and makes them more effective. It is very much like a man who eats his dinner in peace and then digests it with a feeling of well-being which in turn aids digestion, just as worry impairs it—though of course trees never worry. When, at intervals, the spirit comes out of the tree, it is usually drawn forth for various reasons. For example, one might see a human being whom he likes, and come out to look more closely at him and express his liking. Often when I have sat under a tree the spirit has come out to express its affection, though, of course, in rather vague terms, and it may even follow one for a few yards. At night these beings seem to have more free time and opportunity for social life. They all come out of their barks, and if the person upon whom they have bestowed their affection is staying in a house and the tree is not too far away, the tree spirits may come out and go in search of him. I think one reason why most people feel afraid at night in a forest is because all these beings seem to have emerged from their trees, so that one feels surrounded by unseen presences. Many people feel as if thousands of eyes are peering at them which, as a matter of fact, is quite true! I do not think that tree spirits would harm any one in a forest, but their vibrations and feelings are so different from ours that it often gives us shivers up and down the spine.

It is of course possible for a tree to have an aversion to a person and feel dislike, and a case of this sort happened when I was a little girl. Though I cannot vouch for all the details of the story, as I did not witness the incident, I did observe the tree spirit to whom the story was ascribed. There was an ancient tree in a garden in Java, but its branches were endangering a house, so some Javanese were delegated to trim it. Each time anyone went up the tree or on the roof for this purpose something happened to him—either his leg was broken by a fall, or his arm was thrown out of joint. Because of all these accidents, the upshot was that nothing happened to the tree, for the men refused to do the work. They attributed the accidents to the malignant influence of the old Kashmir nut-tree spirit. I can vouch for the fact that when I was a child I did not like to play under that tree, although I was at the same time fascinated by the strong and powerful looking old tree spirit. He did not like human beings at all, for he remembered a time when he was surrounded by trees and not by houses, and he really blamed human beings for his isolation and loneliness. When he projected himself toward people he looked rather like a thin grey-faced ape of huge dimensions, perhaps fifteen feet tall. When within his tree, he was much taller, for it seems that the operation of densifying the body outside the tree draws the matter of his subtle vehicles into a smaller volume.

On the whole, however, trees generally feel quite affectionate toward people. In fact, they are distinctly different from garden fairies in this respect. They have the same kind of feeling of loyalty as a dog does, but they are more dignified, and do not gambol and romp about as dogs do. This loyal affection is probably due to their rooted condition. An instance of this kind of affectionate response happened to be witnessed by some one besides myself, and was experienced, furthermore, by dozens of others who did not quite understand what it meant.

At a school in California where we were invited to the commencement exercises of the graduating class, the children performed a play about fairies. One girl, who had been very happy at the school, took the part of the spirit of a fine live oak. At a certain moment she emerged from behind the tree as though she came from within it, and was to address the tree as her home in terms of affection. When she came to the words, "Dear old tree," she said them with real sincere feelings, which were especially intense because she was going to leave. Because the play was about fairies and performed by children, and because the audience was sympathetic and attuned, when she said those words, they were an appeal to the *real* spirit of the tree. He responded by coming out with a rush of affection so strong that the whole audience was stirred, and many people had tears in their eyes though they did not know why. The girl who had called him out was also greatly affected. This was a clear case of the natural feeling of trees for humanity, when people are of right mind toward them. In this case, the spirit of the tree put on an appearance of a tall, benign being radiating good will. How very different from the spirit of the Kashmir nut-tree.

The differences between the various kinds of tree spirits are not so marked as, say, between varieties of dogs. I have already described elsewhere the spirit of a hickory tree, so it may be of interest to give you descriptions of an oak tree, a pine, and a birch. In a small forest I have observed a beautiful oak—a kind tree, whose spirit is about fifteen feet tall with a human outline more Western or European in feature than those previously described. His face is more oval and regular, and he is better looking and more "human." In color he is dark tan and his hair is black, but his eyes are green and he has patches of green about his body. He floats out from his tree

with a certain calm dignity, and takes an interest in the surroundings and in the fairies about him, who are somewhat
different from those seen in the garden.

The birches, on the other hand, are much more feminine
in appearance and manner. They are slender, like elongated
Burne-Jones[1] figures. Their coloring is a little darker shade
than that of their bark, being a brownish grey, their hair is
brown, and they have misty grey eyes. They have sweet, gentle
dispositions, and their movements are rather quick and fluttery,
reminiscent of the movements of the leaves of a birch tree. I
have never seen any tree spirits which are not in some degree
brown in color, although the variations are many, from the
red-gold of the redwood trees to the grey-brown of the birch.
Evidently this is the basic color type, but there is also a relation
between the color of the bark and the color of the spirit in
any individual tree—its color probably deriving from the fibre
and bark.

The pine spirit is a dark person, with rather square features
and a great deal of dark green about him. He gives one the
impression of being honest and frank, and pours out a radiant
feeling of harmony. He is not so tall—this particular specimen
is perhaps ten feet, but sturdy and powerful looking, with black
hair (coarse, as usual) and black eyes. He withdraws from his
tree with great deliberation and gazes about in a penetrating
manner. His quality is not as vigorous as that of the oak, who
may be said to give a real impression of virility.

It seems that the slenderness of form which characterizes
all these spirits has some relation to the trunk of the tree and
its life currents. For the spirit of a young tree is a tiny sliver
of a thing, and its form enlarges as the tree itself grows bigger.
(These spirits of young trees have little intelligence, and
come outside their barks only when older ones make it clear
that it is the thing to do.) In general, a tree spirit's form is
rather rounder when he is within the tree, conforming to the
tree's contour. When he comes out he flattens a good deal,
just as a human body is narrower through than across.

I also observed a young maple tree which grows nearby,
on the edge of a wood. He displays the "American Indian"
character much more than the others. His general appearance
is decorative, rather like pictures of a young Indian buck.
Whereas the hickory tree gave an impression of a staid old
Indian warrior, this maple has the springing quality of youth.

Dora van Gelder

His color is, in general, a yellowish brown, with variegations of rich red and yellow, evidently correlated with his autumn leaf colors. Instead of hair, he has a sort of autumn-leaf headdress which makes him look very gay, and he is quite evidently proud of this stylish effect!

The house in which I am writing this has a few trees around it, mainly birches. The wood begins close by, and it is easy to contrast the life of the scattered trees encountered in or near a city with the conditions here, where the trees near the house are practically part of the woods. The isolated hickory, cut off from his fellows, has less of the life of his own kind, in fact almost none, so he has to find his interests in human beings and animals, with the result that his mind grows more than his emotions do. Here, the woods gives the trees a sense of kinship with their own kind and thus they are more interested in what goes on among themselves than in human beings, although they feel very kindly toward people. But between the house and the edge of the wood a number of birches have lately been felled for fire wood, and the rest of the trees resent it and do not feel so friendly to human beings. Trees dislike being cut down more than fairies resent their plants being destroyed, for of course the life of the tree spirit is closely bound up in the life of the tree.

In this woods, which is fairly close to civilization, yet far wilder than a city park, there is a feeling of expectancy. The life of a tree is not at all certain, and human beings do interfere. This particular forest gives one a feeling of youth. The trees all live together and feel kindly toward one another, but they take a definite interest in the human beings around, and they think of these beings as aliens, apart from themselves. Human beings tend to think of trees as firewood or shade or decorative objects, but very seldom as beautiful individuals or as anything which is at all alive. The trees feel this and it arouses in them a close community spirit for they realize that they are of one kind and we are another.

I should make it clear that trees react to things very slowly, and it takes them a long time to assimilate new experiences. Their understanding is limited, of course, so when we speak of them as thinking or feeling this or that what it means is that they react in a manner which is half-somnolent in comparison with human beings. And of course there are differences among individual trees. Nevertheless, when a forest has been cut down ruthlessly, the trees that remain have strong feelings of a mixed character—injury, loss and a sense of isolation, even though there is in nature a great sense of philosophic calm, and of the inevitability of things. Our idea of a woods is a nicely cleared place, but the ideal according to trees and fairies is a place where there are trees and a great deal of underbrush and wild life. The trees and the fairies feel a close link, and there are fairies who frequent those places where underbrush and flowers and grass grow together. But if everything is too tidy they are not attracted. Our ideals and those of the woods' life could be reconciled if we could intersperse our cleared land with large areas of wild growth. Many people may think this a sentimental point of view because (they will say) it is necessary to cut down trees in order for us to be able to live. There is, of course, some truth in this, but, nevertheless, in our western civilization we are both wasteful and ruthless, and the needs of the land and of the forest do not appeal to the average commercial person. I have been all over the north-west of the United States—at present the greatest lumber territory of the world—and I have seen miles upon miles of absolutely barren country with only the tree stumps standing. It gives one a sense of nightmare to see the burned out stumps without any signs of living, to see no fairies where once their life was rich and full, and to know that magnificent cedars, spruce and pines were slaughtered and even left to rot.

On the Pacific Highway near Vancouver there is a magnificent piece of first growth timber. When I first saw this it was one of the most beautiful forests of trees I have ever seen in my life, rich with fairies and a sense of tremendous happiness. But when I passed it again I experienced a sense of deep horror because half of those magnificent trees had been cut down, and where there was once beauty, ugliness and barren-ness reigned. The feeling of the few trees which remained was one of expectant terror, looking hopelessly on and waiting to be cut down, for we must remember that trees cannot run away. This lumber company had been offered, I am told, a large sum of money by the government and private individuals or equivalent forest elsewhere if they would not cut down this particular forest. It was one of the rare bits of first growth timber left in that part of the world. Think of the loss to thousands of people right on the Pacific Highway who were thus cut off from passing through the very heart of such a magnificent forest!

The wood at our doorstep here in New Hampshire is characteristic of the summer growth all over the United States, except in the far West and the extreme South. The tree spirits we have described are happy in their existence and full of a sense of enjoyment. They like standing in the soil and feeling the sunshine pouring down upon them and the wind blowing through their leaves. It gives them a sensation of dancing. Trees love the wind and even a wind storm, for it offers them a kind of excitement as they keep themselves erect and steady, and yet are swayed by the power of the storm. They do not like being blown down, but they take this philosophically, as it is to them like a battle in which one or several may be marked as victims, for to them this is a natural end of life. The rank growth round about them is alive with fairies. The animals scurry about bent on business and pleasure, and the trees take all this in, interested in the smallest details of the woods life, and feeling a happy and tender sense of protection toward all the plants and animals, for after all they make it all possible.

Naturally, in a wood like this the fairy life is particularly rich. Here are all the kinds we have seen in the garden, with slight differences because life in the woods is different from garden life. There are more varieties of fairies. There are, for example, tiny fellows about a foot tall, of a rich golden brown color, which have human outlines as vague as that of a tree spirit. Their faces look much more like little monkeys than like human beings, and they live in the mossy part of the woods, looking after small ferns and mosses. Then there are a great many of the brown and gold small gnomes variety mentioned elsewhere, as well as some lovely deep blue fairies about eighteen inches tall, which flit about among the underbrush. There are also a few water fairies down in the brook. They are tiny, slender things which look like translucent pale blue water, quite human in appearance even though only ten or twelve inches tall. Fresh water fairies seem never to get so fat and roly-poly as the ones who inhabit the sea. The numerous lakes and ponds have the same kind of water fairy, but these are rather bigger, from about a foot and a half to two feet tall. But there are never so many fairies in fresh water as in the sea, which appears to be their ancient home and birthplace. Here and there in the forest are fairies almost of the standing of angels, which are of human size and form, perfectly colored in yellow and green. These help to direct the woods' life. Over all, an angel is brooding—over the fairies, the trees, the hills and streams, which are part of his life and are his trust. He is a powerful personality and the valley is just as much part of his body as the trunk of a tree is the body of a tree spirit, except that in this case the angel has intelligence and emotions as powerful as our own, and he is as much a being as we are, if not more so. When he takes form he looks like a beautiful human being, a clean-shaven youth with fine dark hair and powerful aquiline face, his body enveloped in a lovely apple green. His presence permeates the life of the forest and valley.

I shall close this chapter with a description of the wonderful redwood forest in northern California—not the familiar parks of southern and central California, but the primeval growth of the northern part of the state. This is an ancient unique forest of giant redwood trees. These trees are extremely impressive, because one feels that they are so old and have seen so many ages go by that they know the secrets of life. Each one has a distinct individuality. One particular tree spirit looks like an immensely tall American Indian of red and gold, as if cast in bronze. His height, over thirty feet, is in itself very impressive! He has dark pin-point eyes and coarse black, straggling hair, and he carries with him a tremendous feeling of power and calm and serenity of spirit as one who has seen so much of life, its changes and chances. This immense country is covered with them, and the fairies of the forest, who are somewhat strange looking, are cast in the same mold as the tree spirits. They, too, look like Indians or strange caricatures of Indians, with nut-brown faces and little black eyes and the same red-gold bodies. Even they are tall for fairies—three to four feet. Over all broods this feeling of immense antiquity. There is little variety of undergrowth (at least at this season), so the invisible life consists of but these two species, but of them there are a great many. The tree spirits, and even the fairies to some extent, have together reached an incredible age. Some of the trees were born one, two and even three thousand years ago, and their life is centered in the tree-tops, much more than with ordinary trees. They are aloof, not only because they belong to the ages gone by but also because they are so immense. They have seen countless people pass beneath them, they have seen innumerable things born and die, so that to them everything that exists is just passing and transient. It is very difficult to communicate with these trees because their thoughts are concerned with remote ages and happenings and it takes time for them to become interested in new things. The fairies, however, were glad to talk to me; they wanted very especially to know about motor cars, for they were consumed with curiosity about the mechanism and its use. They thought it was so funny an idea for people to sit in little square boxes in order to move about, for their notion of motion is flying. They have always known that human beings walk about, and considered them slow, but cars they thought peculiar. The fairies and the trees rather resented the roads being cut through their country, even though in that particular spot they did not cut down the trees to make the roads. At the same time, they were rather interested in this new (to them) civilization. Could we only imagine what the life of these trees must have been! The fairies and animals all have lived together and helped one another as far as was natural for hundreds of years, and the trees which overshadow all have had an inner social life of a strange sort. The trees used to emerge from their tops and look out over the world and communicate to each other what they observed. They told one another about the people they saw, but there was no feeling that those older races were alien, as our modern civilization is to them. People and trees understood one another in those remote times, and saluted one another when they passed. This was a strange thing to observe when a scene from the past was called for me by one of the trees. They appreciated this intercourse with humanity in the past and were doubtful about the future, but they had learned through their thousands of years of experience that even life and death pass away, and so they await their end philosophically. If each of us could go out into the forest and see and under-stand these beings we would have a better comprehension of the spiritual power of life itself, which is after all the essence of religion. They are such strange, splendid, noble, aloof beings! If only I could give some idea of what it is they talk about and think over out of their past! But it is immensely difficult to convey the quality of the forest life which these tree spirits experience. They learn from the cell life within their own bark the difficulties of survival. They see the life around them and know death intimately, as the trees next to them often fall and die, struck by lightning. But just as in the case of the fairies, the trees learn through all this experience that life never dies and is never wasted. They cannot move about and therefore we think of them as having less life experience, but that is where we are mistaken. It is not through rushing about that one learns, but from taking into oneself the experiences from without and thus feeling the pulse of life beating within. Humanity tries to escape from experience which is often suffering. When it rains we go to shelter; when death comes we put away the sight of it. The trees let life beat against them, and try to withstand it. Trees are the greatest realists I know, and these grand old giants are the kings of all trees.

Notes

1. Sir Edward Coley Burne-Jones (1833-1898); English painter and designer.

20
Devic Life of the Mountains

GEOFFREY HODSON

Geoffrey Hodson was a well-known and respected clairvoyant who investigated the unseen worlds in nature. His works include descriptions of great nature devas whose consciousness permeates features of the landscape, such as mountains and oceans. Below is a discussion of some of these beings in New Zealand where Hodson lived.

The reigning Devaraja appears several hundred feet above the mountain top and draws my attention to the "ladder" or "steps" of intercommunion from and between the Devaraja within the crater—the very active Hephaestus-like being— the mountain Deva itself, and also a still greater Mahadeva presiding over the whole area of Tongariro. This includes Mt. Ruapehu and other mountains extending for some thirty miles in all directions from the Chateau Tongariro. This great one is, in its turn, at one with the major landscape Mahadeva of the earth as a whole—an angelic presence of immeasurable stature.

Within the lower portion of the aura of this latter planetary Devaraja, there shines a blend of grass-green and deep sky-blue. From where the spine would be there rises out of the center of the earth the planetary Kundalini-Shakti, a mighty power indeed. Closely examined, this triple force is seen to flow upward, Kundalini-like, with a very wide cylindrical uprush of "fire" enclosing the threefold current. This ascends far above the high aura and upper radiations into areas beyond my range of vision towards, I venture to presume, the Logos of our planetary scheme. This "ladder" extends upwards into the Solar Logos itself, whom I can only faintly and very reverently conceive of as a vast, sky-filling, intensely glowing radiance of golden power and light.

I am only able to describe the Mahadeva for whom Mt. Ngauruhoe is, as it were, a physical focal point or "throne" as a center of power whose responsibilities extend beyond New Zealand, and so beyond my capacity to observe. Outwards

244

from the "shoulders" I gradually note forces sweeping out and raying forth, some slantingly, from the upper part of the "body," while the heart chakram is a most wonderful sun-like, whirling center of outrushing, brilliantly colored power— purple, green, roseate pink, red, and golden, with many other hues produced by the blendings of these shades.

I can only bow in reverent homage before this great one, in gratitude for the privilege of being granted awareness of its presence while visiting the volcanic mountain above which the Devaraja would seem to be stationed, or rather enthroned.

The mountain's mass itself is clearly being subjected to an inertia-reducing, responsiveness-increasing condition, a quickening of the evolution of both the life and the substances associated therewith. Hosts of salamanders or nature spirits of Fire of varying degrees of development and stature are seen to be collaborating in this planetary "blacksmith's" work.[1] Thus the whole interior of the volcano—especially where I am observing it at the level of the lower slopes and earth surface—is being intensely "worked upon" by salamanders and the volcanic Deva in charge of them, in order to participate in the great planetary and systemic urge or increasing drive to bring about the evolution-quickening procedure. I have come to believe this quickening fulfills the whole purpose of the existence of the universe, all its beings, greater and lesser, and all its component parts.

I presume that volcanoes differ from all other mountains in that the element of Fire from deeper down within the planet is in them actively employed by devic ministrants for the carrying out of this wholly impersonal, universally operative urge towards evolutionary unfoldment. The consciousness of members of the devic hierarchy, from nature sprite to archangel, I now perceive consists of laughter-filled joy. This could be a yogic ideal for human attainment. Admittedly this can be very difficult, if not impossible, especially for those who are enduring karmic sadness, whether physical from ill-health or psychological from sufferings of the heart and the mind.

These Fire Devas appear to be "digging" into and loosening the structure of the etheric and physical "lining" of the crater, and even beyond it for several yards into the interior. The life-principle in the atoms and molecules of the substance glows increasingly as this occult, devic ministration continues.

The process takes place deep within the crater even below the base of the mountain where—using the Blacksmith simile—the great planetary forge is burning, this being a continuance of the same activities deeper into the earth.

On further observing the great Devaraja of Mt. Ngauruhoe, I find on the left side where the "hip" would be the principal colors are grass-green near the "waist" and then a brilliant sky blue for the whole of the "hip," extending to below the "knee" area. This blue spreads out for at least one hundred yards on the left side of the Deva in all directions, especially from the "shoulders" to up above the "head" from where it extends at least two hundred feet and blends with a brilliant white radiation from the whole aura.

The left side of the aura below the blue is radiant with a rosy-red glow, which expands skirt-like right round the lower portion of the aura and reaches out for at least one hundred yards. This white radiance also descends below the "feet" deep down towards and into the crater. The upper right side of the devic aura is also sky blue at the regions of the "shoulders" and "neck," with the radiant rose below that area.

The "throat" chakram is very bright, the colors being chiefly white and gold, while through the crown an uprush of fiery power is shooting along the "spinal" area, Kundalini-like, and far up above the "head," reaching into heights beyond. In the center of the "head," radiant at the place where the eyes would be, is an outraying white and sky blue force, with other colors blended within the enormous funnel of the brow chakram. Deep within, I now gradually learn, is a profound stillness of consciousness, far beyond the limitations of personality and concrete thought. At this level the Devaraja is wonderfully crowned with a golden uprushing radiance, shot through and at places glowing with the same rosy-red coloring —a godlike crown indeed!

Although the higher consciousness would seem to exist in poised stillness, the more formal mind is aware throughout this region and, I venture to suggest, reaches out as far as Rangitoto (Auckland Harbor) and Bream Head Mountain (Whangarei Harbor Heads) and the Kundalini fire and volcanic fires within both of them. The system of correspondences is actively at work, and the range of communication is virtually planetary. Indeed, the words come to mind: "A Devaraja of the embodied and incarnated Kundalini Shakti of the planet, of which order many others exist and function in New Zealand."

Notes

1. See Geoffrey Hodson, *The Kingdom of the Gods,* (Adyar: Theosophical Publishing House, 1980), 211.

Part Five

Living with Unseen Lives

What a thing it is to sit absolutely alone,
in the forest, at night, cherished by this
wonderful, unintelligible,
perfectly innocent speech,
the most comforting speech in the world,
the talk that rain makes by itself all over the ridges,
and the talk of the watercourses everywhere in the hollows!
Nobody started it, nobody is going to stop it.
It will talk as long as it wants, this rain.
As long as it talks I am going to listen.

Thomas Merton

Many nature-lovers accept that Gaia is an interconnected web of living beings—some of whom, like plants and animals, we can see and others whose living presence announces itself more subtly. If this is so, what can we do to interact with these beings to our mutual benefit? As the essays that follow attest, the means of cooperating cocreatively with nature and its inhabitants are both practical and accessible.

For one thing, we can garden. The fields, meadows, woods, and streams of Perelandra, the open-air nature laboratory founded by Machaelle Small Wright in rural Virginia, are dedicated to furthering the dynamic interaction between humanity and nature. Home gardeners, David Valbracht suggests, can forge a similar bond with "all the participants in earth processes, sensible and supersensible." We can also spend time in forests and other wild places. As Henryk Skolimowski writes, such "unstructured environments" are important for "deep psychological reasons." In journeying to forests and other wilderness places, Skolimowski continues, we "return to the source of our origin" and, in so doing, "nourish the core of our being."

Communicating with animals, plants, thunderclouds, and other natural forces is not the province of shamans only, as Serge King explains. "Peaceful intention, positive imagination, and a clear mental verbalization" allow even ordinary men and women to merge with the spirit of a dolphin or a rose and to coax it into mutual cooperation. Instead of formal meditation, John Seed suggests, we can "lie down in the forest . . . and imagine an umbilical cord reaching down into the earth," visualizing ourselves as being "one leaf on the tree of life." Finally, of course, we can take part in rituals, such as Geoffrey Hodson's powerful "Invocation to the Angels" which concludes this section.

In all of these ways we can learn, as Thomas Merton did, to hear the "most comforting speech in the world"—the musical voices of Gaia and her creatures.

21

Discovering Intelligence within Nature

MACHAELLE SMALL WRIGHT

We live in a world of high technology and expertise. We have countless teams of exceptionally qualified research scientists who are dedicated to finding the answers we need in order to live a healthier life on a healed and thriving planet. We look to these people to tell us what we can do in our lives in order to achieve that healthier life on a healed planet. Yet, despite all this earnest technology and research, I am saying that we now need to turn our attention to nature itself, recognize the intelligence inherent in all natural form on Earth and allow it to teach us what we need to know in order that we may apply that information to our life and our technology, and pull ourselves out of the present ecological mess.

The nature intelligence I speak of contains within it truth—a truth that has been present since the beginning of time and available to us all down through the ages. It is not exclusive to the gifted. It is a vast universal truth that is present around us everywhere. Our doorway to this truth is through nature itself. Many have opened the doors. Individuals such as myself who live in tiny rural areas around the world, such as Jefferson-ton, Virginia, have tapped into the truth within nature purely because of a personal need to understand something more about life. On a larger scale, we have the world-famous Findhorn Community in Scotland which began its growth and development twenty years ago on a foundation of discovery of the co-creation between man and nature. But these examples only serve as affirmations to you that, indeed, there is truth, and it is available to us all, no matter who we are and where we live.

I first consciously tapped into this truth in 1976 when, after a series of events, I decided I wanted to become a student of nature and be taught by nature. I immediately discovered that there is an extraordinary intelligence inherent in all forms of nature—plant, animal and mineral; that contained within this intelligence are the answers to any question we could possibly have about nature—its specific rhythms, its true ecological balance, how this balance can be achieved with the help of humans (and in some cases, despite our interference), the deeper role nature plays on Earth, its various relationships with mankind. This information is just sitting there for us. All we have to do is decide we want to hear it—which can at times be a gutsy decision on our part, since what nature has to teach is not always the easiest thing for us to take—learn how to tap in and receive the information.

I also quickly learned that the desire of the intelligences within nature to touch in with us, to communicate and work with us, is intense. The quality of our life and of all life forms on Earth depends on our willingness to learn how to act and move in such a way that we enhance life-quality, not damage or destroy it.

22

Forests as Sanctuaries

HENRYK SKOLIMOWSKI

Forests and the Original Geometry of the Universe

We all know how intricate are the relationships between a single tree and the forms of life that live in it, and around it. But why are trees so important to human beings who are after all—as forms of life—so distinct and different from trees? Though distinctive and different, human beings are part of the same heritage of life.

The reason that trees and forests are so important to us, as human beings, has to do with the natural geometry of the universe. We must therefore distinguish between man-made geometry, stemming from Euclidean geometry, the geometry we learn at schools, from the natural geometry, especially the geometry of the living forms.

When Euclid was inventing his geometry, which has become the basis for man-made forms, the Greek reason was already corrupted by Aristotle's analytical and classificatory approach to the world. With Socrates and Plato the Greek world is still held in unity and harmony. With Aristotle, we begin to divide and chop and atomize—put things into separate compartments, where they are identified by special labels called definitions.

Euclid and his geometry only reinforces the tendency to atomism, separatism, thinking in neat logical categories—here are the axioms, here are the rules of derivation, here are the theorems derived from the axioms through the accepted rules of derivation. All very neatly and rigorously defined. A triumph of the rational Western mind which is going to depend so much on the power of formal reasoning, on the meaning of axioms which will become the ultimate bricks out of which other things are to be constructed.

What should not escape our notice, in particular, is Euclid's emphasis on the importance of the point, and of the straight line. Let us be aware that we never see the point because the point as such is invisible; we hardly meet a straight line in nature. Yet the architecture of the human world, or to be more precise the architecture of the world as constructed by modern man, is founded on the straight line and those invisible points.

Let us put the proposition in general terms: the geometry that dominates our lives, when we live in a city, in a modern house, or when we drive an automobile, is the geometry derived from the abstract system of man-made geometry. It is a geometry which, after a while, constrains and suffocates us.

We have distinguished natural geometry from man-made geometry. But what is natural geometry? The forms by which and through which the universe has evolved, the forms by which life has evolved. What are these forms? These forms are circular, spiral, round, womb-like. When we contemplate the architecture of the universe: the galaxies and the atoms, the amoebas and the trees, then we immediately see that the dominant forms and shapes of nature and of the universe are round and spiral and so often amorphous.

The dancing universe does not move in straight lines. It moves in spiral, circular and irregular motions. The life dancing in, and through the universe, is not choreographed by the computer and its linear logic. The quintessential symbol of life is that of the womb.

All life has emerged from the primordial womb which is irregular, amorphous, full of connecting loops and spirals. We, individual human beings, were conceived and nursed in the wombs of our mothers. Natural geometry had conditioned our early impulses. Natural geometry has shaped our early growth. Natural geometry has formed our bodies which are but an expression of this geometry. Now, look at your own body and see it in terms of natural geometry. Your body is full of irregular shapes—round, oval, asymmetrical. There is hardly any straight line within the architecture of our body. The head is such a funny irregular egg. The hands and legs are irregular cylinders. The eyes and the mouth, the neck and the stomach are but endless variations on the theme of natural geometry.

Being nursed and conditioned, shaped and determined by natural geometry, we respond to it in an intuitive and spontaneous manner. Why do we rest so well in the presence of a tree? Because in it we find an outlet for our natural geometry. The communion with the trees, being surrounded and nursed by them, is for us a return to the original geometry of life. That is why we feel so good in the act of this communion. We were born and nourished by natural geometry and to this geometry we long to return. By dissolving ourselves in the geometry of the tree, we resolve tensions and stresses accumulated through, and thrust upon us by artificial geometry. We must clearly see that artificial geometry of man-made environments is full of tension and stress.

To dissolve in the primordial matrix of life—this is sanity.

To enter the communion with the shapes which spell out organic life—this is a silent joy.

To lose oneself in the forms soaked in the substance of life—this is a fundamental renewal.

Trees and forests are important for deep psychological reasons. In returning to the forest, we are returning to the womb not in psychoanalytical terms but in cosmological terms. We are returning to the source of our origin. We are entering communion with life at large. The existence of the forests is so important because they enable us to return to the source of our origin. They provide for us a niche in which our communion with all life can happen.

The unstructured environments which we need for our sanity and for our mental health, as well as for the moments of silent brooding without which we cannot truly reach our deeper selves, should not be limited to forests only. Rugged mountains and wilderness areas provide the same nexus for being at one with the glory of the elemental forces of life. Wilderness areas are life-giving in a fundamental sense, nourishing the core of our being. This core of our being is sometimes called the soul.

To understand the nature of the human being is ultimately a metaphysical journey; in the very least it is a transphysical journey. Transphysical translated into the Greek language means metaphysical. The metaphysical meaning of forests has to do with the quality of spaces the forests provide for the tranquility of our souls. Those are the spaces of silence, the spaces of sanity, the spaces of spiritual nourishment—within which our being is healed and at peace.

We all know how soul-destroying and destructive to our inner being modern cities can be; and actually are. The comparison alone between the modus of a technological city and the modus of a wilderness area informs us sufficiently about the metaphysical meaning of the spaces of forests, of the mountains, of the marshlands.

Though the trees are immensely important to our psychic well-being, not every tree possesses the same energy and meaning. The manicured French parks and the primordial

Finnish forests are different entities. In the manicured French parks we witness the triumph of the Cartesian logic and of Euclidean geometry, while in the Finnish forests, immensely brooding and surrounded by irregular, female-like lakes we witness the triumph of natural geometry.

What is natural and what is artificial is nowadays difficult to determine. However, when we find ourselves among the plastic interiors of an airport, with its cold brutal walls and lifeless plastic fixtures surrounding us, on the one hand, and within the bosom of a big forest, on the other hand, we know exactly the difference and without any ambiguity. In the forest our soul breathes, while in plastic environments our soul suffocates.

The idea that our soul breathes in natural unstructured environments should not be treated as a poetic metaphor. It is a palpable truth. This truth has been recognized on countless occasions, and in many contexts—although usually indirectly and semi-consciously.

We go to a lovely old cottage. The old wooden beams supporting the ceiling attract us immensely—as no concrete and iron beams will ever do. We go to a modern flat, undistinguished otherwise except that there is a lovely wooden panelling along the walls of the rooms. We respond to it. We resonate with it. We do so not because we are old sentimental fools, or for aesthetic reasons alone, but for deeper and more fundamental reasons.

Life wants to breathe. We breathe more freely when there are other forms of life which can breathe around us. Those old beams made of oak in the old cottage breathe. Those panellings made of wood in the modern flat breathe. And we breathe with them. Those plastic interiors, and those concrete cubicles, and those tower blocks, and those rectilinear cities do not breathe. We find them 'sterile,' 'repulsive,' 'depressing.' These very adjectives come straight from the core of our beings. And those are not just the reactions of some idiosyncratic individuals, but the reactions of all of us, at least a great majority of us.

A plastic interior may be aesthetically pleasing. Yet after a while, our soul finds it uncomfortable, constraining, somewhat crippling. The primordial life in us responds quite unequivocally to our environments. We have to learn to listen carefully to the beat of the primordial life in us, whether we call it instinct, intuition, or the wholistic response. We do respond with great sensitivity to spaces, geometries and forms of life surrounding us. We respond positively to the forms which breathe life for these forms are life-enhancing. Life in us wants to be enhanced and nourished. Hence we want to be in the company of forms that breathe life.

It is therefore very important to dwell in surroundings in which there are forms that can breathe—the wooden beams, the wooden floors, the wooden panellings. Lucky are the nations that can build houses made of wood—inside and outside. For the wood breathes, changes, decays—as we do. It is also important to have flowers and plants in our living environment. For they breathe. To contemplate a flower for three seconds may be an important journey of solitude, a journey of return to original geometry—which is always renewing. We make these journeys actually rather often, whenever plants and flowers are in our surroundings. But we are rarely aware of what we are doing.

Forests and spirituality are intimately connected. Ancient people knew about this connection and cherished and culti-vated it. Their spirit was nourished because their wisdom told them where the true sources of nourishment lay.

Sacred Forests in History

Ancient people were intimate with their surroundings. They so often weaved themselves into the tapestry of life sur-rounding them so exquisitely that we can only admire their sensitivity and their wisdom. They had a very special under-standing of the places, the locus genius of their territory.

Forests were of course of great importance to ancient people, and almost everywhere in the world trees grew, some forests were marked as special enclosures, indeed as sacred. These forests were to be protected, and never desecrated. In the seminal book of Sir James Frazer *The Golden Bough* (1935), we have an impressive and eloquent evidence of how people, from the paleolithic era onwards went on about preserving and worshipping their forests; how they set out certain forests as sacred. "In them no axe may be laid to any tree, no branch broken, no firewood gathered, no grass burnt; and animals which have taken refuge there may not be molested."[1]

In the world of classical Greece, and then of Rome, these special groves and forests were usually enclosed by stone walls. This enclosure was called in Greek *Temenos*, a cut-off place, or a demarcated place. A better translation would be "a sacred enclosure." Indeed a periodical entitled *Temenos* started to be published in England in the late 1970s explicitly evoking the spirit of Temenos as a sacred enclosure, and calling for the creation of sacred spaces.

In Latin the term for these demarcated places was *templum*. Templum was of course the original root of the word 'temple.' To begin with, those sacred enclosures were the sanctuaries in which religious ceremonies took place. They were in fact open air temples. When later on temples were erected as monumental buildings with columns and all, sacred groves and forests did not cease to exist. They were still cherished and protected. They inspired the sense of awe, the sense of the mystery of the universe, a higher sense of in-dwelling, being close to gods. The Roman philosopher Seneka so writes in the first century A.D.:

"If you come upon a grove of old trees that have lifted their crowns up above and shut out the light of the sky by the darkness of their interlacing boughs, you feel that there is a spirit in the place, so lofty is the wood, so lonely the spot, so wondrous the thick unbroken shade."[2]

This sense of the mystery of the universe, which some places evoked more than other places, led ancient people to celebrate and protect these places. They felt that in those places their life was enriched and deepened. In sacred groves and forests they felt close to gods and other sublime forces of nature. This sense of the mystery of the universe has, by and large, been lost by modern Western man. But not entirely so.

When we go to Delphi, on a crisp spring day, at the time when the hoards of tourists did not desecrate the place yet, and when in peace and tranquility we identify ourselves with the spirit of the place, we feel a tremendous power emanating from the surroundings.

The sense of the sacred resides in us all. But now it requires very special circumstances for this sense to manifest itself. Our jaded bodies, our overloaded senses and overburdened minds make the journey of transcendence—to the core of our being—rather difficult nowadays.

For the ancient people the sense of the sacred was enacted daily. The whole structure of life was so arranged that the human being could not only experience the sacred but was encouraged to do so. It is rather different in our times.

In the sacred groves and forests of ancient Greece, particular species of trees were dedicated to particular gods. Oaks were in the domain of Zeus, willows of Hera, olives of Athena, the laurel of Apollo, pines of Pan, vine of Dionysus. But this identification was not rigid. The ancient Greeks were generous and flexible people. In various localities, due to specific traditions, different trees could be dedicated to different deities. On the island of Lesbos, for instance, there was an apple grove dedicated to Aphrodite.

Many of the sacred groves contained springs and streams and sometimes lakes. The pollution of these springs and lakes was absolutely forbidden. There was usually a total ban on fishing, with the exception of priests. It was believed that whoever would fish in the lake Poseidon and would catch fish would be turned into the fish called *fisher*.

In Pellene there was a very special sacred grove, dedicated to Artemis the savior, which no man could enter except the priests. This was rather unusual. The common rule was that ordinary people could enter the grove providing they came ritually clean, not guilty of any serious crimes, especially blood guilt.[3]

The tradition of sacred groves and forests was maintained by the ancient people throughout the world. Sacred groves in India are as ancient as the civilization itself. Indeed they go back to the prehistoric, pre-agricultural times. While the idea and the existence of sacred forests and groves did not survive in the West—as we have progressively become a secular society—those groves survived in India until recent times. However, with the weakening of the religious structure of beliefs, the very idea, and hence the existence of the sacred groves and forests have been undermined in India. Yet there are still some sacred groves in India—left, particularly among tribal people.[4]

One of my favorite definitions of the forest is that given by the Buddha. For him the forest was "a peculiar organism of unlimited kindness and benevolence that makes no demands for its sustenance and extends generously the products of its life activity; it affords protection to all beings, offering shade even to the axeman who destroys it."

The native Americans or American Indians have been particularly sensitive to the quality of places. For them to worship a mountain or a brook or a forest was quite a natural thing, for every plant, every tree as well as Mother Earth and Father Heaven were imbued with a spirit.

In the cosmos infused with spiritual forces, delineating special places as particularly important and sacred was as natural as it was inevitable. These special places were also the places of ritual and ceremony, the ones in which the sacred was enacted in daily life; and in the act, the essential mystery and divinity of the universe reaffirmed.

In the Western world the churches and shrines served this purpose—of connecting man with the sacred. But that was some time ago. As we had become progressively secularized so we have lost the sense of the mystery of life and the sacredness of the universe. The churches are now hollow and reverberate with nothingness, for the spirit is gone from the people. The churches are being closed. In England alone two thousand of the existing sixteen thousand churches have been closed. It is reported that only three percent of the people regularly attend the Anglican church. And so the Bishop of Durham proclaims: "It is not now the case that England is a Christian country." Is it not similar in other so called Christian countries?

The original temple or templum or Temenos have lost their meaning, for our hearts so often are cold, and our minds have lost the touch with the mysterious and the sacred. As we have impoverished the universe of the sacred, so we have impoverished ourselves. As we have turned sacred groves and other forests into the timber industry, we no longer have natural temples in which we can renew ourselves.

Towards a Spiritual Renewal

We are now reassessing the legacy of the entire technological civilization and what it has done to our souls and our forests. Out problem is no longer how to manage our forests and our lives more efficiently in order to achieve further material progress. We now ask ourselves more fundamental questions: How can we renew ourselves spiritually? What is the path to life that is whole? How can we survive as humane and compassionate beings? How can we maintain our spiritual and cultural heritage?

The wilderness areas, which I call life-giving areas, are important for three reasons, Firstly, they are important as sanctuaries. Various forms of life might not have survived without them.

Secondly, they are important as givers of timber that breathes and out of which will be made beautiful panels and beams that breathe life in our homes.

Thirdly, and most significantly, they are important as human sanctuaries, as places of spiritual, biological and psychological renewal. As the chariot of progress which is the demon of ecological destruction moves on, we wipe out more and more sanctuaries. They disappear under the axe of man, are polluted by plastic environments, are turned into Disneylands.

The rebuilding of sanctuaries is vital to the well being of our body and the well being of our soul, for the two act in unison. We have lost the meaning of the Temple (Templum) in now deserted churches. We have to recreate this meaning from the foundations. We have to re-sacralize the world, for otherwise our existence will be sterile. We live in a disenchanted world. We have to embark on the journey of the re-enchantment of the world. We have to recreate rituals and special ceremonies through which most precious aspects of life are expressed and celebrated.

Forests still inspire us and infuse us with the sense of awe and mystery . . . that is when we have time and the quietness of mind to lose ourselves in them. And here is an important message. Forests may again become sacred enclosures where great rituals of life are performed, and where the celebration of the uniqueness and mystery of life and the universe is taking place. It depends on our wills to make the forests the places of the re-sacrilazation of the world. The first steps in this direction were taken by the famous Polish director, Jerzy Grotowski, who has abandoned the theatre in order to make nature and particularly forests the sacred grounds for man's new communion with the cosmos.[5]

While I was at Findhorn in 1979, I met the legendary Man of Trees, Richard St. Barbe Baker. By the time I met him he was in his nineties. A beautiful man in his old age, emanating the uprightness, calmness and solidity of big trees. From early childhood his passion was to plant trees. And he planted literally millions of them throughout his busy and productive life—all over the world. During his talk at Findhorn, he led meditation of a special kind. He asked us to imagine that each of us is a tree. We stretched our arms as if we were trees . . . while our feet were solidly grounded in the earth— as the roots of a tree are. For St. Barbe Baker to be in touch with the forest was a form of religion. Each tree was a form of altar for him.[6] We must develop a similar spirit of reverence and empathy for the trees and forests. For they are true sanctuaries.

Let me finish with a short poem.

Of Men and Forests

Forests are the temples.
Trees are the altars.
We are the priests serving the forest gods.

We are also the priests serving the inner temple.
Treat yourself as if you were an inner temple
And you will come close
To the god which resides within.

To walk through the life as if you were
In one enormous temple,
This is the secret of grace.

Notes

1. Sir James Frazer, *The Golden Bough,* Vol. 2, p. 42.
2. Seneka, *Epistoles,* 4,12,3.
3. For further discussion see: J. Donald Hughes, "Sacred Groves: The Gods, Forest Protection, and Sustainable Yield in the Ancient World," in *History of Sustained Yield Forestry,* N. K. Steen, Ed., 1983.
4. For further discussion see: Madhav Gadgil and V. D. Vartak, "Sacred Groves in India—a Plea for Continued Conservation," *The Journal of Bombay Natural History Society,* Vol. 72, No. 2, pp. 314-320, 1975.
5. See Jerzy Grotowski. *On the Road to Active Culture,* 1979; and his other writings.
6. See especially: Richard St. Barbe Baker, *My Life, My Trees,* Findhorn Press, 1979.

23

Healing the Earth and Humanity

DAVID VALBRACHT

In former ages the spiritual leaders of society were responsible for both medicine and agriculture. Medicine for both the human body and the earth derived from the sacramental functions of the priest. Only an individual attuned to the divine had the capacity to perceive accurately the cause of disease and to formulate a plan for restoring health. Healing was based on spiritual understanding and on a recognition of the intimate relationship between humanity and the earth. The health of one depended on the other. If an individual or a society became ill, out of balance, the source of healing was thought to lie within the earth; plants, for example, provided forces to assist healing. Similarly, cures might require an individual to move, so that one might be exposed to different forces. Springs or natural sanctuaries were also recognized as places conducive to healing. Conversely, if the earth became ill, balance had to be regained through the activities of people; ceremonies or a change in settlement or agricultural practices might be required to restore the health of the planet.

As humanity gained independence from the earth, the connection between human beings and the earth weakened and eventually was lost. Old cures no longer worked under new conditions. The ability to perceive the effects that the destruction of the earth was having on human health was also lost. Preoccupation with physical matter resulted in new systems of healing in which the human being and the earth were seen as separate and as composed merely of physical substances. As a result, agriculture and medicine concentrated on developing methods to analyze component substances and to supplement them as necessary. Only in recent years have the limitations of synthetic drugs and chemical fertilizers become widely acknowledged. Now new systems of healing for humanity and the earth are required.

Such new methods for healing will be based on a clear understanding that human beings and the earth are spiritual organisms which must retain a connection with the wider sphere of the universe. Both need not more physical nourishment, but a deeper link with the forces and beings of the spiritual world. To accomplish this, new organs of perception must be developed. Human sense organs need to be enhanced in order for evolution to continue; likewise, the earth's senses must continue to evolve. The health of the earth and of humanity depend on their continued connection.

The Development of
New Human Organs of Perception

In order to work towards physical and spiritual healing, we must attend to the development of new organs of perception. By doing so, we create an objective basis for the restoration of the earth. Recognizing the underlying spiritual nature of the earth, we also understand that all changes to the earth affect its spiritual body. Earth modifications must be based not only on economics or tradition, but on a recognition of the evolving patterns of the earth organism. This requires that new spiritual sense organs emerge out of the spiritual body of the human being. We seek these organs and renewed abilities not out of curiosity, but in order to heal the earth and ourselves.

Several steps can be taken to prepare for the development of these spiritual organs of perception. Up to this point in history, the evolution of consciousness has been part of an orderly process guided from above. With the emergence of human freedom comes the opportunity for individuals to take responsibility for their own development. The conditions of our day require a new understanding of the earth and humanity which comes not out of past revelation but from individual discovery. Research can then be based on objective spiritual observation with newly developed spiritual sense organs.

A fundamental preparatory step in such development is the elimination of prejudice. Present attitudes which reject the existence of spiritual forces hinders clear observation and thought. They encourage one to see only those things which fit preconceptions of what is acceptable. The belief that early peoples were ignorant and ill informed, because a translation of their perceptions does not fit into our way of seeing the world, prevents us from understanding them. Assumptions that improvement of our present situation is impossible, or that Western civilizations are inherently destructive and less spiritual than other peoples, hinder necessary activity. What is required is eliminating preconceptions and developing confidence in our capacity for recognizing the truth.

Frequent involvement with nature is another important step towards developing higher perceptions. Among the many possible activities that encourage the awakening of sensitivity to nature is gardening. In this activity one steps out of the role of passive observer and becomes an active participant in natural processes. Besides the objective improvement of part of the earth, this activity forms a bond with all the participants in earth processes, sensible and supersensible. A gardener experiences directly the human ability to improve conditions and to find a place in the world.

Artistic activity can also be an important preparation. The development of artistic sensitivity, which seeks to comprehend meanings beyond surface impressions, is a step towards perception of the supersensible. Artistic activity can awaken a deeper understanding of nature in an individual and refines one's perceptive abilities. Artistic activity also encourages an individual to be sensitive to the nuances of nature and builds a connection to the supersensible world.[1]

The study of the results of investigations into the supersensible realm can also be helpful in developing new organs of perception. The many descriptions of the supersensible world of nature provided by Rudolf Steiner,[2] for example, may assist in the development of an individual's spiritual sense organs. The goal of such study is to awaken in an interested individual the same perceptual abilities used in the research. Study of the results of such research challenges one to re-evaluate one's conception of the world and of the self and may encourage one to work to eliminate self-imposed boundaries to our perceptual abilities. Any new thoughts based on the results of spiritual research can nourish our developing organs of perception.

We can also undertake exercises to assist directly in a deeper perception of nature. Throughout history such exercises have matched the particular conditions of the time; with the development of modern consciousness, new forms of exercises have been developed. Several exercises suggested by Rudolf Steiner are noteworthy in that they use the observation of nature to enhance our spiritual sense organs. Steiner's exercises are a natural extension of the precise methods of observation used by modern science. Science, however, limits its scope of observation to physical phenomena. While spiritual science acknowledges the importance of the methods of natural science and the human capacities which this approach has nurtured, it also seeks to eliminate the boundaries to its application and to adapt the objective scientific attitude to the realms lying beyond the normal physical senses. Exercises like Steiner's can reveal the spiritual essence which lies behind the forms of each plant, stone, and animal.

Directing one's attention to the phenomena of plant growth and development is one exercise suggested by Rudolf Steiner. One should observe a growing, thriving plant as carefully and intensely as possible. Then apart from the physical impressions of the plant, one should give oneself over to the feelings and thoughts that accompany these observations, which are usually allowed to slip away unnoticed. One should attempt to shut out the rest of the world and allow only these impressions of the phenomena of blossoming and thriving to grow within one's soul.

One can then turn to the phenomena of fading and dying in plants and again pass from an intense physical observation of the plant to the feelings and thoughts that the phenomenon of dying produces within the soul. By alternating between observations of something that is growing and blossoming and something that is fading and dying, the faint feelings accompanying these phenomena are strengthened. Such simple exercises reveal that behind the physical phenomena of nature lie faint impressions of worlds beyond our normal senses. Through such exercises one strengthens the developing organs of supersensible perception and allows nature to reveal its secrets.[3]

The Development of the Sense Organs of the Earth

The earth must also have healthy sense organs in order to remain connected with the wider universe and obtain required nourishment. A human stays in contact with the environment through sense organs such as the eyes and the largest sense organ, the skin. The earth also has individual sense organs and an all-encompassing organ—the soil. The plants and animals of a region serve as some of the earth's organs of perception. They reveal the health of the land and help

266

to maintain a proper relationship between the earth and the universe.

The true basis for the health of the earth and its plants, animals, and human beings is the soil itself. As a sensitive gardener recognizes, the soil is not just powdered minerals; it is a universe of life. Efforts to increase the sensitivity, and thus the health of the earth, must begin with increasing the health of the soil. The needs of this enveloping sense organ are more than physical. What is necessary is nourishing the life and the consciousness of this realm in order to make the soil more "intelligent." One possible means for accomplishing this task is using bio-dynamic preparations, such as those employed by farmers around the globe. These preparations are, in fact, homeopathic medicines for the earth; their purpose is to help in the healing of the earth's primary sense organ.

Further progress can be made by properly organizing the use of the earth's surface. A recognition of the earth as a living being leads to the understanding that like all organisms, the earth is arranged into systems and individual organs. The earth in its primeval state reflected this organization. Earlier cultures established complex patterns of habitation and agriculture which respected the organic differentiation of earth regions. Only modern industrialized societies have ignored this necessity. Land use must be consciously modified to accommodate the effects of human population. Old patterns are not sufficient for the earth in its present condition. We must use all our perceptive capacities to develop the required new patterns.[4]

Steps like these are means by which the earth can regain its health and again become a fit realm for the spirit beings appropriate for this age. It is especially important to provide for the nurturing of the earth in such times as these, when technology is rapidly developing new forces destructive to the environment. Each identifiable form and force in nature has, standing beyond it, a spirit being. Much as plants and stones have emerged out of spiritual substances and retain a connection to the spiritual world, machines and other technological innovations must have a spiritual counterpart. The machines of our day have visibly affected the landscape and human health through their electromagnetic emissions and chemical residues. As we seek to reduce the physical effects of these developments, we should remain aware of the possibility of supersensible effects as well. As in all processes of healing, the best procedure is to sustain and support the naturally beneficent forces of our earth.

When we view the intimate relationship between earth and humanity, we recognize that the health of each depends on the other. We seek healing for the earth as well as for humanity. Each step that is taken benefits both. Human beings, having regained their spiritual sight in a new form, will be prepared to participate in the healing of the earth. This healing will be guided by a perception of the spiritual geography of the earth, rather than by abstractions or tradition. The earth, having regained its relation to the wider spheres, awakens. The fruits the earth provides can then truly nourish humanity, furthering its evolution. When humanity and the earth are approached as one system, human beings' growing independence serves both.

Our goal cannot be to restore humanity or the earth to primeval conditions. The dying process we experience represents a maturation of the earth necessary for the emergence of humanity and the development of the new forces of freedom which were its task to develop. Change has provided an opportunity for an evolution of consciousness for both humanity and the earth. The forces developed during this period will be called upon in the further evolution of both.

New forms of medical practice have emerged to provide health care alternatives. These new approaches recognize that the individual's health must be considered in a holistic fashion—that symptoms in one area of the body have a relation to the totality of the individual and his or her environment.[5] Out of these new forms of practice have come a renewed awareness that the health of an individual is also a response to the environment; health is not possible in a sick world. We need to show the same concern for the health of the earth as we do for our own health. This requires an attitude that acknowledges our connection to the earth. A new healing art will emerge to assist in this work. Farmers and gardeners will join with scientists and physicians to contribute to the practice of a new earth medicine. The geophysician will work with the human physician to insure the health of our world.

Notes

1. Art as a path towards a deeper understanding of nature is demonstrated in Joshen Bockemuhl's, *Dying Forests: A Crisis in*

Consciousness. Methods of drawing that encourage a connection with the natural world are described in *Drawing From the Book of Nature.*

2. Rudolf Steiner's fundamental description of the relationship between the earth and mankind is contained in *An Outline of Occult Science.* In this work Steiner explains the nature of spiritual scientific research and its relation to natural science and gives some of the results of this research.

3. Rudolf Steiner describes a modern method for the development of supersensible organs of perception in *Knowledge of the Higher Worlds and Its Attainment* as well as in *An Outline of Occult Science* and *Theosophy.* These and similar exercises are presented in the chapter "The Stages of Initiation" in *Knowledge of the Higher Worlds.* A systematic examination of the anthroposophical path of schooling is contained in *Rudolf Steiner and Initiation* by Paul Eugen Schiller.

4. Rudolf Steiner describes the basis for a new agriculture in a lecture course given in 1924 and published in English as *Agriculture.* The bio-dynamic approach to agriculture which has developed from this beginning is described by Herbert Koepf in *Bio-Dynamic Agriculture: An Introduction.* Another introduction is provided by Wolf Storl in *Culture and Horticulture: A Philosophy of Gardening.* This approach to agriculture is being developed in the United States by the Bio-Dynamic Farming and Gardening Association, PO Box 290, Kimberton, PA 19442 which publishes a quarterly journal, *Bio-Dynamics.*

5. Some descriptions of medical approaches initiated by Rudolf Steiner and continuing to be developed today are found in *The Anthroposophical Approach to Medicine* by F. Husemann, MD, and Otto Wolf, MD, and in *Anthroposophical Medicine* by Victor Bott.

24
Working with Nature: A Kahuna View

SERGE KAHILI KING

In old Hawaii, and to some extent in modern Hawaii, people were very close to Nature. Of course, this is not surprising. Taro farmers had to be intimately acquainted with the sources of fresh water, the best rocks to use for terraces, the growing cycle of their plants, and the phases of the moon. Fishermen had to know the right plants to use for making nets and lines, the habits and behavior of the fish they sought, and the weather characteristics of winds and clouds. Manual craftsmen needed a thorough knowledge of stone and wood, both as tools and as materials to work on. Herbalists had to be familiar not only with the appearance and qualities of hundreds of plants, but with the healing aspects of fish, salt, and clay, too. And sea-going nomads had to know the secrets of wind, waves, clouds, birds, sun, moon, and stars. But the Hawaiians were more than just close to Nature in terms of knowledge and proximity. Rather, they were neighbors in a living community.

The Aliveness of Nature

For the ordinary Hawaiian of former times, noble or commoner, all of Nature was alive: animals and plants, of course, but also rocks, mountains, valleys, clouds, stars, wind, rain, and everything else. Nature was not just alive, but as consciously aware as any human being. Therefore, in order to maintain a good relationship with any particular part of Nature, human beings had to treat it with respect, just as they would a human neighbor. From experience people knew that for most occasions, the only show of respect needed was simple acknowledgment: a greeting to the fisherman or clothmaker who lived next door, or to the sun that warmed your skin or the moon that lit your way at night; a flower to your girlfriend or to a waterfall for its beauty; a song or a dance to your chief or to the nourishing rain; and something special to those whose assistance, favor, or protection you needed—a pig for the *kahuna lapa'au* to heal your child, a chicken to the man who helped you build your house, a flower lei for your canoe for its help in catching fish, and some *ohelo* berries to keep *Pele* the volcano spirit happy.

This kind of thinking is generally called *animism*, a name which refers to the idea that everything is "animated" by a soul or spirit which can exist independent of its material form. Animism was a deep-seated, commonly held view all over the world at one time, and we can still find modern traces of it in the naming of boats and cars, moons and mountains. It does not imply worship, only an awareness of spiritual presence.

For the Hawaiians, a spirit tended to stay with one form for its whole existence, unless it was a particularly strong spirit. Rock spirits tended to stay rock spirits, even if they became different rocks; tree spirits tended to remain trees; and human spirits tended to remain human. A very strong spirit, however, might have the ability to take a number of different forms. Pele, the volcano spirit, could take the form of a human woman, young or old, as well as molten lava, and *Kamapua'a*, the pig spirit, could become rain, grass, or the *humuhumunukunukuapua'a* fish. Still, for the ordinary Hawaiian, the only way of communicating with the spirits of Nature was by acknowledgment, offerings, or prayer.

The Skills of the Shamans

Among the Hawaiians, however, some were closer to Nature than others—so close that they could speak with the elements, with plants, and with animals, and so attuned that they could shift their shape into an animal, plant, or element at will and take on their qualities, knowledge, and skills. Some of these people were called *kupua*, a term roughly equivalent to *shaman*. By inclination and practice they were healers, though they did not limit themselves to physical means of healing. A master of shamanic skills was called a *kahuna kupua*.

The most famous of all Hawaiian shaman masters was *Maui Kupua*, often translated as "Maui the Demigod," "Maui the Trickster," "Maui the Magician," or "Maui the Wonderworker." Tales of Maui were told all over the Pacific, and while there were certain local variations, practically the same tales were related by island peoples separated by thousands of miles of ocean and centuries of time.

One Hawaiian tale tells how Maui got the secret of fire from birds on the island of Oahu. A long time ago, according to the story, only mudhens knew how to make fire. One day Maui got tired of eating raw food, so he crept up to where the mudhens lived. When they weren't looking, Maui captured a small mudhen and demanded to know the secret of fire. First the mudhen told Maui the secret was in one plant and then in another, but Maui was smart enough to keep hold of the bird's neck while he tested each answer. Finally, when Maui was so fed up with all the wrong answers that he was about to wring the bird's neck, the bird screeched out that the secret was in the *hau* tree. Maui gave the mudhen one last chance and happily produced fire by rubbing two pieces of *hau* wood together. But he was so angry at the bird for misleading him for so long that he struck its head with a fire-brand. That's why mudhens all have a streak of red feathers on their head to this day.

This story has several interesting levels of meaning. One is that mudhens live in the marshy lands where the soft-wooded *hau* trees grow. Another is that the Hawaiian word for mudhen, *alae*, has connotations of "redness" and "rising up," terms reminiscent of fire; and the *hau* tree has flowers that turn red-orange at the end of the day, when fires are needed. More important for our purposes is that the shaman communicated directly with an animal to learn something useful for human society. A modern view would probably be that humans discovered that *hau* trees burned intensely when struck by lightning; the mudhens were included in the story because of their association with the area and the symbolic red of their crest. But shamans would say it was equally possible that a shaman like Maui communicated directly with the birds to learn about the effect of lightning on the *hau*. In other stories Maui talks to various kinds of birds, to fish, to bats, to trees, to water, to wind, and to the sun either to learn from them or to get them to do what he wanted.

Many more tales are told in Hawaii of beneficial interactions between humans and Nature. Among the most numerous are stories of owls as protectors, guardians, and helpers. In an Oahu story a man had gathered eggs from owls' nests, but was so touched by the crying of the mother owl that he returned the eggs. In gratitude the owl promised to help him if he needed it. The day came when the man and his family were under attack from an evil chief. Thousands of owls flew to his assistance and drove off the enemy. To this day there are many place names in the Waikiki area that commemorate this great event. Equally important in Hawaiian lore are the stories of shark helpers who protect against other sharks, help to gather fish, warn of storms, and save swimmers from drowning, and of special human spirits who transform into sharks so they can be helpers to their human family.

How To Communicate With Nature

Of course, a major question that arises is how people actually do speak to Nature, once you accept communication as possible. It's highly unlikely that mudhens, owls, and sharks would understand human language, and barely acceptable that humans would understand theirs. (What is the language of a shark, anyway?) What I learned in my own training as a *kupua* may shed some light on what is behind the stories of shamans "speaking" to animals and other aspects of Nature.

Although in stories it is made to seem as if a human and an animal are having an ordinary conversation, the communication is actually much more telepathic. On the part of the human this includes a combination of intent, imagery, and perhaps some words to help keep the focus. One time I was standing on the lanai of our center in Kilauea, Kauai, looking at a big wasp who was inside beating his head against a window trying to get out. I spoke to the wasp to get his attention (or to focus my own—take your pick), and with my mind traced a bright pathway from his position around a post and out the open door about ten feet from where he was. Then I told him to follow the path and he would be outside. Instantly, he took off and followed the exact path I had traced right out the door. On another occasion I was at a large gathering in Minnesota—an outside picnic which seemed in imminent danger of being deluged by rain. I was requested to do something, so I asked the wind to hold off the storm until we had finished our picnic. That is, I spoke words with my mind and made a mental picture of what I wanted. And the wind very nicely cooperated. Some students of mine have been able to get wild deer to approach them within a few feet, and others have attracted wild dolphins to play with them in the ocean. Peaceful intention, positive imagination, and clear mental verbalization are what make the connection. Of course, we still don't know what is actually taking place when Nature responds to such focus, anymore than we know what is actually happening when we cause electricity to flow through a wire. Theories abound, but all we really know in the latter case is that when we set up certain conditions, electricity happens. In the case of human-Nature communication, all we really know is that when we set up certain conditions in our mind, Nature responds.

I, my family, and my students have communicated with Nature successfully so many times that we accept it as being as natural as breathing. We speak to the wind to calm down the turbulence during airplane flights. We speak to the rain to leave an area or to come to an area. We speak to whales, dolphins, and turtles so they will appear and delight us with their presence. We speak to our plants so they will grow better and to our cars so they will run better. Everything is part of Nature, and everything responds.

Shape-Changing through Spiritual Merging

So far, though, we've been discussing only telepathic communication. But what about the idea of shape-changing that is so much a part of traditional lore all around the world? Is it purely fantasy, or is there something to it? And what does it have to do with working with Nature?

According to my experience and training, this phenomenon is both real and practical, but it is not easy to describe. Through observation, experimentation, and practice, the earliest shamans discovered and passed on the knowledge that if you acted as if you were something else—an element, a force of Nature, an animal, or a plant—and if you were able to put your whole mind and body into the acting, something very peculiar would happen. First, you would find yourself "knowing" things you had not learned through ordinary experience. Acting the part of an eagle, for instance, you might suddenly know a great deal about the habits and behavior of eagles and how the earth would look from a thousand feet in the air. Acting as a buffalo or a fish, you might know where the best feeding places are and the best time and direction for migrations. Secondly, you would find that if you gently "leaned your will" in a desired direction while acting as a particular force, animal, or whatever, the entity itself would tend to move in that direction. The shamans who did this also found that any such influence had to be both gentle and positive (from the point of view of the entity being influenced) for it to work at all. So in a rain dance, the storm clouds had to be coaxed to come hither and drop their rain—they could not be forced; and in a hunting dance, the deer had to be persuaded to come within range of the hunters—they could not be coerced.

In Hawaii this skill is called *kulike* a rough translation of which is "to make subconscious patterns." This ability was and is used for fishing, agriculture, weather, tidal waves, and lava flows by those who know how to do it. And even among them, as it always has been for every shaman, the rate of success is highly dependent upon one's merging skills, persuasive ability, and the will of the entity being influenced. When an experienced practitioner is deeply involved in acting the part of an aspect of Nature, then he or she may appear to observers to take on more and more of the aspect's appearance. A man may objectively look like a man, but truly seem to be an animal at the same time. A woman may clearly be a woman, and just as clearly be a butterfly. It is very similar to the ability we see in the best actors of stage and screen, except that the purpose is different. And it is said that a real master of the art can concentrate so well that he or she can actually change physical form and become the aspect focused on in all physical respects. However, in all my travels and adventures, I have never witnessed nor experienced a shape-changing that could be explained only by a physical transformation. It is theoretically possible, from a shaman point of view, but if it happens, it must be extremely rare, because it serves no useful purpose in working with Nature that cannot be accomplished by much easier methods.

My first experience in *kulike* took place in West Africa under the guidance of a Hausa shaman. One night in a hut in northern Dahomey (now Benin), he guided me into a very deep trance and helped me to merge my spirit with that of a cooperative leopard. I spent the rest of that night as the leopard, hunting, feeding, resting, observing, and feeling tremendously, vibrantly aware, alive, and full of energy. In that experience I learned a great deal about leopards and their incredible sense of power in the present moment. In fact, some of the leopard's pattern must have rubbed off on me, because for several years after my return from Africa, numerous people told me that I reminded them of a leopard in some ways.

In a more practical vein, one of my students told me that she was picking roses and getting pricked by the thorns until she merged with the spirit of the roses. Then she could pick them without harm, even when she tried to get pricked.

Shape-Changing through Astral Projection

Another type of shape-changing employed by shamans can be used for observing events in Nature at a distance or for influencing the behavior of animals, birds, fish, and the like. It is called in Hawaiian *ho'okakaola* ("to send out a visible astral body"). This kind of shape-changing probably accounts for many of the traditional legends. In this case the shaman creates a visible thoughtform, that is, a pattern of energy formed by thought and charged with emotion or intent, which follows the will of the shaman and serves as his or her eyes, ears, voice, and even distant body. This technique will sound familiar to anyone who has studied European, Native American, or other shamanic lore, but it does sound very strange to anyone whose experience has been limited to the Western scientific tradition. And even to someone who can admit to the reality of telepathy, and to *kulike* as an extended form of it, *ho'okakaola*, or "astral projections," can seem rather far out. But to many millions of people around the world, it is something very real.

Although the form created and sent out could be that of the shaman, it is more commonly that of a bird or an animal, especially when working with Nature. To draw upon my West African experience again, it was common knowledge in Dahomey that one of the presidents of the country would visit the north in the form of an antelope to check on the behavior of the people and the state of the land. And my Hawaiian uncle would often appear to me in the form of a bird, usually an owl, and he would use the same form to communicate with other animals. Seldom is enough energy put into the astral form for moving anything physically, though. Usually the ability to be seen and/or heard is enough.

Simple, but not Easy

We are all part of the life of Haumea (the Hawaiian equivalent of Gaia), whether we are human or not, and we are all influencing each other all of the time, whether we are conscious of it or not. The shaman perspective is that as long as there is influence anyway, why not make it both conscious and positive? After all, while we are working with Nature, Nature is also working with us.

But in order to work effectively with Nature, we must learn to be at peace with ourselves. It is one thing to talk about using techniques like telepathy, spiritual merging, and astral projection to learn from and influence Nature, but it's quite another thing to use them in such a way that you get results. As humans we have learned to shut out sensory data that we don't like, but Nature is very, very aware. If we approach it with anger, fear, or a desire to control, then we will get nowhere. But if we approach it with peaceful minds and loving hearts, then technique doesn't even matter. As a Hawaiian proverb states, in expressing the universality of love:

> *He manu ke aloha, 'a' ole lala kau 'ole*
> (Love is like a bird; there is no branch
> that it does not perch on.)

25

The Rainforest as Teacher

JOHN SEED

John Seed gave up his practice of insight meditation after the rainforest suddenly took over as his teacher of truth. In the last decade, since hearing the call of the wild, Seed has become a leading environmental activist as well as a theoretician and teacher of deep ecology.

In 1979, although I had no knowledge of, or conscious interest in, the issue, I got involved in a demonstration to save a rain forest located about five miles down the road from where I lived. Somehow I found myself involved in what turned out to be the first direct action in Australia—or in the world for that matter—in defense of the rain forests. All of a sudden, the forest was inside me and was calling to me, and it was the most powerful thing I have ever felt. Very soon after that I stopped meditating. My practice just dropped away. I wasn't looking inside anymore. And I didn't have any particular explanation for this. I must say, at first it caused me quite a lot of anguish, and for awhile the only reason I was sitting was some kind of vague dread or guilt that if I stopped something terrible would happen. But all the other motivation to meditate had gone, and pretty soon the guilt was gone too, and then I was just out there in the world of direct action. I was getting a very strong message from the rain forest and I followed it.

I receive great spiritual nourishment from the forest itself. Furthermore, I have the scientific understanding that we humans spent 125 million of the last 130 million years evolving within this rain forest, and that our cells and our very psyche are infused with the intelligence of the forest. The fact that the forest communicates so strongly to me is not surprising.

What also turned me toward the forest were the statistics I began reading from the United Nations Environment Program and from various ecologists, which indicate that we are the

This article is excerpted from an interview with John Seed by Wes Nisker in *Inquiring Mind*, a semi-annual journal of the Vipassana Community, P. O. Box 9999, North Berkeley Station, Berkeley, CA 94709.

last generations of human beings that are going to be in a position to turn this thing around—to prevent the destruction of complex life on earth. That kind of information burnt away all the distractions in my life, the kinds of things that at one time had been obstacles to my meditation practice. But again, it was not so much the intellectual knowing as it was just being in the forest. That experience was what made it possible for me to apply myself to the environmental work with a kind of urgency and commitment that I was never able to apply to my sitting practice.

I find myself surrendering completely to the rain forest. The closest thing to meditation practice for me now is to lie down in the forest when it's dry, cover myself in leaves, and imagine an umbilical cord reaching down into the earth. Then I visualize myself as being one leaf on the tree of life, both as myself personally and as a human being, and I realize that the sap of that tree runs through every leaf, including me, whether I'm aware of it or not.

I don't believe this to be a mystical notion. It's very matter of fact. In reality, every breath of air we take connects us to the entire life of the planet—the atmosphere. I feel it very physically. I'm part of the water cycle. The sun lifts the water up into the atmosphere and then it comes down, lubricating and giving life to everything. Eighty to ninety percent of what I am is just this water.

I help organize and lead gatherings called the Council of All Beings, and the exercises we do at these gatherings give us a sense that we are not so much a personality as an intersection of these great cycles. We begin to break the illusion of being separate from the rest of creation. I can lay on the ground and feel the vibration of this earth which gave rise to me and which has sustained my ancestors and everything else for four thousand million years in incredible intelligent harmony.

It's only recently that I as a human being have lost the ability to dance to that tune which promises hundreds and thousands and millions of years of continued evolution. I started creating my own tune, the human tune, which has become so loud in my ears that I can't hear the sound of the earth's cycles or the music of the spheres. We need to check into those other tunes through ritual and ceremony.

When I first started doing this, I felt so separate from nature that I thought it was going to be a huge undertaking; that it would be a vast voyage before I could reconnect. But to my amazement, I found the illusion of separation to be very flimsy, and that there are just a few conceptual filters that prevent us from reuniting with the earth. Just hold your breath for two minutes and you will understand the illusion of separation. There's no separation possible. We're constantly cycling the water and air and earth through us. Furthermore, we don't walk on the earth. The air is part of the earth. We walk *in* the earth. It really helps if we realize these things.

Recognizing our connection with nature is very simple and accessible regardless of where we are living. We may think we're surrounded by concrete and plastic, but then we think a little further and realize that the concrete is sand and the bodies of shellfish. The plastic is a product of the rain forest laid down during the carboniferous era 130 million years ago and turned into oil. Look just under the surface and the unnaturalness of things starts to disappear.

That's what we work on in the Council of All Beings. We present a series of rituals and ceremonies intended to dispel the illusion of separation and alienation. All indigenous cultures have, at the very center of their spiritual life, similar kinds of ritual and ceremony that acknowledge and nurture human interconnectedness in the larger family of life. What has happened to modern humans is that we have become arrogant. It stems perhaps from the Judeo-Christian idea that we are the center of it all, the crown of creation, and the rest of the world is just resources. We look at the nature rituals and ceremonies of indigenous people as nothing but primitive superstition and pagan mumbo jumbo. We think we're enlightened, and that means we are above nature, and out of that arrogance we are threatening to destroy ourselves.

Everything about our society is based on this idea of ourselves as specially created apart from the rest of nature. We don't have to believe this intellectually to be completely enthralled by it. As long as we think of "the environment" we are objectifying it and turning it into something over there and separate from ourselves. Even if we don't believe in any particular theory of economics, our whole life is conditioned by an economic system based upon the principle that the earth has no value until human labor is added to it. The earth is just a bunch of dirt, and we are so clever we can mold that dirt and turn it into spaceships and into great long electric wires to carry our messages. We think we are the miracle, and we've refused to recognize the miracle of the dirt which composes us. Any miracle that we have is only miraculous because we are made of this incredible dirt—miracle dirt which will agree to do everything we ask of it. We refuse to recognize any of that. All that we know is "aren't I fantastic?" That's our downfall.

Of course, everything dies, and we're going to have to let go of this planet sooner or later. The sun is going to go into nova in four thousand million years, and then the earth is going to fry up in a crisp. So what am I going to do about it? Tear my hair?

Once I was swimming at sunrise on the coast of New South Wales when I was attracted to a rock that was covered with incredible life: sea weed, crabs, shellfish. And as I began to embrace this life, all of a sudden I was embracing the living rock underneath, and I could feel the molecular continuity between the rock and the life it was supporting and my own physical being. I experienced that all of the molecules and atoms were the same, and that somehow the rock had the potential and, I would have to say, the desire or the propensity to transform itself into all kinds of soft stuff, like sea weed and human flesh. I realized that the sharp distinction between cellular life and what preceded it was actually just in my mind. The universe was miraculous and seamless. The miracle didn't start when humans came along or for that matter when life began. When a bolt of lightening fertilized the bowl of molecular soup, it was ready and waiting. I have a visceral understanding of this process, and a deep feeling of connection. Therefore I don't have a great deal of anxiety about the result.

I was afraid to accept that realization at first. I struggled against it. I was afraid that I might lose my motivation by letting in the good news that everything was all right whatever happens. The atoms which had done this before, for whatever imponderable reasons, were obviously capable of doing it again. And nothing I did could touch those bigger processes.

But my motivation to save complex life was undiminished by this realization. Somehow I have surrendered the interests of my personality. I say regularly to my DNA, "Just tell me what to do. I'm working for you now." I'm not working for "the man" anymore.

The music that evolved me for four thousand million years—I can hear that again. It says to me, "Save the planet. Save complex life. Protect biological diversity. Try and keep gene pools intact wherever possible. That's what I want you to do."

Meanwhile, what I notice is that when I live committed like this, my life is full of joy. I was sitting on a train in Tokyo on my way to do a Council of All Beings and I looked around at the people on the train, the wealthiest people in the world, and saw that they were so unhappy. I don't want that life. My life feels very joyful and exciting to me right now. In this day and age, if you end up with a joyful and exciting life, feeling at one with all things, you really can't complain, regardless of the outcome.

For information about John Seed's workshops write to R. G. Steinman, Rainforest Information Center, 9009 Fairview Road, Silver Springs, MD 20910.

26

Invoking Angelic Beings

GEOFFREY HODSON

The ceremonies consist of a morning invocation to the Angels and an evening service of thanksgiving.

For this purpose the following suggestions are made: A shrine, in or out of doors, should be set apart and, where possible, used exclusively for this purpose; it should be consecrated by an appropriate ceremonial, which would have as its object the invocation of the power of the angels and the establishment of a centre and atmosphere in which contact and co-operation would be possible. The initial ceremony could be performed by a priest of the religion of the country, who is sympathetic to the ideals expressed, or by an occultist possessing the necessary knowledge and power.

In the east, should be an altar upon which worshippers should place (*a*) fragrant flowers, gathered freshly each day, (*b*) religious symbols, (*c*) a picture or statue of the Founder of the religion, (*d*) holy water, (*e*) incense, and (*f*) candles. The minimum—where other things are unobtainable—would be flowers and a single object of beauty.

Essential conditions are complete cleanliness, an atmosphere of utter purity, and a single desire for mutual co-operation of angels and men for the helping of the world.

Joy, simplicity and beauty should characterise all the ceremonies, preparations and arrangements.

All participants in the ceremonies should be clothed in simple robes of colour corresponding to that of the group of angels whose aid is being invoked; all undergarments should be white. One of the participants should officiate and act as link between the two corresponding groups of angels and men.

Groups of Angels	Colours To Be Worn
Guardian angels of the home	Rose and soft green
Healing angels	Deep sapphire blue
Angels of maternity and birth	Sky blue
Ceremonial angels	White
Angels of music	White
Nature angels	Apple-green
Angels of Beauty and Art	Yellow (the wisdom colour)

Prayers may be offered for particular purposes. Where more than one group of angels is invoked, the officiant for each should be robed in the appropriate colour and perform the appropriate ceremony.

Procedure: Once begun the services should be maintained regularly and are best performed immediately after the morning and evening ablutions. The presence of children—who should wear white—is desirable.

All should enter in procession, the children leading, the officiants last. The children should sit in a half-circle, facing the altar, in front of the elders, leaving a passage in the centre for the officiants.

Where very young, aged, sick people or pregnant women are present, they should be placed nearest the altar, the rest, with the exception of children, standing in straight rows behind them.

Each officiant, one for each group of angels, will advance to the altar in turn, repeat the appropriate invocation, during which he will lift the bowl of flowers above his head, following them with his eyes. When taking his special part in the cere-mony, the officiant should use all his powers of thought and will to summon the angels. (The measure of effectiveness in all ceremony is proportionate to the amount of knowledge, will and thought-power employed by the officiant.)

All present will join with him, to the utmost of their capacity, following intently the meaning of the prayer.

No undue physical strain should be produced by the effort made, but ceremonies should not be allowed to degenerate into mere repetition of formulae. At the same time, an intense feeling of joy in, and a sense of anticipation of, the companion-ship of the angels must be steadily maintained.

* * *

At the evening service of thanksgiving, after the prayer, let the officiant hold up the bowl of flowers, offering their beauty and their sweetness to the angels, and pouring through them deep love and gratitude from his heart towards the angel hosts. Let all present similarly pour out their love through the officiant and the flowers; then sit in silence, giving thanks and making their private prayers; then go directly to bed.

When it is not possible for the young, the sick, the aged or the pregnant to be present, the group or a part of the group should go straight to their rooms from the shrine, bearing a second bowl of flowers, which has been standing on the altar during the ceremony. Then, facing the patient, the particular ceremony required should be repeated—invoking angel guardians for the young and aged, building angels for the pregnant, healing angels for the sick. Where only one room is thus visited, the bowl of flowers should be left on a small shrine in the room; where a number of visits are called for, the flowers should be distributed among the rooms, placed in vases on the respective shrines. Where an appropriate object of beauty cannot be procured for these shrines, flowers will suffice.

* * *

At risk of repetition it should be made clear that this conception must be preserved in its simplest possible form, entirely free from all sensationalism or elaborate ceremonial; nor should any attempt be made to obtain close personal contact with individual angels, or to employ them from motives of personal gain, interest or curiosity. Such endeavours would almost invariably lead to disaster, and must be rigorously avoided. It should be as natural to work with angels as with human beings, or as with domestic animals; and qualities of SIMPLICITY, PURITY, DIRECTNESS and IMPERSONALITY must characterise all who would successfully take part in such endeavours.

A knowledge and appreciation of the teachings of the Ancient Wisdom should make depression and similar moods impossible. Complete confidence in the Divine power and Divine justice characterise the angel hosts, and if men would work with them they, too, must attain those qualities. The ability to judge the importance of a temporary circumstance by seeing its relation to the whole, to the completed scheme, must be developed, so that it becomes impossible to be unduly elated, cast down, or overcome by any particular event or succession of events. The power to work on, with utter faith, with complete certainty, in spite of the apparent failure of any particular endeavour, must be sought; for thus the angels work. Christians would do well to remember and repeat frequently the Collect for the day of St. Michael and All Angels.

* * *

Let me picture to you what may still come, give you a vision of that which lies ahead.

Picture a vast plain, in a far clime, under a clear sky, where

285

thousands and thousands of your people gather—and, with them, the sick, the aged, the young—and form, in great figures on the plain, stars, triangles, pentagons, invoking us, until, descending to your earth, we come, visible, as robed in flesh— a glorious descent into your midst. Not we alone, but with us members of your race, coming from the ranks of Those to whom earth can teach no more. There we come among the multitude, to heal, to guide and to inspire, and, ere we depart, with promise of early return, to pray with them, uplifting all to the feet of Him Who is the Father of us all, our Logos and our Lord. In every land, to every people, thus might we come.

Invocations and Prayers
MORNING INVOCATIONS

Devas of Ceremony

Hail, brethren of the devic hosts!
Come to our aid.
Give us your fiery devic power
As we give you our human love.

Fill every place with power and life!
Share with us the labours of this earth,
That the life-force within be set free.

Music

Hail, devas of Music!
Come to our aid.
Sing to us your songs of joy;
Fill us with divine harmony.
Awaken us, that we may hear your voice;
Attune our ears to your song;
Ensoul our earthly music with your light.
Share with us the labours of the earth,
That men may hear the melodies you sing.
Beyond the realms of Space and Time.

Guardian Devas of the Home

Hail, Guardian Angels of the Home!
Come to our aid,

Share with us our work and play.
Be with us that we may hear your wings.
And feel your breathe upon our cheek;
Come close, and sense our human love.

Take our hands in yours,
Lift us for a while
From the burden of this flesh.

Grant us to share with you
Your wondrous freedom throughout space
Your vivid life in sunlit air,
Your great intensity of joy,
Your unity with Life.

Help us so to work and play
That the time may be brought near
When all our race
Shall know you well,
And hail, you brother pilgrims
On the path to God.

Hail, Guardian Angels of the Home!
Come to our aid,
Share with us our work and play,
That the Life within may be set free.

Building Angels

Hail, devic hosts who build!
Come to our aid;
Help this new birth
Into the world of men.

Strengthen the mother in her pain;
And send your gracious angels
To attend the bed of birth,
And usher in the dawn
Of this new life.
Give to the coming child
The blessing of our Lord.

Hail, devic hosts who build!
Come to our aid;
Help this new birth into the world of men,
That the divinity within may be set free.

Geoffrey Hodson

Healing Angels

Hail, devas of the Healing Art!
Come to our aid.
Pour forth your healing life
Into this . . . (place or person).

Let every cell be charged anew
With vital force.
To every nerve give peace.
Let tortured sense be soothed.
May the rising tide of life
Set every limb aglow,
As, by your healing power,
Both soul and body are restored.

Leave here (or there) an angel watcher,
To comfort and protect,
Till health returns or life departs,
That he may ward away all ill,
May hasten the returning strength—
Or lead to peace when life is done.

Hail, devas of the Healing Art!
Come to our aid,
And share with us the labours of this earth,
That God may be set free in man.

Angels of Nature

Hail, devas of the earth and sky!
Come to our aid.
Give fertility to our fields,
Give life to all our seeds,
That this our earth may be fruitful.

Hail, devas of the earth and sky!
Come to our aid;
Share with us the labours of our world
That the divinity within may be set free.

Angels of Beauty and of Art

Hail, angels of the Hand of God!
Come to our aid.

Impress upon our worlds
Of thought, of feeling and of flesh,
A sense of Divine Beauty.
Help us to see the vision of the Self,
To recognise in all created things
The Beauty of the Self;
That through the Beauty we may find,
Hid deep behind external veils
Of colour, line and form,
The Very Self,
Thus, having helped us,
Inspire us with the power
To give expression in our lives
To all that we have seen—
To the Good, the True, the Beautiful.

Grant that we may see and know
You, the angels of His Hand,
That, seeing, we may learn to share
Your task of shedding beauty on the world.

Hail, angels of the Hand of God!
Come to our aid.
Share with us the labours of this earth,
That the beauty within may be revealed.

EVENING HYMNS OF PRAYER AND THANKSGIVING

May blessings from above
Flow forth and beautify the human love
Which we in gratitude pour forth
To you, our angel helpers of this day.
Accept our love and grateful prayers
And help us, so to live and work,
That ever, day by day,
Your hosts shall find us growing
Akin to you.

We crave this night your guardianship for all,
Be with the young, the aged, and the sick;
Surround their beds with wings of light and peace,
Cherish them, we pray, until the dawn.
And, as the sun once more returns
To give us life and warmth and light,

289

Let us again prelude our work
With salutation and with praise
To Him Who is the Father of us all;
That, hand in hand and side by side,
His human and His angel sons
May labour in His Name
To bring about the glorious day
When, in our world and theirs,
His Will alone shall reign.

AMEN

Night gathers to its close our earthly day,
And now we gather here, our angel guest,
To offer thee our love and gratitude;
To thank thee for thy service.

May Those Who labour ever night and day,
Pour down upon thee blessings manifold,
Send thee Their super-human love and grace;
May Their compassion fill thee, and Their life,
Till, overflowing, streams of love shall fall
From Thee to us, flow back from us to thee,
Binding our hearts in bonds of brotherhood,
Uniting us by links of love divine.
We pray thee, ever answer our call,
For we would ever open our hearts to thee.
Come closer, blessed messengers of God,
We would hear Him in the beating of thy wings.

In silence, in serenity of heart and mind,
We greet thee, at the closing of this day;
May He enfold thee in His everlasting arms
Till His radiance and His joy shine through thee.

Be with the children, blessed one, this night;
Be with the aged and the sick;
By each bed a guardian angel stand
That all may sleep in peace, waking betimes
To feel thy guardian presence with them still.

AMEN

QUEST BOOKS
are published by
The Theosophical Society in America,
Wheaton, Illinois 60189-0270,
a branch of a world organization
dedicated to the promotion of brotherhood and
the encouragement of the study of religion,
philosophy, and science, to the end that man may
better understand himself and his place in
the universe. The Society stands for complete
freedom of individual search and belief.

THE POWER OF PLACE

James A. Swan, Ph.D.

Stonehenge ... the Himalayas ... the sacred river Ganges ... the Great Pyramid of Giza ... these places affect us profoundly. But until now, few have explored why such places are revered. In this provocative work, James Swan has collected essays on sacred places and their effect on human beings. **In an age when you may feel you have lost your connection to the planet, this book will help you discover your own relationship to the life around you.**

> *"Jim Swan continues his expert efforts to educate us about our relationship to the earth."*
> —Marilyn Christiano, Editor, *Voice of America*

> *"... it's exciting, beautifully produced, highly intelligent, and fun. A superior work."*
> —Joseph Terrano, *Friend's Review*

> *"Jim Swan should be commended for creating a multi-cultural overview of the role of sacred places in all people's lives."*
> —Zoh M. Hieronimus, 21st Century Radio's Hieronimus & Co.

> *"This book is an important step on the path of creating a modern "Land Ethic" that cherishes humanity, other living creatures, and the land that sustains all life."*
> —Evelyn Martin, former director with the American Planning Assn.

> *"A superior anthology of articles. An intelligent, lucid excursion into the power of heart and mind, soul and place."*
> —*The Book Reader*

Jim Swan is currently Associate Professor of Anthropology at the California Institute of Integral Studies and with his wife Roberta is co-producer of Spirit of Place symposia series. He was one of the founding members of the Division of Environment and Population Psychology at the American Psychological Association. Swan has published over 100 articles in magzines such as *Shaman's Drum*, *Audubon*, and *Environmental Health Digest*.

NATIVE HEALER

NATIVE
HEALER
INITIATION INTO AN ANCIENT ART

Medicine Grizzlybear Lake

Medicine Grizzlybear Lake

Many claim to be healers and spiritual teachers; the author is both. Here he explains how a person is called to be a medicine man or woman and the trials and tests of a candidate. Lake gives an exciting glimpse into the world of Native American shamanism. He was trained by numerous Native American teachers, including Rolling Thunder, and has conducted hundreds of ceremonies and lectures.

"... very interesting account of a native American Indian healer's apprenticeship and practice..."
— Serge Kahili King
author of *Imagineering for Health* and *Earth Energies*

"... wonderful reading and full of important psychological, anthropological and spiritual information."
— James A. Swan, Ph.D., author of *The Power of Place*

"... it is a joy for me to read this work of Medicine Grizzlybear..."
— Brooke Medicine Eagle

"... a rare opportunity ... to learn about shamanism from somebody who has been taught, trained, studied, and practiced in both worlds and societies. I therefore highy recommend it ..."
— Rolling Thunder, Inter-tribal Medicine Man

"I highly recommend his book to all those who are feeling the expansion of spiritual awareness in their hearts and those who wish to understand the direct tradition of shamanism whose course is the same throughout many nations of indigenous people."
— Dhyani Ywahoo, Spiritual Director, Sunray Meditation Society

"In Native Healer *we are reminded that healing is a powerful culturally endorsed ritual whose practitioners use skills and wisdom accumulated for centuries to help patients garner their most powerful self-healing responses."*
— Carl A. Hammerschlag, M.D., author of *The Dancing Healers*